D1579083

STUDYING SCOTS LAW

THIRD EDITION

Hector L MacQueen, LL.B, PhD, FRSE

Professor of Private Law, University of Edinburgh

Published by
Tottel Publishing Ltd
Maxwelton House
41-43 Boltro Road
Haywards Heath
West Sussex
RH16 1BJ

Tottel Publishing Ltd
9-10 St Andrew Square
Edinburgh
EH2 2AF

ISBN 978 1 84592 359 4
© Reed Elsevier (UK) 2004
Third edition 2004
Formerly published by LexisNexis Butterworths
Third edition reprinted by Tottel Publishing Ltd 2006
Reprinted 2007, 2008

All rights reserved. No part of this publication may be reproduced in any material form (including photocopying or storing it in any medium by electronic means and whether or not transiently or incidentally to some other use of this publication) without the written permission of the copyright owner except in accordance with the provisions of the Copyright, Designs and Patents Act 1988 or under the terms of a licence issued by the Copyright Licensing Agency Ltd., Saffron House, 6–10 Kirby Street, London, EC1N 8TS, England. Applications for the copyright owner's written permission to reproduce any part of this publication should be addressed to the publisher.

Warning: The doing of an unauthorised act in relation to a copyright work may result in both a civil claim for damages and criminal prosecution.

Crown copyright material is reproduced with the permission of the Controller of HMSO and the Queen's Printer for Scotland. Parliamentary copyright material is reproduced with the permission of the Controller of Her Majesty's Stationery Office on behalf of Parliament. Any European material in this work which has been reproduced from EUR-lex, the official European Communities legislation website, is European Communities copyright.

British Library Cataloguing-in-Publication Data
A catalogue record for this book is available from the British Library

Typeset by The Partnership Publishing Solutions Ltd
Printed and bound in Great Britain by
CPI Antony Rowe Limited, Chippenham, Wiltshire

STUDYING SCOTS LAW

Third Edition

Dedication

In memoriam David Williamson, OBE, QC, WS

6 May 1949 – 27 January 2004

cricketer, golfer, solicitor-advocate, part-time sheriff and friend

Preface

This book is intended to help, inform and advise people wishing to pursue a career in law in Scotland, those who are in the early stages of a course in law (whether or not they are minded to have a career in the field), or those who have a general interest in Scottish law and its distinctive legal system and want to learn a little more about it. The first edition, published in 1993, was written at a time of great change in the legal profession; so was the second, published in 1999. These changes have continued into the twenty-first century, as have changes in the structure of the legal system generally, the nature and forms of legal education, the publication of legal materials (most notably on the Internet), and the funding of the higher education system generally. This third edition has thus, like its predecessors, required a surprisingly large amount of work to be done to be brought up-to-date. I hope that the revisions ensure that the book continues to serve its purpose, although the pace of ongoing change makes it necessary to say that the position is stated as it stood in April 2004. Shrouded in particular doubt at that time again was the future of student funding in higher education, thanks to the possible effects in Scotland of the variable 'top-up' fees proposed for introduction in 2006 in England and Wales under the Higher Education Bill 2004. I hope that I have provided enough sources of further information to enable the reader to make a good start with any necessary updating. In particular the website addresses to which I have tried to refer at relevant points throughout the book should be consulted in addition to my own descriptions and comments.

The work of revision could not be accomplished without the willing aid of a number of friends, some of whom were going round the course for a third time. They include my Edinburgh colleagues Alan Barr, Lorand Bartels, Sandra Eden, Bob Lane, Stephen Neff, and Clare Stephen; Liz Campbell, Director of Education and Training, Law Society of Scotland; Kenneth Campbell, advocate, Director of Training and Education, Faculty of Advocates; Iain Macphail, Sheriff Principal of Lothian and Borders; and Anne Passmore. Other individuals and organisations also responded willingly and promptly to inquiries. My thanks to them all. They are not responsible for errors of law, fact or opinion in the text. Wife and offspring gave their usual unstinting support and advice, and I am glad to report that the neither of the two children who have so far entered Scottish universities has done so as a student of law. It remains to be seen whether the youngest will help me maintain this record of success.

The book is dedicated to the memory of David Williamson: see the appreciations of his life, work and character in the March 2004 issue of the *Journal of the Law Society of Scotland* and in 2004 *Scots Law Times* (News) 55. In many ways (although he would have disliked the very idea) he was a role model for readers of this book. I am grateful to Dee for allowing me to celebrate his memory in this way.

Hector MacQueen
Old College, University of Edinburgh
30 April 2004

Contents

Table of statutes

Table of statutory instruments

Table of treaties

Table of cases

The Scottish legal system

The primary aims of this book are to provide an account of the educational and training requirements for entry into the Scottish legal profession, and to give some guidance on the study skills needed to fulfil these requirements successfully. But it is impossible to come to grips with this subject without some knowledge and understanding of the legal system in Scotland and of the profession itself. This is particularly so when in recent years both system and profession have been undergoing major changes. Part I is therefore given over to a somewhat compressed account of the Scottish legal system.

CHAPTER I

The law in Scotland

INTRODUCTION

1.01 There are three major legal systems in the United Kingdom. One is in England and Wales, another is in Northern Ireland, and the third, and the one with which this book is primarily concerned, is in Scotland. Although these legal systems share a legislature in the Westminster Parliament for the making of new laws, each of them has long had its own structure of courts, its own ways of qualifying as a lawyer, and its own legal rules. In addition, Scotland now has its own Parliament in Edinburgh, while Northern Ireland (not to mention Wales) has an Assembly. The reasons for these legal divisions of the United Kingdom are historical; we need only concern ourselves with Scotland.

1.02 There is an independent Scottish legal system today because until the Union of the Crowns in 1603 and the Union of the Parliaments in 1707 Scotland was an independent sovereign state. When King James VI of Scotland became James I of England and Great Britain in 1603, there was considerable interest in the possibility of establishing a single legal system for the newly-united kingdoms, while during the Cromwellian interlude of the 1650s the possibility moved some way towards an actuality. The 1707 Act of Union showed a recognition that the establishment of a single legal system and body of law for the whole of the United Kingdom was not really a practical proposition. Article XVIII provided for the continuation of Scots law after the Union, excepting only the 'Laws concerning Regulation of Trade, Customs and ... Excises', which were to 'be the same in Scotland, from and after the Union as in England'. Change to Scots law was allowed under the article, but in matters of 'private right' such change had to be for the 'evident utility' of the Scottish people. Only in matters of 'public right' might the aim be simply to make the law the same throughout the United Kingdom.

1.03 Article XIX of the Union laid down that the principal Scottish courts, the Court of Session and the High Court of Justiciary, should 'remain in all time coming' as they were then constituted, subject only to regulations for the better administration of justice which the new British Parliament might choose to make. The article also stated that all the other Scottish courts should remain, 'but subject to Alterations by the Parliament of Great Britain'. If you have already taken the point which flows from the absence of qualification to this last quotation, namely that such alterations to the other courts do *not* have to be for the better administration of justice, you are well on your way to thinking like a lawyer. A final point in article XIX was that Scottish cases were not to be dealt with in the English courts 'in Westminster-hall', which likewise continued their pre-Union existence.

1.04 These articles remain as the formal basis for the continuing existence of an independent Scottish legal system and law. This is why when you live and work in Scotland you are governed by laws which may well be and often are quite different from those found in the other parts of the United Kingdom. It is also why, when you study law in Scotland, it will probably be Scots law that is the basis for your course. This is very important if you want to be a lawyer. If you take a law degree in Scotland, the quickest route to final professional qualification thereafter will also be in Scotland. If you think you want to practise law in England and Wales, or in Northern Ireland, you are probably best to take your degree in the jurisdiction concerned. But this is not absolute. Dundee University offers both a Scottish and an English law degree. Also, for reasons and by routes to be discussed later (see paras **8.09–8.12**), a Scottish law degree can be used to obtain professional qualifications elsewhere in the United Kingdom (not to mention the rest of the world). So you need not feel that you are restricting yourself to a purely Scottish legal career when you embark upon a Scots law degree. Of course, if you have no intention of becoming a lawyer, then the question of where you took your law degree matters a great deal less.

1.05 The remainder of this chapter sets out in simple terms some of the major characteristics of the Scottish legal system as it has taken shape since the 1707 Union. The choice of topics has been dictated by what is needed for understanding some of the discussions later in the book. The main perspective chosen is a historical one, which offers the easiest way of explaining some of the quirks in a system which, having developed slowly over time rather than being produced according to a grand overall design, is not always straightforward.

THE SCOTTISH LEGAL SYSTEM:THE LEGISLATURE

European, UK and Scottish legislative bodies

1.06 In modern terms, a legislature is a body which has the function of making new law. Within the United Kingdom, as already indicated, until 1999 this role was mainly carried out by the Westminster Parliament (website: http://www.parliament.uk/), and the Scottish legal system had no legislature of its own after the Union of the Parliaments of England and Scotland in 1707. The United Kingdom's accession to the European Communities on 1 January 1973, implemented by the European Communities Act 1972, had meant the addition of a further legislative authority in the legal system. The European Community makes law principally through the Council (of Ministers), but generally this body can act only on a proposal from the Community's executive (or civil service), the Commission (website: http://europa.eu.int/comm/index_en.htm). The elected European Parliament, based in Strasbourg and with offices in Brussels (website: http://www.europarl.eu.int/home/default_en.htm), has an increasingly important role in Community legislation, including the opportunity to request the Commission to introduce legislation, to amend Council draft legislation under the co-operation procedure, and to reject it altogether under the co-decision procedure. The European Parliament also checks that the proposed legislation is within the competence of the Community and complies with all mandatory procedural and substantive rules[1].

1   The European Union, created by the Maastricht Treaty 1992, is founded upon and embraces the European Community (which therefore continues to exist) and two other 'pillars' (ie common foreign and security policy and police and judicial co-operation in criminal matters). These Union competences are not subject to the democratic and judicial controls of the Community system. It is therefore still correct to speak of 'Community' rather than 'Union' law.

1.07   In May 1999 the Scottish Parliament, which had been set up under the Scotland Act 1998, began to sit in Edinburgh[1]. The initial sessions of its 129 members (MSPs) were in the Church of Scotland Assembly Hall on The Mound. In 2004, after a long and expensive construction saga, a purpose-built home opened at Holyrood. From the beginning the Scottish Parliament has had an excellent website (http://www.scottish.parliament.uk/). Under Schedule 5 of the Scotland Act the Parliament has power to make laws on any topic not specifically reserved to the Westminster Parliament, which also retains the power to legislate in the areas otherwise devolved to Edinburgh. This reflects a traditional theory about government in the United Kingdom known as the 'Supremacy of Parliament' (ie Westminster), which means that Parliament is legislatively omnicompetent, the courts must apply the laws it makes no matter how abhorrent or repugnant they may be, and other bodies can only legislate so far as allowed to do so by Westminster. However, many people now think that this doctrine is out of date or in need of modification. It first had to be adjusted when Britain entered the European Community in 1973. A fundamental principle of Community law is that national law is subject to Community rules, and where the two are inconsistent, the latter prevails. There are now several examples of British statutes being over-ridden in our courts on this ground. Accordingly the supremacy of Parliament has ceased to be absolute. A further constraint was introduced when the Human Rights Act 1998 came into force on 2 October 2000. Under this Act a court can declare Westminster legislation to be incompatible with the European Convention on Human Rights (ECHR), in effect requiring Parliament to change the law in question to make it compatible with the Convention. In practice, Westminster also does not legislate very often in the areas which have been devolved to the Scottish Parliament, and so there is a further, factual, limitation on the supremacy of Westminster. The Scottish Parliament is also able to repeal or amend Westminster legislation which is among the devolved matters.

1   At the same time there came into existence the Scottish Executive, the civil service supporting the Scottish Ministers who form the governing group in the Scottish Parliament. See the Scottish Executive website: http://www.scotland.gov.uk/. There is also still the Westminster Government's Scotland Office in Whitehall, much reduced in significance compared to the former Scottish Office: see its website: http://www.scottishsecretary.gov.uk/index.htm.

1.08   It has been argued for many years that in Scotland there is another limitation upon the supremacy of Westminster, arising from the provisions of the 1707 Union already referred to (above, paras **1.02–1.03**). Thus the legislation providing for Britain's accession to the European Community was challenged on the grounds that it was not for the 'evident utility' of the people of Scotland (*Gibson v Lord Advocate* 1975 SC 136), while claims were also made that the community charge or poll tax legislation for Scotland (the Abolition of Domestic Rates etc (Scotland) Act 1987) and the Skye Bridge toll charges infringed the Act of Union by not making, in a matter of 'excise', ie taxation, equal provision with respect to England (*Murray v Rogers* 1992 SLT 221; *Fraser v MacCorquodale* 1992 SLT 229; *Robbie the Pict v Hingston (No 2)* 1998 SLT 1201). The Scottish courts have always rejected such claims when made, but have never said that it is absolutely impossible to challenge legislation on the grounds of inconsistency with the Act of Union. It remains to be seen whether a successful challenge will ever be brought.

1.09 The supremacy doctrine will not apply to the Scottish Parliament in its own right, since legislation beyond its devolved powers or contrary to either Community law or the ECHR will be challengeable in court and is not to be given any effect as law. So far the legislation passed by the Scottish Parliament has survived challenges made to it in court[1].

1   See *A v Scottish Ministers* 2002 SC (PC) 63; *Adams v Scottish Ministers* 2003 SLT 366 aff'd 2004 GWD 18-384; *Whaley v Lord Advocate* 2004 SLT 425.

Legislative procedure

(a) Westminster Parliament

1.10 The Westminster Parliament is bicameral: that is, divided into two chambers, the House of Commons and the House of Lords. Before any new measure, or Bill, can become law, it must be passed by both Houses and receive the Royal Assent (this last stage being a formality in modern constitutional practice). The laws passed at Westminster are known as Acts or statutes. Statutes can also confer power on bodies other than Parliament (eg a government minister or a local authority) to make law for defined purposes: there is a vast amount of such subordinate legislation, or statutory instruments, every year. In carrying out its legislative function, Parliament may make a statute which is applicable to Scotland only, and not to the rest of the United Kingdom (although this is much less likely since devolution). The easy way to identify such a statute is because the word 'Scotland' appears in its title: eg the Law Reform (Miscellaneous Provisions) (Scotland) Act 1990 or the Age of Legal Capacity (Scotland) Act 1991. But the absence of such an identifier in its title does not mean that the statute is inapplicable to Scotland, and there is no practice of inserting 'England and Wales' into statute titles even when the legislation is indeed limited to that jurisdiction. Instead you usually have to look for a section saying that the statute is not applicable to Scotland. It is also perfectly possible for a statute to be applicable throughout the United Kingdom. Examples you are likely to encounter on a law course include the Companies Acts, the Finance Acts (which lay down the law on general taxation) and the Consumer Credit Act 1974. Very often, however, these United Kingdom statutes are cast in the technical language of English law, and a Scots lawyer reading them has to look for the section of the Act, usually headed 'Application to Scotland', in which these terms are translated into Scottish legal terminology. The Parliamentary draftsmen who write the text of statutes refer to such sections as 'putting a kilt' on the legislation. A further legislative technique is to deal with both Scotland and the other countries in one statute, but to give each jurisdiction its own part or parts within the text. Examples of this which again you are likely to encounter in law studies are the Unfair Contract Terms Act 1977 and the Insolvency Act 1986.

(b) Scottish Parliament

1.11   The Scottish Parliament is unicameral, and Bills need only be passed by its single chamber and receive the Royal Assent to become Acts. There are complex pre-legislative procedures designed to ensure as far as possible that legislation passed by the Scottish Parliament is within its devolved competence. The committees of the Parliament also play an important role in the scrutiny of legislation in draft. An Act of the Scottish Parliament (asp) is usually identified in its short title by the appearance in it of the bracketed word 'Scotland' – for example, the Adults with Incapacity (Scotland) Act 2000. Some asps do however only have the word 'Scottish' to indicate their origin – for example, the Scottish Local Government (Elections) Act 2002. Asps may also be cited by year and their numbers in the sequence of passage in that year, eg the two Acts just mentioned are respectively asp 2000, no 4, and asp 2002, no 1. The appearance of this reference after the short title will tell you whether the Act comes from Holyrood or Westminster. Such Acts can only extend to Scotland or, more accurately, can only form part of Scots law.

1.12   One further point worth mentioning briefly is that Acts of the pre-1707 Scottish Parliament still form part of the law so far as not repealed at

Westminster or, from 1999 onwards, at Holyrood. Further, those not so repealed are not necessarily protected from challenge in the courts. It is also possible to argue in court that pre-1707 legislation has 'fallen into desuetude', that is, disuse, and is no longer observed. Most of the pre-1707 Acts which have not already been repealed or held in desuetude are probably now unlikely to be subject to this kind of challenge, but one never knows when an obscure old law may be dug up if it will serve someone's purpose to do so. In these circumstances a doctrine of 'desuetude' can be useful; on the other hand, sometimes ancient law can provide helpful solutions not available in more modern sources[1].

1 See for example *Britton v Johnstone* 1992 SCLR 947, reviving the Curators Act 1585.

(c) European legislative procedures

1.13 The foundation documents of the European Union are the Treaty of Rome 1957, and its subsequent amendments by the Single European Act 1986, the Treaty on European Union made at Maastricht 1992, the Treaty of Amsterdam 1997, and the Treaty of Nice 2001[1]. Under these treaties, the two main forms of Community legislation are Regulations and Directives. Regulations are *directly applicable* as law throughout the Community, often giving citizens enforceable rights. Directives require only member states to take action in their own legislatures within a certain period, but may nonetheless have *direct effect* in giving citizens rights as well in the event of faulty or non-implementation by their member state. In the United Kingdom, Directives are typically carried through by a statute or by statutory instruments using powers under the European Communities Act 1972, with the Scottish Parliament or Executive also having responsibility in devolved matters. Community legislative power is gradually being extended, although the Treaty of Maastricht recognised (but did not define) a principle of 'subsidiarity', whereby decisions are to be taken as closely to the citizen as possible and in areas outside its exclusive competence the Community will act only if the objectives in question cannot be sufficiently achieved by the member states themselves. The political problem lies, of course, in defining when the objective cannot be sufficiently achieved by the member states and can be best achieved by the Community.

1 These may be replaced by the Constitution of the European Union, which was under debate at the time of writing (April 2004).

Background to legislation

1.14   What lies behind the production of legislation? A whole variety of factors political, social and economic may be at work, depending on what it is the legislation is trying to achieve. Part of the function of government is to identify problems which require change or addition to the law. Usually, when a government intends to introduce legislation, its proposals are preceded by consultation and discussion papers in which the problems are set out and options for new law put forward. The aim of these documents is to obtain general comment and criticism which can be taken on board before draft legislation is put to the legislature. This is the opportunity for interested persons and pressure groups to have their initial say on the matter; these opportunities continue for as long the legislation is being debated in the legislature. Of course interested persons and pressure groups do not have to wait until government decides to take action; a crucial part of the political process is persuading government to take action. If the government is unpersuadable, or unwilling to find time to take action, attention may shift to individual members of the legislature, who can also propose new legislation. One of the problems in this is that a great deal of the most important subject-matter of the law is not very interesting politically – few votes are usually to be won in dealing with technical difficulties in the law of contract or trusts, for example – but reform may nonetheless be very necessary. In 1965, to help keep the more technical areas of the law up-to-date in the United Kingdom, the then-government established the Law Commissions, one for England and Wales and one for Scotland. The Scottish Law Commission, which is based in Edinburgh (website: http://www.scotlawcom.gov.uk/), works to programmes of law reform, monitoring particular areas of law, issuing consultation papers on problems and possible reforms, and reporting to government with legislative proposals and draft Bills. Many important legislative changes in Scots law have followed from the activities of the Commission.

THE SCOTTISH LEGAL SYSTEM: THE COURTS

1.15   As we have seen, while the 1707 Union got rid of the then Scottish Parliament, it preserved the Scottish court system. In 1707 the principal courts were the Court of Session and the High Court of Justiciary. The latter dealt with criminal cases and the former with non-criminal, or civil, cases. (The distinction between civil and criminal will be explained later on: see paras **1.33–1.38**.) Both courts continue to function to this day[1]. The Court of Session sits in Parliament House in Edinburgh, just behind St Giles Kirk on the High Street. The building incorporates the hall where the pre-1707 Scottish Parliament met, which is well worth a visit in its own right. The High Court of Justiciary also sits in Parliament House, but in addition the Court goes 'on circuit' in other towns. In 1999 special legislation was passed to enable the High Court to sit in the Netherlands for the trial of the two Libyans accused of bombing the jet airliner which exploded over Lockerbie in December 1988, killing 279 people. This was, however, a very unusual case, because it is an old tradition that criminal trials should normally be held in the area where the crime was committed. Ordinarily this means that the High Court has to travel on three circuits apart from its Edinburgh or Home sittings: West (Glasgow, Stirling and Oban), North (Perth, Dundee, Aberdeen and Inverness) and South (Ayr, Dumfries and Jedburgh). In Glasgow, the court sits almost permanently.

1 The Scottish courts have a website: http://www.scotcourts.gov.uk. The site also contains information about the sheriff courts, for which see further below, paras **1.21–1.24**.

The Court of Session

1.16 Traditional accounts of the Court of Session date its foundation to 1532. In fact, the court has a much longer history than that. Its origins lie in petitions to the king by his subjects seeking justice. In the fifteenth century the king dealt with these petitions according to the advice of his council, a relatively informal group of advisers made up of senior churchmen, lords and other laymen. The growing number of petitions forced the council to set up special sessions to deal with them. Increasingly certain lords of council came to specialise in its judicial work. By the beginning of the sixteenth century, the 'Lords of Council and Session' were an established grouping, meeting regularly and clearly constituting an institution for the dispensing of justice. The date of 1532 is nevertheless important, because in that year the Pope agreed to let King James V have certain church resources to set up a College of Justice in Scotland. The Lords of Council and Session, headed by a Lord President, formed this new College, but there was no real break with the past in this development, although the Lords now became Senators of the College of Justice. Gradually there also arose a distinction between the Lords Ordinary, who held permanent paid appointments as judges in the court, and the

Extraordinary Lords, who held office at the King's pleasure and were not paid; the latter were to continue until abolished in the eighteenth century.

1.17   After 1532 the Lords of Session firmly established their court as the most important civil court in Scotland. From 1532 on there were 15 Lords, headed by the Lord President. All 15 sat together to determine cases, but generally one would be deputed to take the evidence in the cases before the court reached its decisions. This led to the evolution of the Outer and Inner Houses of the court. The Inner House was where the Lords sat together in an inner room of their building (originally either Edinburgh's Tolbooth, the site of which is marked by the 'Heart of Midlothian' outside St Giles Kirk, or the west end of St Giles itself; then from 1638 the present location of Parliament House); the Outer House was a room near the front where the evidence was heard by the deputed Lord. In the early nineteenth century, this system was rationalised. Some of the Lords came to sit permanently in the Outer House, not only hearing the evidence but deciding the case as well. Henceforth the term 'Lord Ordinary' would only be applied to the judges of the Outer House. The Inner House became a court to which litigants could appeal against the decisions of the Lords Ordinary in the Outer House. Two divisions of the Inner House, each ultimately consisting of four Lords, were created: the First Division, in which the Lord President presides, and the Second Division, in which the Lord Justice-Clerk presides (for whom, see para **1.19** below). These Divisions were of equivalent status.

1.18   This remains in essence the structure of the Court of Session. If you begin an action in the court, you start before a Lord Ordinary in the Outer House. In 2002, 4,855 causes were initiated in the Outer House[1]. To assist with the disposal of this and criminal business (for the extent of which see below, para **1.20**), the 32 Senators have been supplemented by an increasing number of Temporary Judges since 1990[2]. Any appeal against the Lord Ordinary's decision (technically known as a reclaiming motion) goes to one of the two Divisions of the Inner House, where normally three of its judges will consider the matter. In 2002, the Inner House received 204 appeals. Today there are often Extra Divisions in order to get through the case load efficiently. However there are still reminders of the days when the whole court sat together, as it remains possible to convene the Lords, or an odd number of them above three, to reconsider particularly difficult cases or deal with matters of high importance. The decision is then described as a decision of the Whole Court. For a good example, see *Law Hospital NHS Trust v Lord Advocate* 1996 SC 301, which considers when, if at all, life support for a PVS (persistent vegetative state) patient might be withdrawn.

1   Statistics about civil courts here and in later paragraphs are derived from *Civil Judicial Statistics* 2002 (the latest available in April 2004), accessible on the Internet at: http://www.scotland.gov.uk/library5/justice/cjs02-00.asp.

2   See, for a holding that such judges are not contrary to the fair trial provisions of the ECHR, *Clancy v Caird* 2000 SC 441, and note that the number of such judges is now about 20.

The High Court of Justiciary

1.19   The High Court of Justiciary has a longer formal history than the Court of Session. It can trace its origins back to twelfth-century royal officers called justices or justiciars, who enjoyed both a criminal and a civil jurisdiction. In the Middle Ages there were normally two justiciars, one for Scotland north of Forth, one for Scotland south of Forth. Each went on circuit or 'ayre' through the parts of Scotland for which he was responsible, administering royal justice to the king's subjects. Gradually the civil jurisdiction of the justiciars disappeared, confining their activities to criminal matters. By the sixteenth century, there was only one justice or justiciar, known as the Justice General because he had responsibility for all Scotland; but most of the work of holding trials was done by others known as justice deputes. There was also the Justice Clerk, so called originally because he was the clerk to the court – that is, responsible for its records. In the seventeenth century the Lord Justice-Clerk moved 'from the Table (that is, the well of the court) to the Bench', and became a judge. In 1672 the Justiciary was reorganised with a court sitting permanently in Edinburgh, headed by the Lord Justice-General and the Lord Justice-Clerk, and Commissioners of Justiciary, appointed from among the Lords of Session, carrying out the circuit work. In 1830 it was laid down that the office of the Lord Justice-General should be combined with that of the Lord President, and in 1887 it was provided that all the Lords of Session should also be Lords Commissioner of Justiciary. There may now also be Temporary Judges. The final major change giving rise to the court as we know it today was the establishment in 1926 of a Court of Criminal Appeal within the High Court. This followed the notorious miscarriage of justice in the Oscar Slater case, which was exposed by the creator of Sherlock Holmes, Sir Arthur Conan Doyle, leading to the release of a man wrongly convicted of murder in 1909 and imprisoned for nearly 20 years[1]. The Court of Criminal

Appeal sits in Edinburgh, and hears appeals not only from the High Court as a trial court but also from the lower courts with a criminal jurisdiction.

1   See *Slater v HM Advocate* 1928 JC 94.

1.20   Trials in the High Court follow what is called *solemn* procedure, meaning that they are always before a judge and a jury of 15 persons. In 2001/02 there were 332 trials in the High Court and 602 more cases were disposed of on the day of the trial without witnesses giving evidence. In 2002, 2,470 appeals from the High Court and lower criminal courts were lodged with the Court of Criminal Appeal[1].

1   Statistics on the criminal courts here and in later paragraphs are derived from the *Annual Report of the Crown Office and Procurator Fiscal Service 2001/02* (accessible at: http://www.crownoffice.gov.uk/), Scottish Executive *Criminal Proceedings in Scottish Courts 2002* (accessible at: http://www.scotland.gov.uk/stats/bulletins/00312-00.asp), and Scottish Executive Justice Department *Criminal Appeal Statistics 2002* (accessible at: http://www.scotland.gov.uk/stats/bulletins/00285-00.pdf).

The sheriff court

1.21   The 1707 Union preserved other existing Scottish courts in rather less absolute terms than for the Court of Session and the High Court of Justiciary. Of those which have survived to modern times, much the most important is the sheriff court. The sheriff has a very long history in Scotland, going back to the early twelfth century. Originally he was the king's officer in a particular district, and by the end of the thirteenth century Scotland was divided up into a number of these districts, which were known as sheriffdoms (usually co-extensive with the counties which survived as a unit of local government until 1975). The sheriff or, increasingly, his depute, presided over a court which dealt with judicial business arising in the sheriffdom. The office of sheriff became heritable in noble families in many instances, and generally the sheriff depute did the court work. In 1748, following the 1745 Jacobite Rebellion led by Bonnie Prince Charlie, heritable sheriffs were abolished, and the sheriff depute effectively became the sheriff, often having under him sheriffs substitute. In the nineteenth century it became possible to appeal to the sheriff depute from the decisions of his sheriffs substitute. In the twentieth century the judicial titles were rationalised, with the sheriff depute being re-designated as sheriff principal, and the sheriffs substitute becoming simply sheriffs.

1.22 Today there are six sheriffdoms in Scotland, each with its own sheriff principal. The sheriffdoms are in turn divided into sheriff court districts, each having its own sheriff court building. Like the Lord Ordinary in the Outer House of the Court of Session, the sheriff is a judge of first instance in civil matters, sitting alone. There are relatively few civil cases which cannot be begun in the sheriff court so long as the court has jurisdiction over the defender by virtue of his residence in the sheriffdom, and over the subject matter of the action. The main excluded topics are declarators of nullity of marriage and reduction (ie nullification) of documents. The court has privative jurisdiction in civil actions for under £1,500. Procedure varies: most actions will follow what is called *ordinary* procedure, but there also exist the less formal *summary* cause and *small claim* procedure for actions of up to, respectively, £1,500 and £750 in value. A grand total of 46,605 ordinary causes, 36,465 summary causes and 32,256 small claims were initiated in the sheriff courts in 2002. To assist the sheriffs permanently based in particular sheriffdoms, there are now over 100 part-time sheriffs who may sit from time to time in any sheriffdom. These replaced the previous 'temporary' sheriffs, whose dependence on the head of the criminal prosecution service (the Lord Advocate – see further para **1.36** below) for their continuation in office was held to disable them from holding an objectively fair trial, contrary to Article 6 of the ECHR[1].

1   See *Starrs v Ruxton* 2000 JC 208; *Millar v Dickson* 2002 SC (PC) 30.

1.23 The sheriff's decisions may, in most cases, be appealed to the sheriff principal of the sheriffdom or, in ordinary causes only, to the Inner House. In 2002 only 80 appeals were initiated from a sheriff direct to the Inner House, while there were 399 to the sheriff principal. The appeal to the sheriff principal is unusual in that the appeal is from one single judge to another, contrary to the usual situation where the appellate court is made up of a greater number of judges than decided the case at the previous level (evident, for example, in the hierarchy of Outer House (1 judge), Inner House (3), and House of Lords (5), for the last of which see further paras **1.25–1.26**). This norm reasserts itself in the event of a further appeal from the sheriff principal, which will be heard by three judges in the Inner House. This seems to be a relatively rare event; there were only 15 such appeals in 2002.

1.24 The criminal jurisdiction of the sheriff court is also wide, but it is excluded from the major crimes (murder, rape, treason and piracy) which must be tried in the High Court of Justiciary. Most other criminal cases can be tried in the sheriff court, but its powers of sentence are limited according to the procedure adopted in the prosecution. Procedure may be *solemn*, before a jury, as in the High Court, or *summary*, before the sheriff sitting alone. The maximum sentence of imprisonment which a sheriff sitting with a jury can impose from 1 May 2004 is five years. If a person convicted in the sheriff court is thought to merit a longer sentence, the case is remitted to the High Court, which alone has the requisite powers to give it. The prosecutor may also decide in advance of a trial to bring the prosecution in the High Court rather than the sheriff court if it is thought that the greater sentencing powers of the High Court ought to be used in the event of conviction. By contrast, very petty crimes will often be prosecuted in the local district court, where procedure is always summary and the judge (known as a justice of the peace) is not a lawyer. (Note however that in Glasgow district courts the judge is a lawyer and is known as a stipendiary magistrate[1].) In 2002 there were 41,745 summary disposals in district courts, and another 79,031 in the sheriff court. This compared with 3,282 solemn disposals in the sheriff court and 892 in the High Court. Appeal lies to the High Court of Justiciary as the Court of Criminal Appeal from both the sheriff and the district court. There were 2,018 such appeals in 2002.

1   In March 2004 the Summary Justice Review Committee recommended to the Scottish Ministers the abolition of the district court and its replacement with a new 'summary sheriff' with power to imprison for up to 12 months and to fine up to £20,000: see: http://www.scotland.gov.uk/library5/justice/sjrcrm-00.asp.

The House of Lords

1.25   There have been four major additions to the Scottish court structure since 1707. The first of these is the Appellate Committee of the House of Lords, to which there is an appeal from the Inner House of the Court of Session. Between 1988 and 2002 the number of Scottish appeals to the House of Lords per year varied from 2 to 15. The House of Lords is better-known as the upper chamber of Parliament, but it also has a judicial function in which it is headed by a government minister, the Lord Chancellor, and an appointed judge known as the Senior Law Lord[1]. This combination of judicial with legislative and executive functions has been questioned and may be the subject of reform designed to keep the different branches of government more clearly apart (see further below, para **1.31**). The origins of the present system lie in the pre-1707 English Parliament. Before 1707 the question of whether an appeal lay from the Court of Session to the Scottish Parliament was a controversial one which induced an advocates' 'strike' in 1674, but in the Union negotiations it seems to have been quietly assumed that there would be an appeal to the new British Parliament. Although the House of Lords was an English court before 1707, it did not sit in Westminster Hall (see above para **1.03**). Nothing, therefore, was said about the matter in the 1707 Union itself, but immediately after the Union was concluded, the practice of appealing from the Court of Session to the House of Lords began and was accepted. The House is also the final court of appeal in the English and Northern Irish legal systems, and its judges, known properly as Lords of Appeal in Ordinary and sometimes also as Law Lords, are drawn from all three jurisdictions. Formerly the Lord Chancellor presided in the court when he sat, but now that honour falls to the appointed Senior Law Lord, or if he is not sitting, the most senior in terms of length of service. At one time the whole House of peers was eligible to hear appeals but since the beginning of the nineteenth century professional judges have been appointed as the Law Lords, and now they alone are entitled to deal with appeals to the House. There are no more than 12 full-time Law Lords, of whom two are Scots lawyers. Since an appeal is normally heard by five Law Lords, and decisions are by a majority, this can mean that on a Scots appeal the views of the Scots lawyers in the House can be defeated by the contrary opinions of their English and Northern Irish brethren[2]. In practice the non-Scots on the panel usually defer to the Scots, and controversy is more likely to flow from the fact that the two Scots sitting in London can effectively over-rule what may be the unanimous view of the Court of Session in Edinburgh[3].

1   The Appellate Committee of the House of Lords has a website: http://www.publications.parliament.uk/pa/ld199697/ldjudgmt/ldjudgmt.htm.
2   See eg *Cleisham v British Transport Commission* 1964 SC (HL) 8.
3   See eg *Sharp v Thomson* 1997 SC (HL) 66; contrast *Burnett's Trustee v Grainger* 2004 UKHL 8, 2004 SLT 513 (HL).

1.26   Although in England, Wales and Northern Ireland the House of Lords hears criminal appeals, there is no similar appeal from the High Court of Justiciary. Curiously this point was not finally determined until as late as 1876[1]. There have been suggestions from time to time that the establishment of such an appeal would be of benefit to Scots criminal law, but the development seems an unlikely one.

1   *Mackintosh v Lord Advocate* (1876) 3 R (HL) 34.

The European Court of Human Rights

1.27   The United Kingdom was the first country to ratify the European Convention on Human Rights 1950, and has been subject to the jurisdiction of the European Court of Human Rights in Strasbourg since 1966[1]. The Court's role is to adjudicate in claims that a member state has infringed a person's Convention rights, and there have been a number of cases emanating from Scotland[2]. The Human Rights Act 1998 enables issues about Convention rights to be aired in domestic courts as well, but the jurisdiction of the Strasbourg court continues. Although British courts must take the decisions of the European Court of Human Rights into account in reaching their own decisions, there is no other direct relationship such as an appeal or a reference for guidance (see further para **1.28** below).

1   For the court's website, see: http://www.echr.coe.int/.
2   See eg *Campbell and Cosans v UK* (1982) 4 EHRR 293; *McMichael v UK* (1995) 20 EHRR 205.

The European Court of Justice

1.28   The next major addition to the Scottish court system came about when the United Kingdom entered the European Community in 1973. The Community is a legal order within the European Union (see above, paras **1.06**, **1.13**), dependent on laws to achieve its political, economic and social goals. When disputes arise about the application of these laws, therefore, it is necessary for them to be resolved in courts. The courts of the member states must apply Community law, even where it conflicts with the law of the member state concerned. However, there may be questions about the *validity* of Community law, and national courts have a duty to refer such questions to the European Court of Justice. Again, when issues about the *interpretation* of Community law arise, the national court has a power (and, if it is a court of last instance, a duty) to refer the point to the European Court of Justice for a preliminary ruling on its meaning. Such references are not the same thing as an appeal, since once the European Court has made its ruling, the case is returned to the national court, which then has to apply the ruling in making its decision. There have not been many references from Scottish courts to the European Court (only 10 from Scotland between 1973 and April 2004, whereas, at the time of writing, Austria has produced 234 since its accession in 1995). As the Community expands its scope, more Community law questions may arise requiring an answer[1]. On the other hand, national courts are not bound to refer

Community law points to the European Court unless they are courts of last instance, and as knowledge, understanding and experience of Community law increase, so national courts should feel increasingly confident of their own powers of interpretation.

1   For important examples of Scottish references, see Case C-394/96 *Brown v Rentokil Ltd* [1998] ECR I-4185, and Joined Cases C-20 and 64/00 *Booker Aquaculture Ltd v Scottish Ministers* [2003] ECR I-7411.

1.29   The European Court sits in Luxembourg and is made up of one judge from each of the member states. Of the four British judges to have served on the court so far, two were Scots lawyers: Lord Mackenzie Stuart (1973–1988) and David Edward (1992–2004). In addition to the judges, there are eight Advocates-General, whose function is to assist the court in reaching its decisions by presenting reasoned submissions on cases brought before it. The court's jurisdiction is not confined to references from national courts; it also deals with disputes between the Community's other institutions, on the one hand, and between member states, commercial enterprises and its own staff on the other. For the court's website, see: http://curia.eu.int/en/. With the growth of the court's workload beginning to over-burden it, a new Court of First Instance was established in 1989 to deal with some of the cases, but this does not (yet) include questions referred by the national courts. Decisions of this court may be appealed on points of law (*Pourvoi*) to the Court of Justice.

The Judicial Committee of the Privy Council

1.30   The latest addition to the Scottish court system is the Judicial Committee of the Privy Council, which under the Scotland Act 1998 is the court of last resort in the determination of disputes about the legislative competence of the Scottish Parliament and other 'devolution issues'[1]. Because devolution issues include the acts of the Lord Advocate as the public prosecutor of crime (see below, para **1.36**), this jurisdiction has meant Scottish criminal cases going to London for the first time. In 2000, 13 such appeals were lodged, the first year of the court's operation in this capacity, but only 2 in 2001 and 3 in 2002. A new Law Officer who under the Scotland Act has considerable responsibility in bringing devolution issues to the attention of the courts is the Advocate General. The first holder of that office is Lynda Clark QC, and there is a website: http://www.scottishsecretary.gov.uk/ags.htm.

1   See further its website: http://www.privy-council.org.uk/output/page5.asp. For statistical information see http://www.privy-council.org.uk/output/Page34.asp.

A United Kingdom Supreme Court?

1.31   In February 2004 the UK government introduced a Constitutional Reform Bill under which the office of Lord Chancellor would be abolished, and the devolution jurisdiction of the Judicial Committee of the Privy Council merged with that of the Appellate Committee of the House of Lords in a new Supreme Court for the United Kingdom. The new court would replace the Appellate Committee of the House of Lords completely. The Bill proved controversial, and the outcome of the debate was unclear at the time of writing (April 2004).

Other courts and other ways of dealing with disputes

1.32   There are many other courts within the Scottish legal system – for example the district court, which deals with petty crime (but see above, para **1.24**, note 1), and the Lyon Court, which deals with questions of armorial bearings – but a knowledge of these not being essential for the purposes of this book, you should go to the standard works of reference for further information about them. It is worth knowing, however, that the courts do not provide the only forum for the resolution of disputes in Scotland. In various areas of the law Parliament has established specialist tribunals in place of the courts. Examples which you are likely to encounter in the course of your studies of law include the Lands Tribunal for Scotland, Employment Tribunals, the Copyright Tribunal and Social Security Appeal Tribunals. In addition, there is private dispute settlement of various forms, avoiding altogether the use of instruments of dispute resolution provided by the state. Arbitration, where disputing parties agree to allow a third person to determine the matter, is probably the best-known. Other forms of dispute resolution, such as mediation and conciliation in which a third party strives to bring the parties to an agreement ending their dispute, are becoming more significant. These other forms are often known as 'Alternative (or Appropriate) Dispute Resolution' (ADR). Lawyers are commonly involved in all these procedures, and are also long versed in the negotiated settlement of disputes on behalf of clients. The difficulty with studying these extremely important mechanisms for bringing disputes to an end is that they are private; unlike the decisions of the courts, the results are not usually published and made available for outsiders to assess. This, of course, is often a major advantage from the point of view of the participants. But you should be aware that the courts do not provide the only way of deciding disputes in society, and that the practice of law will frequently involve the use of the other methods available.

STRUCTURE OF THE LAW

Criminal law and civil law

1.33 The discussion of the courts illustrates a general point about law which is often not well understood by the public at large. Law is not just about criminals and wrongdoing. Indeed, the great bulk of the law has nothing to do with criminal matters (or indeed the courts). But the fact that there is a separate structure of courts to deal with *criminal law* shows how important a part of the law it is, dealing as it does with the maintenance of good order, the infliction of punishment by the state upon wrongdoers, and the maintenance of individual liberty. This last is very important. Recent instances of miscarriage of criminal justice in England have shown how necessary is that part of the criminal law which deals with the protection of the accused, in particular the need for proof beyond reasonable doubt. Many of the English convictions recently reversed rested on the evidence of confessions to the police which on their own would have been insufficient for conviction in Scotland, because in the Scots law of criminal evidence, evidence must be corroborated – that is, there must be at least two independent sources – before a conviction can rest upon it[1].

1   This of course does not mean that miscarriages of justice never occur in Scotland. The Scottish Criminal Cases Review Commission was established in 1999 to consider cases of this kind and where appropriate refer them to the High Court of Justiciary for reconsideration: see the Commission's website: http://www.sccrc.org.uk/.

1.34 Those parts of the law which are not criminal law are usually referred to as forming the *civil law*, and lawyers will talk of being either civil or criminal practitioners. There are a number of aspects to the distinction other than the different court systems, but they should not be over-stressed. For example, criminal law is concerned with the conduct which people should not pursue if they wish to avoid various forms of punishment, while a good deal of civil law provides rules about the steps which people should take to achieve a desired result: making a contract for the sale of a house, for example, or setting up a company. However, civil law is also concerned with conduct which should be avoided. Its response to such conduct is not the punishment of the wrongdoer, but the compensation (usually through some financial award) of the person who suffers loss or injury as a result. For example, civil law says that people should pay their debts, and enables the unpaid creditor to claim payment through the courts, with the back-up that if the debtor still fails to pay the courts will supervise a seizure of his assets to satisfy the claim. On the other hand, criminal courts have powers over and above their penal ones to order convicted persons to compensate their victims, and are also being encouraged to use more imaginative forms of sentencing to prevent over-crowding of the prisons. Community service is one example.

1.35 Both civil and criminal law may be invoked in response to particular events. Suppose for example that, driving carelessly, I knock down a pedestrian and severely injure her. There may well be a criminal prosecution here but in addition the pedestrian can sue me in the civil courts for damages which will compensate her for her losses and suffering following the incident. The reason that civil claims in respect of criminal acts are infrequent is because often criminals have no assets, which makes suing them for damages not worthwhile. In road accident cases, however, civil action is worthwhile because the driver has to be insured by law. If the driver has no insurance, the injured person may recover compensation from another organisation, the Motor Insurers Bureau (MIB), set up by the motor insurance industry and operating under an agreement with the Government[1].

1   Website: http://www.mib.org.uk/index.asp. Note also that a party injured by criminal violence (which does not include a traffic offence) may be able to get compensation from a government body, the Criminal Injuries Compensation Authority, website: https://www.cica.gov.uk/.

1.36 Another important point of distinction between the civil and the criminal law is that generally criminal prosecutions are conducted by the state, while civil court actions are brought by the person affected by the wrongdoing. Criminal prosecution in Scotland is ultimately in the hands of the Lord Advocate and the Solicitor General for Scotland, the Law Officers of the Crown in Scotland. The Lord Advocate heads the Crown Office, a central government department based in Chambers Street in Edinburgh (website: http://www.crownoffice.gov.uk/). Criminal prosecutions in the High Court are in the name of the Lord Advocate (Her Majesty's Advocate, or HMA) but are usually actually conducted by Advocates Depute appointed from the Faculty of Advocates (see below, para **2.45**). At the level of the sheriff and district courts, however, prosecution is in the hands of the procurators fiscal, of whom there is one in each sheriffdom heading the fiscal's office. The fiscal is also in charge of the criminal investigations of the police, giving rise to the familiar phrase in news reports that 'the police have sent a report to the Procurator Fiscal'. It is the fiscal who takes the initial decision on whether or not to prosecute. An Advocate Depute will make the final decision on whether or not a prosecution should take place in the High Court, but will not be involved in any cases which the fiscal decides to prosecute summarily.

1.37 Yet even this distinctive characteristic of Scottish criminal law is subject to the exception that private prosecution, usually by the victim of crime, remains possible in Scotland where the public prosecutor, for whatever reason, has exercised his discretion not to prosecute. This was made clear by the sensational Glasgow rape case in 1982, where the victim raised her own prosecution after the Crown Office, concerned that she was not fit to give evidence, had decided not to go ahead[1].

1   See *X v Sweeney* 1982 JC 70.

1.38 A final distinction between criminal and civil law might be the greater use of the jury in criminal cases. On the civil side a jury can only be used in the Court of Session and in certain types of case (most notably personal injuries, reduction of wills, and defamation actions). Even in such cases the jury (which would be 12 in number) is rarely employed. By contrast, all High Court prosecutions must be tried before a judge and a jury of 15 persons. But in criminal cases in the sheriff court it is more common for the sheriff to sit alone than with a jury, while criminal procedure in the district court is always summary. (See the statistics quoted at para **1.24** above.) It is worth noting that it is the prosecutor who decides whether a case merits jury trial in Scotland. In England, it is a right of the accused.

Public law and private law

1.39 The distinction between civil and criminal law may be blurred in part but it is important in practice. Another distinction which you will encounter in law is more likely to be of importance in your studies than in legal practice. That is the distinction between public law and private law. You may find these phrases in course names and structures of the law school; you will certainly find them in the syllabi of professional examinations administered by the Law Society of Scotland and the Faculty of Advocates (see below, para **3.03**, Table 1). The distinction lies in the extent to which the law directly involves the state. *Public law* is the law relating to the constitution and government of the United Kingdom, or that affecting relationships between the state and citizens. *Private law* is the law dealing only with relationships between private persons (who might include organisations such as companies, trade unions and charities). In some other legal systems, for example France, the distinction is of significance in practice because actions involving the state are dealt with in different courts and under special rules. It used to be argued that, since in Britain actions involving the state were heard in the same courts and used the same remedies as actions between private persons, the distinction of public and private was meaningless. But the growth of the complex modern state, the development in both Scotland and England of the special procedure known as *judicial review* for use in actions by citizens against the various manifestations of the state, and the fact that many disputes between the individual and the state do now take place in special tribunals (for example, immigration and social security), does suggest that the distinction has increasing relevance in practice as well as in theory.

WHERE AND HOW DO YOU FIND THE LAW?

1.40   Most laymen think of law as a body of rules set out in a text, perhaps in numbered paragraphs, and written in sentences saying, in effect, that if certain events occur a particular consequence will follow. But, although it is useful to think of law as a system of rules, and although much law can be found in texts rather like the ones just hypothesised, in fact the picture this provides is far from complete. Also, even when the law does take the form of a rule book, the rules are often rather difficult to apply because they are not so clear-cut and specific as to mean that getting the legal answer is like feeding a calculation into a computer.

1.41   A great deal of your legal study will be devoted to getting to grips with how to find and determine the scope in particular situations of particular legal rules. Here only the briefest description of where the law is found will be attempted, closely related to the two elements of the legal system already discussed, namely the legislature and the courts.

Legislation

1.42 As should already be clear from the discussion of the legislature, the most important source of law today is legislation: Community Regulations and Directives, Acts of the United Kingdom and Scottish Parliaments, and subordinate legislation produced by bodies which have been empowered to do so. United Kingdom legislation characteristically takes the 'rulebook' form described in para **1.40**, being laid out in numbered paragraphs known as 'sections'. The amount of legislation is enormous, as you can easily gauge by proceeding to the legislation section of your law library and looking at the annual volumes (nowadays several a year) of *Public General Statutes* and *Statutory Instruments* for the United Kingdom and *Acts of the Scottish Parliament* and *Scottish Statutory Instruments* for Scotland, not to mention the *Official Journal of the European Communities* (L Series).

1.43 A quick glance at the contents of these volumes may also suggest some of the problems faced by those who would like to know what the law is on any given subject. Legislation is often cast in detailed technical language or deals with some complex field of activity knowledge of which is taken for granted, with in addition a great deal of internal and external cross-referencing; alternatively it may be put in a very general way, as for example provisions requiring actions and decisions to be based on imprecise criteria of 'reasonableness'. What does it all mean? It is rare for a statute to be a wholly self-sufficient text, and it requires interpretation.

1.44 So often lawyers have to look beyond the legislative text to discover what it means. A very important source will be decisions of the courts on what the statute means; in practice, of course, it is possible to consult many other aids, in particular any of the preparatory material published before and while the statute was a Bill in Parliament such as Law Commission reports, parliamentary debates, and what textbook and other writers on the law think the statute means. In addition, it is quite common for there to be a general professional opinion on what a statute means, even though there is no direct support for it in any written source.

Decisions of the courts (cases)

1.45 So where the law comes closest to being a rulebook, it is nonetheless clear that the rulebook does not provide all the answers in itself. Nor indeed is legislation all the law. There is a great deal of law which is not referable in any way to legislation, usually known as the '*common law*'. This is the law which is to be derived mainly from the decisions of the courts. Here we are certainly not dealing with rulebooks. If you go to the section of the law library containing what are usually grouped under the heading 'Law Reports' and take a volume off the shelf, you will find inside a series of narratives and legal analyses, usually with an opening summary, which constitute reports of cases decided by the courts. The heart of these reports is found in the section which gives what the judges in the case said in justification of the result which they reached on those facts. These judicial opinions are discursive and argumentative in nature; the judge is reasoning his way to a conclusion. The result looks nothing like a rulebook or a statute. Yet it is from this material that lawyers will derive law to be used thereafter.

1.46   Later on (see paras **10.21–10.30**), we will look at how this is done, and at how the status of the case as a source is affected by the status of the court deciding it in the judicial hierarchy described earlier in this chapter (see paras **1.15–1.31**). For the moment, the point to make is that using this material requires certain skills, and it is these skills, among other things, which you should get from your studies. It is also worth noting that with the constant flow of cases as well as legislation the law is never static, and that while lawyers are always looking backwards at what the legislature and the courts have done, in the process they are also moving forward.

Legal writings

1.47   Legal writings – in textbooks and legal journals and periodicals – play an important part in interpreting, synthesising and explaining case law just as they do with legislation. But such legal writings are generally not, according to traditional dogma, sources of law like statutes and cases. Instead they are said to be persuasive according to the reputation of the author. There was once a convention, known as the 'Better Read When Dead' rule, that a book could not be cited in court while its author was still alive, on the ground that only when dead would he be stopped from changing his mind! This has been abandoned, but there are still a number of old books by long-deceased writers which you will see cited in Scottish cases, even though they might be thought to have been superseded by more up-to-date works. Examples of such elderly but authoritative works include *Gloag on Contract* (2nd edition, 1929), *Macdonald's Criminal Law* (5th edition, 1948) and *Rankine on Land Ownership* (4th edition,

1909). In some ways, such books come very close at points to being sources of law in the formal sense.

Institutional writings

1.48 Certain very old books have achieved the status of formal sources of law. These are the so-called institutional works. The main examples are:
— James Dalrymple Viscount **Stair**, *Institutions of the Laws of Scotland*, first published in 1681, most recent edition the 6th published in 1981;
— John **Erskine**, *Institute of the Law of Scotland*, first published in 1773, 8th edition 1871;
— George Joseph **Bell**, *Commentaries on the Mercantile Law of Scotland*, first published in 1800, 7th edition, 1870; and
— David **Hume**, *Commentaries on the Law of Scotland respecting Crimes*, first published in 1797, 4th edition 1844.
All are remarkable works of synthesis and analysis in their respective fields, and they have achieved their status because they are thought to state the common law of Scotland as it was before about 1800, when the modern legislative and law reporting systems really begin. Accordingly if no more recent source can be found, the institutional works stand as the law. Fortunately the courts are not absolutely spell-bound by this idea; see, for example, *S v HM Advocate* 1989 SLT 469, when the High Court of Justiciary overruled Hume's view that in law a man could not rape his wife.

1.49 The institutional writers established a tradition in Scotland whereby writers produced books covering the whole of private law. Modern examples include *Gloag & Henderson's Introduction to the Law of Scotland*, first published in 1927 and now in its 11th edition (2001), and D M Walker's *Principles of Scots Private Law*, first published in 1970 and now in a four-volume 4th edition (1991). These are much used for ready reference by practitioners. Much more ambitious than either is *The Laws of Scotland: Stair Memorial Encyclopaedia*, a 25-volume work completed in 1996 and now being updated in regular supplements and reissues. Although none of these works are formal sources of law, they have great influence in shaping the law as it is generally understood.

Other sources of law: Roman law

1.50 There are some other sources of law. The status of many of these is a result of the history of the law. For example, the law of the ancient

Romans has been an important source historically in Scotland, as in most western legal systems, because the Romans were the first to evolve many of the legal concepts upon which western law has been based. Roman legal writings and ideas were preserved in the *Digest* and *Institutes* compiled in the sixth century at the command of the Emperor Justinian, and rediscovered in the eleventh century. They have proved a fertile source of material for lawyers ever since. This was particularly true in the medieval and early modern periods, in Scotland as elsewhere, and as a consequence there took place in Europe what is usually known as the *Reception* of Roman law into the developing national systems, meaning that even today European legal systems have certain features and characteristics in common (sometimes caught in the Latin phrase, *ius commune Europaeum*). Unsurprisingly, given that the law of a long-dead society was being transplanted into wholly different worlds, the borrowing sometimes produced results that would have surprised the Romans, and this medieval and early modern version of Roman law is sometimes known as the Civil Law (note, avoid confusion with the use of the phrase 'civil law' to mean non-criminal law (above, para **1.34**), the context usually making clear in which sense the phrase is being used if capitalisation of the initial letters (the technique used in this book) does not). The Reception of Roman and Civil Law continues today – a modern example is a case in which the Court of Session made extensive use of Civilian authorities in deciding whether the expense of the destruction of a house by fire fell on seller or buyer when at the time of the fire they had concluded a contract of sale but the formal transfer of ownership had not gone through (*Sloans Dairies Limited v Glasgow Corporation* 1977 SC 223). But generally nowadays, although many rules of Scots law began as borrowings from Roman or Civil Law, it is not necessary to refer directly to the Roman or Civilian texts, as the law is best understood through the specifically Scottish sources.

Other sources of law: English law

1.51   Another important source, both historically and in contemporary practice, is English law. For historical reasons, English law is often referred to as 'the Common Law'. Once again confusion is possible with the usage of 'common law' denoting non-statutory law (above, para **1.45**). The context usually makes clear in which sense the phrase is being used if capitalisation of the initial letters (the technique used in this book) does not. In the medieval period, the feudal land law of Scotland was much influenced by that of England; from the eighteenth century on, the same has been true of commercial law; and in more recent times the law of obligations (contract, delict and unjustified enrichment – see further below, para **3.06**) has often drawn heavily on English cases. Again, as with Roman law, the borrowing has sometimes seemed based on misunderstandings of the English position. In 1852 Lord Justice-Clerk Hope commented that he was 'confident that we do not understand nine out of ten of the English cases which are quoted to us and that in attempts to apply that law we run the greatest risk of spoiling our own by mistaking theirs'[1]. The risk remains today. Of all Western legal systems, England's is the least influenced by Roman law, but in its turn it has had great influence in those parts of the world formerly under the sway of the British Empire. As a result the western legal tradition is sometimes said to be divided between those systems most influenced by Roman law (Civil Law or Civilian systems) and those most influenced by English law (Common Law systems), with the division characterised by radical differences of method and philosophy making one side incompatible with the other. The sharpness of the division can be over-drawn and 'mixed' systems like the Scottish one may show that accommodation between them is more than a possibility.

1   *McCowan v Wright* (1852) 15 D 229 at 232.

Other sources of law: Canon law and Udal law

1.52 The picture would be incomplete without reference to two other historical sources, the influence of which is still felt in modern Scots law. First, until the Reformation of the sixteenth century the unified western church laid claim to exclusive competence in certain legal matters which were held to affect the welfare of the Christian's soul, including marriage, divorce, defamation and wills. Many of the rules of modern Scots law find their origins in this law of the Church, which is known as the Canon Law: for example, marriage by cohabitation with habit and repute, whereby couples who have not been through any formal marriage ceremony may nonetheless be held to be married. The law of evidence and court procedure also shows many signs of canonical influence.

1.53 Second, Orkney and Shetland became part of the Scottish kingdom only in the fifteenth century, having previously been part of Norway and Denmark. Norse law continued in the Northern isles, notably with respect to the 'udal' law of landownership. The most recent of many cases on this subject took place in the Court of Session in 1990, when the issue was the right of the Crown to charge rent to fish farmers whose farms were anchored to the seabed off the Shetlands. In general Scots law the Crown owns the seabed but it was argued by the farmers that this was not so under udal law, which still applied. Sadly, however, the Court held for the Crown and the application of the general law[1].

1   *Crown Estate Commissioners v Shetland Salmon Farmers Association* 1991 SLT 166.

Other sources of law: modern comparative law

1.54   From time to time the Scottish courts look at the contemporary law of countries outside the United Kingdom, in order to gain some idea of parallel developments in other jurisdictions when some new or radical movement in the common law is proposed[1]. Usually these references are to the case law of other English-speaking systems (notably Australia, Canada, New Zealand, South Africa and the United States). But in *Caledonia North Sea Ltd v London Bridge Engineering Ltd* 2000 SLT 1123 (the Piper Alpha case), for example, Lord President Rodger referred to the Civil Codes of France and Germany. The Civilian tradition of Scots law coupled with the European character of Community and human rights law should make such references more common in future, while many lawyers are also beginning to draw upon the law of other 'mixed' legal systems such as South Africa, Louisiana and Québec, which often have striking similarities with Scots law.

1   See for example *Morgan Guaranty Trust Co of New York v Lothian Regional Council* 1995 SC 151, *Law Hospital NHS Trust v Lord Advocate* 1996 SC 301 and *McFarlane v Tayside Health Board* 2000 SC (HL) 1.

1.55   In 1949 Lord President Cooper gave this famous description of Scots law: 'an original amalgam of Roman Law, Feudal Law and native customary law, systematised by resort to the law of nature and the Bible, and illuminated by many flashes of ideal metaphysic'. Perhaps not every Scots lawyer would put it quite this way, but it remains true that Scots law is a product of a long history and many influences. The process continues with the growing significance of European Community and human rights law.

CHAPTER 2

The Scottish legal profession

INTRODUCTION

2.01   In one sense it is true to say that there is no such thing as 'the' legal profession in Scotland. Instead lawyers usually talk about the 'two branches' of the profession. There is traditionally a great divide between the *solicitors*, on the one hand, and the *advocates*, on the other, paralleling the division between solicitors and barristers in England. The origins of the distinction, which are very old, need not concern us here. It can be summarised very simply: all lawyers who are not advocates are solicitors. But modern developments have begun to blur some of the old distinctions between the two branches of the profession.

Rights of audience in the courts

2.02   Advocates are those members of the profession who, by virtue of their membership of the Faculty of Advocates, have a right of audience in the Scottish courts. Formerly this right of audience was exclusive so far as concerned the higher courts – that is, the Court of Session, the High Court of Justiciary and the House of Lords. What this meant was that someone wanting to raise or defend an action in these courts would have to be represented there by an advocate unless prepared to act without professional assistance (that is, be a party litigant). Solicitors could appear only in the lower courts. However, legislation in 1990 – the Law Reform (Miscellaneous Provisions) (Scotland) Act 1990 – removed the advocates' exclusive rights of audience in the higher courts. Now, subject to conditions as to knowledge shown by passing exams, training, experience and general fitness for the task, a solicitor may be granted such rights of audience by the Law Society of Scotland (the governing body of the solicitors' branch of the profession) and become a *solicitor-advocate*. The 1990 legislation went even further than this by enabling members of professions other than law to conduct litigation on behalf of members of the public in any court in Scotland, provided that their professional body had a scheme for such representation which had been approved by the Lord President and the Secretary of State for Scotland. At the time of writing no such scheme had been put forward by any professional body. It remains to be seen whether this option, granted by the Government to encourage more competition in the market for legal services, will ever be taken up.

Distinctions between advocates and solicitors

2.03   Even with the removal of the fundamental monopoly on rights of audience in the higher courts, there remain a number of important distinctions between advocates and solicitors. You cannot practise as both at the same time, and at present solicitors and advocates cannot work together in partnerships. Solicitors' activities are not restricted to court work. Advocates must always practise as individuals on their own account whereas, while solicitors may so practise if they choose, most work in partnerships with other solicitors, or in the employment of solicitors' partnerships, or in the employment of some other organisation. An advocate in court is required to wear a wig (traditionally made of horsehair but sometimes now made of nylon), as well as dark clothing under a black stuff gown. Out of court, the wig and gown come off, but generally smart, reasonably formal clothing would be retained. Solicitors' working attire would always be like that of any other business or professional person – formal but modern and relatively comfortable.

Solicitors' former 'monopolies'

2.04   The solicitor used to have three 'monopolies' which were in some sense the equivalent of the advocate's monopoly on rights of audience in the higher courts. The first of these was concerned with conveyancing. In very general terms, no-one other than a solicitor could draw up certain documents relating to the transfer of property, in particular land and buildings (including houses), and charge fees for doing so. The key documents were those recording the actual transfer from seller to buyer (the disposition), and the mortgage documents (known in Scotland as the standard security). Also a warrant or application for registration of the transfer in whichever is the appropriate land register (without which there is no transfer of ownership) had to be added to the transfer document and signed by a solicitor.

2.05 A second 'monopoly' enjoyed by solicitors concerned executry services. 'Executry' is the legal term for matters concerned with wills and, in particular, the distribution and administration of a deceased person's estate. For fairly obvious reasons – in particular the protection of the deceased's family and creditors – administration and distribution of an estate can only be carried out by executors, who may be appointed either in the will or by the sheriff court. All executors must further be granted what is known as 'confirmation' by the sheriff court, conditions of which include the provision of an inventory of the deceased's estate and a financial guarantee that the estate will be made forthcoming to interested parties. Under the pre-1990 law, although anybody could draw up a will, only solicitors could draw or prepare any papers on which to found or oppose an application for a grant of confirmation in favour of executors, and charge a fee for the service.

2.06 The legal basis of the conveyancing and executry 'monopolies' was removed by the Law Reform (Miscellaneous Provisions) (Scotland) Act 1990 amidst controversy. Under the Act the Scottish Conveyancing and Executry Services Board was set up to regulate the provision of these services by non-solicitors called qualified conveyancers and executry practitioners. However, the Board was abolished by the Public Bodies and Public Appointments etc (Scotland) Act 2003, and its functions have been transferred to the body also regulating solicitors, the Law Society of Scotland (see further below, para **2.11**). See also the website of the Scottish Paralegal Association, http://www.scottish-paralegal.org.uk/.

2.07 The third 'monopoly' was that only solicitors could instruct advocates. Thus a client embarking upon litigation had first to approach a solicitor, who would then instruct an advocate. This too was changed and now, subject to certain conditions, persons who are members of certain other professional bodies may instruct advocates directly, instead of having first to approach a solicitor. Unlike the position with the ability of such professional bodies to obtain rights of audience for their members (see above, para **2.02**), a number of them have taken the opportunity to gain the right to instruct advocates directly. Examples include accountants, surveyors, architects and engineers.

2.08   The purpose of the 1990 Act and other reforms described above was to increase competition in the market for legal services, in the belief that one effect of such competition is to reduce the charges made to members of the public for legal services. This means that lawyers generally are now under greater pressure than ever before to show that the services which they provide are indeed worth the fees charged for them, and to attract business to themselves as opposed to their competitors in other professions. Other recent changes in the laws governing legal practice have made it a little easier to compete in the marketplace: for example, solicitors are now allowed to advertise, although in such advertisements they are not allowed to compare their fees with, or claim superiority of service over, any other solicitor's fees or services. But they can indicate that they are specialists in particular fields of law. Advocates too may advertise now, although only in a very limited way: see below, para **2.45**.

WHAT DO LAWYERS DO?

2.09   Despite the fact that advertising might be expected to lead to better information about and greater understanding of legal services, the work that lawyers do nonetheless remains something of a mystery to the public at large. The mystery is not really removed by popular television programmes such as *Ally McBeal* or *Kavanagh QC*. These tend to focus on the cut and thrust of the courtroom, in particular the criminal law. Yet in the real world the great majority of lawyers have little to do with either the criminal law or the courts. In the remainder of this chapter we will examine what lawyers do with their time, starting with solicitors, since most lawyers belong to this branch of the profession.

SOLICITORS

2.10   In October 2002 there were 9,742 enrolled solicitors in Scotland, of whom 8,926 held practising certificates.[1] About 7,500 (that is, the great majority) of those holding practising certificates were in private practice, that is to say, in solicitors' firms. Accordingly this part will focus mainly on what happens in private practice, although account will be taken later on of those working in the public sector (that is, for employers such as central and local government, NHS trusts, the Crown Office and the fiscal service), and of those working for private sector employers other than solicitors' firms.

1   Figures in this and succeeding paragraphs about numbers of solicitors come from the *Annual Report and Accounts 2002* of the Law Society of Scotland, accessible at http://www.lawsociety.ws/?acr=memb_soc.

Law Society of Scotland

2.11   The solicitors' governing body is the Law Society of Scotland, which is headed by its annually-elected President and Council and has a permanent Secretary and Secretariat based in Edinburgh. The Society also functions by means of committees dealing with particular subjects; the most important of these for readers of this book are the Admissions, the Education and Training, and the Competence Committees. Further details about the Society can be found on its website: http://www.lawscot.org.uk/ .

Solicitors' firms

2.12   Solicitors' firms, of which there were 2,268 in Scotland in April 2004, are usually partnerships, meaning that two or more solicitors (the partners or principals) have agreed to set up in business together and to share the profits thereof. As already mentioned, however, there are firms which consist of a sole practitioner or principal who has chosen to practise on his or her own account without partners. In both cases, there will be other people involved in the firm, who will be employees paid a wage or salary rather than sharing the profits of the business. At the very least there will be clerical and administrative staff, and normally there will also be legally qualified staff, generically known as 'assistants' and often further dignified with the title 'associates', frequently a sign that the assistants concerned are on the way to being assumed as partners in the firm. Nowadays there will often be 'para-legals' carrying out legal work but not qualified as solicitors. Finally, the firm may have 'consultants', usually but not always retired partners whose services and advice are made available to the partners, perhaps especially in matters affecting clients for whose affairs they were previously responsible. Of holders of practising certificates in October 2002, 5,453 were male and 3,473 female. Also at that time, of all solicitors holding practising certificates, 4,324 were under 40 years of age, 2,217 of this group being women, and 2,107 men.

2.13 A key point about a partnership is that the partners share not only the profits but also the losses of the business, and are all liable for each other's work as well as the work of those they employ. It used to be a distinguishing feature of the professions such as law that practice had to be on one's own account or in partnership, because the client who was negligently served could then sue the principals and recover, not just from their business income and assets but from their personal estates as well. In reality, however, it was and is rare for the partner to lose everything in this way, because the liability will usually be covered by professional indemnity insurance. For solicitors the Law Society of Scotland maintains an insurance policy (the Master Policy) which covers professional liability but which is paid for by the Society's members who are principals in private practice. Thus the client does not receive protection so much from the mere fact that solicitors practise in partnership as from the existence of insurance. Accordingly the old requirement to practise in partnership has disappeared, and it is possible (except for sole practitioners) to set up a solicitors' business in the form of a company (an incorporated practice) or as a limited liability partnership. What this means is that the owners of the business may practise with their personal liability limited to the sums they have actually invested in the business itself; and there are said to be some further advantages to the client as well.

2.14 Most (if not all) solicitors' firms continue as partnerships or as sole practitioners, although at present solicitors may only form partnerships with other solicitors. However there has been discussion of the possibility of 'multi-disciplinary practices' (MDPs), in which solicitors would practise inside the same organisation as other professionals such as accountants, surveyors and brokers. In 1992 the Office of Fair Trading suggested that, while the existing restrictions did not unduly restrain or distort competition in the market for legal services, their removal might enhance such competition. At the time of writing, however, no action had followed from this conclusion. Certainly solicitors' firms do already employ members of other professions within their organisation, and it would seem only a small jump to the MDP in which these other professionals could become partners. Multi-national partnerships, in which solicitors enter into practice with foreign lawyers, are now permitted and many firms have also established 'networks' by which they are linked with legal firms in other countries around the world.

Professional discipline

2.15 All solicitors, partners or not, are subject to the discipline of the Law Society of Scotland, which on receipt of a complaint may prosecute before the independent Scottish Solicitors' Discipline Tribunal. This has power to censure, fine, suspend, or have struck off the Roll of Solicitors any solicitor whom it finds guilty of professional misconduct. If the case is one of inadequate professional services, the solicitor's fees may be adjusted. If any client thinks that a complaint about a solicitor has been badly handled by the Law Society, the matter may be referred to the Scottish Legal Services Ombudsman, a person who is neither advocate nor solicitor and is appointed by the Scottish Ministers (see her website, http://www.slso.org.uk/). Where any person suffers pecuniary loss by reason of a solicitor's dishonesty *as a solicitor*, it is made good from the Scottish Solicitors Guarantee Fund, which is administered by the Law Society. Every solicitor in private practice makes an annual contribution (unless the Fund exceeds a certain sum), and where needed may also be required to make a special contribution to cover the Fund's liabilities. As a few unhappy cases have shown all too clearly, the losses which flow to people from a solicitor's dishonesty can run into millions of pounds, so that the profession as a whole can pay a heavy price for the dishonesty of a small number of its members. Fortunately this sort of thing does not happen very often in Scotland.

2.16 Solicitors also remain liable to sued in the courts for damages for professional negligence, quite aside from any of the other remedies just discussed. It is this liability which is covered by the Master Policy of insurance mentioned earlier (para **2.13**).

What solicitors do

2.17 The size of solicitors' firms, and the work they do, varies greatly, and the remainder of this section offers brief descriptions of the major areas while acknowledging that their relative importance in particular instances may be very different. The headings are derived principally from the traditional departmental structure of the modern larger firm, but it should be remembered that many firms will do no or little work in some of the fields mentioned; some of the smaller or medium-sized firms may have no formal departmental structure as such; and nowadays the very large firms tend to organise themselves in smaller specialist teams rather than in departments. It is also worth noting that the basic realities of working life differ little whichever law firm you happen to work in; correspondence has to be maintained, phone calls made and answered, files updated, and the general tenor of office life anywhere kept up. Computerisation of many functions has taken place. Examples include the storage, retrieval and accessing of legal, client and case information, electronic communications with clients and colleagues, and, of course, accounts and billing. Computers are also increasingly used in litigation support; that is, for the electronic storage and retrieval of large quantities of documents which form evidence in a case. The attraction of a solicitor's job remains the variety of the work which comes into the office each day so that, especially in the smaller, less compartmentalised firm, you never know what is coming next.

Private client

2.18   This heading now covers but is not confined to what have been, and in many firms still are, the classic areas of a solicitor's work, namely conveyancing and executry services. At the heart of both of these lies the drafting of formal documents and the following of certain procedures to achieve the client's desired result, but there is a great deal more to them than that, and the knowledge and skills required are not confined strictly to law. For example, involvement in conveyancing will cover the marketing of property, often through 'property shops' such as the Edinburgh and Glasgow Solicitors Property Centres, and advertising, advising selling clients on pricing and description of their property in such advertising, general advice to buying clients on where to look and what to look for, establishing connections with other relevant professionals such as surveyors and with lenders and insurers, ensuring that the seller does indeed own the property being sold, and negotiating acceptable terms and conditions of sale with the other party to the transaction.

2.19   With wills, the solicitor may need to advise on matters such as the charities through which the client's benevolent intentions can be given effect, and how to minimise the incidence of tax, as well as draft the actual document. On the client's death, the solicitor is often an executor; confirmation has to be obtained and the estate distributed. Closely allied to wills is trust work, where the client sets up a fund or property the income of which is directed towards the benefit of others, whether other members of the family or some charity. This requires legal documentation again, as well as administration.

2.20 Solicitors like to present themselves as general personal advisers, and their skills and expertise may cover other matters, notably in the financial, investment, pension and tax planning arena. The administration of a client's property can include not only the management of an investment portfolio but also such matters as the leasing of domestic property, and planning and building warrant applications for house improvement.

2.21 Additionally, almost any of the problems which the individual may encounter in life – be it with debt, defective goods and services, employment, housing, family matters, social security or the difficulties of old age and mental incapacity – can have a legal aspect on which the private client solicitor may be called upon to advise or act, for example by writing appropriate letters or making telephone calls. In many situations, however, the solicitor's role can come down to straightforward personal support for the client in difficult circumstances, with common sense, tact and sympathy being the chief tools rather than law.

2.22 Much of the work in the private client field was already subject to competition from banks, building societies, insurance companies, mortgage brokers and estate agents before the reforms of the 1990 Act, even though the documentary formalities of conveyancing and confirmation had to be carried through by solicitors. With the documentary formalities executable by others as well, solicitors are under even greater pressure to carry out private client work that is competitive on both price and quality. While this should be good for the clients, it does mean that some firms have had to consider whether the profitability of private client work justifies continuing to provide the service. It is also the case that many firms now employ staff unqualified in law (but possibly qualified in other disciplines such as surveying) to carry out work such as valuing and marketing property. This permits more cost-effective use of legally-qualified staff.

Corporate/commercial/company

2.23 Many of the larger firms place most emphasis on commercial rather than private client work. Two major areas can be identified: commercial property, and what may be known as either corporate, company or commercial work. The latter deals principally with the setting-up, financing, development, expansion and winding-up of businesses. It might include advising entrepreneurial clients on the legal forms within which businesses can be set up – partnerships, companies, franchises; how to raise finance by borrowing, use of public resources, share issues and investment; selling the business, management buy-outs, takeovers and mergers, joint ventures and reconstruction; business taxation; the implications of laws regulating competition for the business; negotiating and drafting contracts for business deals; ensuring that the business complies with the legal formalities of business administration; and, when the business terminates or is in difficulties, ensuring that appropriate winding-up procedures or rescue packages are adopted and carried through.

2.24   Businessmen can be sceptical of the services which they receive from lawyers, and in all the fields just mentioned there is no particular protection which solicitors receive from the competition provided by other professions and institutions. In practice, solicitors often find themselves as members of a team of professional advisers retained by the client, and it is unlikely that the client will direct all its business through the solicitor alone. What is always emphasised is the need to be able to work under great pressure, particularly of time, and to produce results that work. It is essential to react quickly to clients' instructions and to meet commercial deadlines. If the financial rewards for commercial work are high, so are its demands. While no lawyer can afford to be a clock-watcher who believes that the working day finishes at 5 pm and that Saturdays and Sundays are days off, this is even less so for the corporate adviser. Once again, it should be noted that in this kind of work knowledge of the relevant law is not enough to make a competent company lawyer; an understanding of the commercial world and in particular of the marketplaces in which the client operates is essential to enable the law to be applied usefully on the client's behalf.

Commercial property

2.25   Similar points may be applied to commercial property, the work in which is often closely tied to that of the corporate/company/commercial lawyers. Also central to this are concerns like those of the private client conveyancer: the sale, purchase or leasing of property, all of which require documentary formalities as well as more general advice. The difference is that here the property will be put to commercial rather than residential use. Examples of commercial properties include shops and shopping centres, offices and office blocks, factories and industrial estates, hotels, licensed premises and leisure facilities. The client's interests may vary from the search for premises where its own activities can be carried out most effectively, to the creation of commercial properties to sell or lease to others. With the latter, several additional matters may require legal assistance. The funding of development by borrowing, grants and other resources has to be worked out along with planning applications, the impact of environmental controls, and the negotiation and drafting of appropriate construction contracts. In addition there are the commercial factors to be taken into account. How many unfilled office blocks are there in the area? Does the city really need another hotel or shopping centre? The commercial property solicitor needs to be abreast of these matters as well as legal developments in the field.

2.26 Another important aspect of commercial property may be the exploitation of the natural resources of the land – minerals such as coal, oil and gas, water, timber and agricultural produce. The resources of the sea and seabed, in particular oil and fish, should also be mentioned. Many of these resources are of considerable economic significance in Scotland, and there is a good deal of legal regulation from a variety of different points of view. In many firms, this may be a specialist area with its own department or team, notably in respect of agricultural property. Once again the role of the lawyer working in this field will be to help the client in complying with the law's requirements, assisting in taking advantage of opportunities which may be presented, and minimising the impact of misfortune when it occurs.

Litigation

2.27 Litigation is the department which deals with court work, although this description is not really adequate for the range of activity involved. As you can see if you consult the official *Civil Judicial Statistics*, the commonest court actions are those to recover debts, large and small; compensation claims in respect of injuries or even death suffered as a result of accidents at work or on the road or while undergoing medical treatment; and, in the sheriff court, divorce. Actions relating to land are also quite common in the sheriff court; most of these are probably evictions of tenants and defaulters on mortgage repayments. In all such claims, it is not merely a matter of raising or defending the action and going along to court to plead it (or instructing an advocate to do the pleading), although clearly the skills of pleading and examining witnesses are usually essential. The client has to be advised whether or not there are prospects of success in either raising or defending an action, which may involve research in the law itself, and whether the likely expenses of litigation are justified given what the client is likely to achieve. If the client goes ahead, the case has to be prepared, the evidence gathered, certain procedural steps followed at the court, and, perhaps most importantly, the possibility of a negotiated settlement with the other side explored. Any advocate involved will participate in this process as well; a good deal of Court of Session work will certainly involve liaison with the advocate concerned.

2.28　The great majority of claims do not end up being decided in court but are settled by the parties themselves (or, in appropriate cases, their insurers) with the advice and assistance of their lawyers. The obtaining of a favourable advocate's opinion (see below, para **2.48**) is often a powerful weapon in such negotiations. The *Civil Judicial Statistics* show that a large proportion of actions raised are settled out of court; and these figures take no account of the cases that never get near the court. Overall, therefore, a good deal of 'court work' is about the avoidance of going to court at all.

2.29　All this has to be carried through against the background of the law of prescription and limitation (also known as time bar) which sets limits on how much time can elapse between the event giving rise to the claim and the raising of an action in court. These look generous from an outsider's perspective – three years in the case of a personal injuries claim, five years in most other cases – but it is remarkable how often in practice these time limits present problems for the lawyers. The danger in going to court too early with an inadequately prepared case is that it may be thrown out by the judge. So the litigation solicitor has to steer a course between Scylla and Charybdis, and in this way time pressures arise. Another type of time pressure which occurs is where court action has to be taken extremely fast, for example to prevent a wrong being committed or to obtain evidence from another party which would otherwise be in danger of being lost or destroyed. There are special procedures for use in such situations, but the court solicitor has to know what these are and how to implement them.

2.30　Not all litigation work will necessarily involve contested actions. Court procedure may need to be followed in respect of certain types of formal application which may or may not be contested: for example, petitions to adopt children, or applications for a liquor licence. Litigation solicitors will also represent clients in fora other than courts – for example, in tribunals, where matters as diverse as unfair dismissal, immigration, fair rents and social security may have to be dealt with. Solicitors may also have to represent clients in arbitrations, which are commonplace in building and civil engineering contract disputes, for example. As already noted, other less formal methods of dispute resolution are increasingly popular, and this provides another avenue for the litigation lawyer.

2.31 It is worth saying a few words about how litigation is funded, as this is also an important element of litigation practice involving specialties over the interest which any provider of services has in being paid for work done. The starting point is that the client pays for the services, although the expenses of successful litigation may be recoverable from the losing party. But many private clients may be eligible for legal aid, that is funding from the state, the availability of which is dependent upon the means of the client and the merits of the case. An important element of litigation practice is therefore an application to the Scottish Legal Aid Board (website http://www.slab.org.uk/). The rates of remuneration for legal aid work are fixed by the state, and lawyers criticise them as too low to be rewarding unless you have a high volume of such work. But given that there is no overall ceiling on legal aid expenditure, the government has no other means of controlling public spending in this field. The policy question is whether a price can be put on access to justice in this way, since the low rates may mean that fewer lawyers offer legal aid services.

2.32 There are certain classes of case for which legal aid is not available at all (for example, defamation and cases before tribunals, although note that Assistance By Way of Representation [ABWOR] under the Advice and Assistance Scheme is available in relation to some statutory tribunals). This, coupled with the means-tested nature of legal aid, means that for many clients it is either a matter of finding some alternative method of funding a claim or abandoning it on the ground that it cannot be afforded. It is always possible to come to an agreement with the solicitor about fees in advance of raising an action; one form which can be helpful is the speculative action, whereby the solicitor will only receive a fee if the action is successful. Such agreements are increasingly common. If however it is further agreed that the solicitor will receive a specific percentage of any award the client gets, the arrangement, being what is known as a contingency fee or *pactum de quota litis*, is illegal and cannot be enforced. The argument against such arrangements is that the solicitor then has too much of a personal interest in the outcome of the case and will be blind to the duties which are owed to the court and to the client in litigation. The argument in favour is that it concentrates the mind of the solicitor wonderfully well on a successful outcome, and may encourage taking on more cases than the less rewarding speculative action. Contingency fees are found in other jurisdictions, notably the USA, where they are justified by the Constitutional provision that no person is to be denied access to the courts. They may yet be introduced here as a solution to the dwindling support offered by legal aid. A halfway house emerged in 1990, when it was provided that solicitor and client in a speculative action might agree to a limited percentage increase in the former's fee in the event of the action being successful. An increasingly important way of funding litigation is through private legal insurance, which can be obtained, for example, as part of one's household protection.

Criminal legal aid

2.33   Legal aid is also of central importance in criminal defence work, an area of legal practice increasingly the preserve of specialist firms. The pressures from government to contain expenditure upon criminal legal aid are even greater than on the civil side, and to this end, in 1998 a state-funded Public Defence Solicitors Office was introduced in Edinburgh. In 2003 further offices were opened in Glasgow and Inverness. (See the PDSO website, http://www.pdso.demon.co.uk/pdso_home.htm.) The defence of those charged with criminal offences is an essential part of the Scottish legal system, which starts with the presumption of innocence and requires the prosecution to prove its case beyond a reasonable doubt. Were this not the law, one of the crucial elements in the freedom of the individual would have been lost. Inevitably, however, the vast majority of those charged with criminal offences would not be able to afford legal representation without the benefit of legal aid. So administration of legal aid applications forms a central part of the life of the criminal defence solicitor, along with most of the other factors mentioned earlier in the discussion of civil litigation work[1].

1   The Justice Minister announced a six-month strategic review of criminal and civil legal aid provision in October 2003.

2.34   A distinctive feature of criminal work, however, is plea negotiation, whereby an accused agrees to plead guilty to a lesser charge than that being put forward by the prosecutor, or to one of several charges in return for the others being dropped. Such negotiations underlie some of the large number of criminal cases disposed of on the day of the trial without witnesses giving evidence or following an early plea of guilty. The advantage of this to the prosecutor is that the trouble and expense of a trial is thereby greatly reduced, while the client can hope for a lesser sentence than might otherwise be the case; for example, in a rape trial because the victim has been spared the ordeal of testimony. This is not certain, however, as the judge imposes the sentence and is not involved in the negotiation. Were it otherwise, there might be too great an inducement to plead guilty when that is not the truth of the matter.

2.35 The criminal defence lawyer is often asked, 'How can you defend someone you know to be guilty?' The answer is that the lawyer acts on his client's instructions, and that it is the function of the courts to determine guilt or innocence. The lawyer can advise a client, and would probably refuse to act for a client who admitted guilt but nevertheless wished to contest the facts of the charge. It is worth remembering, however, that there are people who have a compulsion to confess to crimes they did not commit, and that there may be defences available to one who committed the wrongful act, such as insanity or self defence. The burden on the prosecution to prove a case is also important here: there may be insufficient evidence against the accused in law (for example, corroboration may be lacking), or the evidence against the accused may collapse under scrutiny, or it may have been irregularly obtained (the result of an illegal search, for example). It is the defence lawyer's duty to bring these matters to the attention of the court, whatever his or her private views about the client may be. Finally, in the event of a plea or finding of guilt, the defence lawyer presents a plea in mitigation, giving factors which might be relevant in reducing the sentence of the court upon the accused. This again requires research and preparation.

Cross-departmental work, teams and specialist units

2.36 Clients' problems do not always fall neatly into the conceptual framework of the law or the departmental structures of the legal office. Private and commercial clients are both affected by taxation, and may be involved in litigation or charged with crimes, for example. Accordingly there is a good deal of interaction between the various areas of work described above. Some of the larger firms set up specialist units or teams to deal with complex areas of law which cut across departmental frameworks. Taxation is an obvious example. Others include construction contracts, a highly technical field which can be relevant to corporate, commercial property and litigation work; intellectual property, which combines the need to be able to produce complicated licensing schemes which are commercially worthwhile, tax-efficient and do not infringe British and Community competition laws, with specialities of enforcement through court action; and environmental law, another difficult and developing branch of law affecting a wide variety of interests.

Solicitors otherwise than in private practice

2.37   Solicitors not in private practice may be employed in either the public or the private sector. Some idea of who the employers are and the numbers of solicitors they employ can be obtained from the figures in the *Annual Report* of the Law Society of Scotland, which numbers solicitors in commerce and the public sector. In 2002, about 1,400 solicitors were employed in the public sector (central and local government, and other public bodies); and 326 were working in 'commerce and industry', that is, they were probably working as 'in-house' solicitors for private sector organisations such as banks, insurance companies and large industrial companies. Some lawyers also work in the voluntary sector, that is, for charities and campaign groups. There is an In-House Lawyers Group which promotes the interests of solicitors not in private practice, whether in the public or the private sector (more details at the Law Society of Scotland website: http://www.lawscot.org.uk/).

2.38   The kind of work which employee solicitors in the public and private sectors do will not necessarily differ greatly from that of their brethren in private practice, but it will typically all be directed towards the interests of one employer rather than a multitude of clients. As a result the in-house solicitor may become an expert in the areas of law of interest to the employer. Most organisations will acquire, own, use and dispose of property, make contracts, raise and be owed money, carry out statutory functions, restructure themselves, sue and be sued, and in all of these matters they will require legal advice to be on hand. That is not to say that all the legal work the organisation needs will necessarily be done by its in-house team. Very often work will be contracted out because it is specialist in nature or is beyond the capacity of the in-house department. The situation will vary from employer to employer according to the nature of its business, even more so than among solicitors' firms, and so more detailed discussion is not attempted here. Further information on the public sector can however be obtained from the relevant authorities themselves (eg Scottish Executive, Crown Office, district councils, NHS trusts) as well as from the Law Society. There is also a lot of relevant information in Fiona Raitt's

Careers in Scots Law: Choosing a Law Degree and a Career (1999; this also covers careers in the private sector and the universities).

Unmet legal need

2.39   In 1980 the Hughes Report on Legal Services in Scotland argued that there was an unmet legal need in that many citizens were unaware of their legal rights, and even where there was awareness rights were not pursued for want of legal services of adequate quality or supply. The Report suggested that there were many areas of law, notably those concerned with social welfare, in which solicitors did not provide an adequate service. Looking at the account of typical solicitors' practice just given, the reader may feel that not much has changed; solicitors' services are still given primarily to those with property, moveable wealth and commercial interests, with a view to enhancing and protecting those assets. There is an element of truth in this view, but it is not the whole picture. Solicitors do not actively turn work away, and for many welfare questions do form a significant part of the total client load. But if there are no clients in a particular field, the solicitor has no incentive to develop expertise in that area. A greater problem may be that potential clients do not think first of the solicitor as a source of help with problems, being deterred by worries about expense or the fact that the solicitors' office is not conveniently located. As a result, many turn first to consumer aid and advice organisations such as the Citizens Advice Bureaux, which provide free assistance to clients and the work-load of which includes many matters to which law is directly relevant. In 2002–03, for example, CABx dealt with 396,208 enquiries, 30% of which were concerned with social security issues, 20% with consumer issues such as consumer debt and faulty goods, 13% with employment problems, and 9% with housing issues such as homelessness and mortgage arrears[1]. Solicitors are often involved in the running of such organisations, notably the Legal Services Agency (http://www.lsa.org.uk/), the Edinburgh Legal Dispensary (see http://www.cpa.ed.ac.uk/leafbroch/ays/), and the Law Centres in Govan and elsewhere (http://www.govanlc.com/, http://www.scottishlaw.org.uk/lawfirms/lawcentres.html)[2].

1   Figures from Citizens Advice Scotland Annual Report for 2002-2003, accessible at http://www.cas.org.uk/Annual_Report_02__03.pdf.
2   For further information about and discussion of unmet legal need in Scotland, see Hazel Genn and Alan Paterson, *Paths to Justice Scotland: What People in Scotland Do and Think About Going to Law* (2001).

ADVOCATES

Faculty of Advocates

2.40   Unlike most solicitors, advocates do not practise in partnership or as companies, a rule which in 1992 the Office of Fair Trading reported did not restrict or distort competition in the market for legal services. An advocate is a self-employed individual, offering certain services to the public, usually although not exclusively through the medium of a solicitor (see above, para **2.07**). But a person only becomes an advocate upon admission to the Faculty of Advocates. Membership confers certain collective benefits but for these the advocate has to pay as part of the costs of his or her practice, and the Faculty also requires its members to have cover under a compulsory indemnity insurance scheme. The main benefits of membership are Faculty Services Limited and the Advocates' Library at Parliament House in Edinburgh. Faculty Services Limited is a company set up by the Faculty, which provides advocates with administrative and back-up services, including the employment of clerks who receive instructions, keep the advocate's diary and negotiate fees. There are eleven clerks altogether in Faculty Services (and one more outside the company). Each clerk (together with one or more deputies) is responsible for a 'stable' of advocates. Faculty Services also deals with the invoicing and collection of fees due to counsel, and provides secretarial and other services. The Advocates' Library, which was formally opened in 1689 by Sir George Mackenzie, then Dean of Faculty, is one of the world's great law libraries, with an immense and historic collection of legal works. The collection was not originally confined to law, and in 1925 the holdings became the basis for the National Library of Scotland, although the Advocates' Library retains the legal collection. The Library, which is in Parliament House, is where many advocates work from, few now choosing to have separate 'chambers' elsewhere in Edinburgh. Many do however work on papers at home, making use of information technology and the increasing availability of legal materials on computer. A number also work in Glasgow for most of their time, because the High Court sits there almost constantly (see above, para **1.15**).

2.41   The Faculty is headed by its elected Dean, who has wide powers to rule on questions of professional conduct and discipline. He (there has not so far been a female Dean) is advised by the Faculty Council, and there are a number of other elected office-bearers: the Vice-Dean, the Treasurer, the Keeper of the Library, the Chairman of Faculty Services Ltd, and the

Clerk of Faculty, the last-named being the one likely to be of greatest importance to those considering a career as an advocate. The Faculty's affairs are overseen by an elected Faculty Council which meets once a month. The Faculty also holds general meetings on issues of importance. In matters of discipline, the Faculty's handling of clients' complaints is now, like that of the Law Society, subject to the scrutiny of the Scottish Legal Services Ombudsman. The Faculty has an informative website: http://www.advocates.org.uk/.

Bar and bench: seniors (QCs) and juniors

2.42   Advocates are often collectively known as 'the Bar', and one talks of 'going to the Bar' or 'practising at the Bar'. The usage flows from the fact that advocates plead at the bar of the court before a judge or judges who sit 'on the Bench' (the judiciary is often collectively referred to as 'the Bench'). An advocate is also frequently referred to as 'counsel' – 'counsel for the pursuer', 'counsel for the defender', and so on. 'Counsel' is also the plural form. All advocates start as junior counsel, but usually after some 10 to 15 years in practice will 'take silk' and become seniors and Queen's Counsel (QCs – KC or King's Counsel when the monarch is male). The 'silk' refers to the different material of which a senior's gown is made. The significance of the distinction is that the senior 'gives up writing' – that is, drafting written pleadings (see below, para **2.47**) and other routine papers – and concentrates on opinion work (see below, para **2.48**) and court appearances. Formerly the senior if instructed was also entitled to have a junior instructed as well, but in 1977 the Monopolies and Mergers Commission reported that this 'two counsel rule' was not in the public interest and it was suspended. The current position is that a senior instructed to appear without a junior has the option to accept or reject those instructions, with rejection being possible in circumstances where otherwise counsel would be bound to accept (see further below, para **2.51**). The senior may insist on the instruction of a junior if the circumstances of the case warrant it, but if instructions to appear without a junior are accepted, then the senior will need to draft the pleadings incidental to the court appearance. The appearance of senior and junior together remains common, as indeed does the appearance of two juniors together.

2.43   There were about 450 advocates in practice in April 2004, and approximately another 280 who, for one reason or another, were not in practice. At that date, 102 of the 450 in practice were women, with 10 being QCs. Although the first admission of a woman to the Bar took place in 1923 (Dame Margaret Kidd, who also became the first female KC in 1949), it was only in 1977 that female members were first invited to Bar Dinners. Nowadays the Bar is a much more open institution, with an intake from all backgrounds.

What advocates do

2.44 Each practising advocate has a box with his or her name in it in the corridors of Parliament House. Instructions and other papers may be placed in this box by solicitors and other persons entitled to instruct as the means of communication with the advocate, or alternatively the advocate's clerk may be contacted. The Faculty operates what is known as the 'cab-rank rule', the gist of which is that the advocate must accept fee'd instructions to act unless prevented by existing commitments or ill-health. The theory of this rule is that it should always be possible to obtain the counsel of your choice. There are, however, a number of circumstances in which an advocate may decline or return instructions, so that the advocate can change during the progress of a case (although not once it is being pleaded in court). But the change can take place right up to the last minute, especially in more routine cases, and one of the features of an advocate's early career is likely to be the instruction to appear given just before the case is called in court. Another reason why change may occur is that the instructing solicitor or the client decides to instruct another advocate, in effect 'sacking' the first. Just as the advocate is independent of the solicitor and the client, so they are independent of the advocate. A dramatic example of this occurred in the murder trial of Peter Manuel in 1958, when Manuel dismissed his counsel in mid-trial, turned down an offer to act from the Dean of Faculty, and conducted his own defence. (See *Manuel v HM Advocate* 1958 JC 41 and Sir Nicholas Fairbairn, *A Life Is Too Short* (1986) pp 110–113.)

2.45 Formerly advocates were not allowed to advertise or tout for business, and therefore had to depend on the reputation which they established, in particular amongst instructing solicitors, to attract work. The ban was removed in 1991, although any advertising must be approved by the Dean. The Faculty now publishes a directory of advocates, available online (see http://www.advocates.org.uk/web/surname.htm), in which members may (but need not) list 'principal areas of interest'. Counsel may not negotiate fees, as this is a matter for the Clerks. Although speculative actions (see above, para **2.32**) may be undertaken, and it may be agreed in such actions that if successful the advocate's fee will be increased by a specified percentage, any form of contingency fee is prohibited as giving the advocate an interest in the outcome of the action which will affect the performance of the duties owed to the court. Advocates are allowed to be employed on retainers, however, by which they agree not to accept instructions to advise or appear for any other party in any proceedings involving the client giving the retainer. This makes them available to act for the retaining client. There are also a number of appointments available as 'standing counsel' to various government departments, along with the positions of Advocates Depute by which advocates undertake public prosecution work for the Crown Office in the High Court of Justiciary, deputising for the Lord Advocate (see above, para **1.36**). An Advocate Depute is practically full-time (40 weeks per year) and receives a salary, but may continue in private civil practice; the attraction is that generally the appointment is seen as a mark of potential further advancement later. The posts are filled, however, by advertisement and interview.

2.46 What then is the nature of the advocate's work? It can be divided up into four main areas: the drafting of pleadings and other formal documents associated with court procedure, opinion work, case preparation (including consultations with clients and solicitors, and negotiations with the other party in the case), and, finally, representation in court and elsewhere. The amount of time spent in each of these areas of work will vary according to the nature of the advocate's practice. The junior is more likely to spend time on drafting than a senior, for reasons already discussed; an advocate with a criminal practice will be more often in court than will one with mainly civil work. In terms of specialisation, it is probably fair to say that there is a specialist criminal Bar but that specialisations have yet to emerge among those concentrating on civil work (although there are a number of informal special interest groups in areas such as personal injury, family law, planning and Community law). This contrasts with the situation in England, where you can find the Chancery Bar, the Patents Bar, or the Construction Law Bar. The difference in Scotland is partly accounted for by the 'cab rank rule', with its requirement that an advocate accept all instructions if available, preventing the picking and choosing of work, and by the fact that by and large and crime (and also perhaps personal injury and family law) always aside, there is not enough work in any one field to permit absolute concentration upon it. But equally, as the 'cab rank rule' enables a choice of counsel to be made, those instructing advocates usually know that some are better than others at dealing with particular kinds of work and will try to get them when necessary. Thus while advocates may not be specialists in the sense of being confined to a particular area of work, nonetheless their practices may come to take on a particular character and be dominated by certain fields.

Drafting litigation documents

2.47   Drafting pleadings and other documents required for litigation is a technical and difficult business. Civil actions are generally raised by a summons or a petition in the Court of Session or an initial writ in the sheriff court. A summons is a command in the name of the Queen addressed to the defender requiring appearance before the Court of Session to answer the pursuer's claim. It has to set out the facts of the case as the pursuer claims them to be, and the propositions of law which justify the remedy which the pursuer seeks on the basis of these facts. A defending counsel will have to draft defences to the summons, setting out the facts which the defender admits, those of which he has no knowledge, those the truth of which he denies, and those additional facts upon which reliance will be placed. Further propositions of law may be made, or it may even be argued that, assuming all the pursuer's allegations of fact are proved, in law they would still not justify the remedy sought. Further exchanges between the parties on these pleadings may then follow. The aim is to identify the issues of fact and law on which the parties actually differ, so that if and when the case comes into court, time is not wasted on matters which are not in dispute. Written pleadings need therefore to focus the issues clearly and concisely, and require considerable skill and knowledge of law to do well. As a case proceeds, it is usually necessary to lodge further documents in process recording the formal steps which have been taken, the drafting of which would again fall to the advocate. Nowadays there are several different ways of starting an action in the Court of Session, many designed to speed up the process in areas such as commercial law, personal injuries and judicial review. Similar steps to accelerate procedure have also been taken in the sheriff courts.

Opinion work

2.48 Opinion work is researching and writing opinions on questions submitted by solicitors, often in the form of memorials to counsel. The solicitor wants to know how the law applies to a particular situation which is affecting a client. This may or may not be in anticipation of litigation; often the motivation for seeking counsel's opinion is to avoid litigation because the answer will make a particular situation clear. The memorial will set out the facts as known to the solicitor and perhaps the goal of the client for whom the opinion is sought. For example, a client has been injured in an accident at work; do the circumstances disclose any possibility of raising an action for damages against the employer for negligence? If so, how much might be recovered? Before giving the opinion, the advocate will have to identify and research the relevant areas of law, consider what the law is and how it applies to the facts and circumstances set out in the memorial, and then write up the conclusions drawn with reasons supported by the relevant authorities, whether in legislation, cases or elsewhere. Very often the advocate will need to know more about the facts before giving a final opinion. As already indicated, the opinion need not give rise to any litigation, but it may well lead to the raising of an action. Again, the raising of an action may be the reason why the defender's solicitor seeks counsel's opinion on whether and how far the action should be defended. In most cases where a contested question of law (as opposed to fact) arises there will have been at least two differing opinions on the matter, which means that it is important to remember that an opinion is just what the name infers: it is the view of a particular counsel, and no more. Another counsel may take a different view, and the difference can only be resolved by a court. Nonetheless, in practice counsel's opinion is a very powerful weapon, especially in settlement negotiations, and many organisations and individuals organise their affairs on the basis of one when the law has not in fact been settled by court decision.

2.49 Less formal than counsel's opinion is the practice of giving advice or notes to solicitors in various situations which may require a view more quickly than is possible usually with an opinion; for example, on the prospects of success in appeals, or on the validity of actions which a client is proposing to take which may involve the risk of being sued later (for example, abandoning a contract). Very occasionally counsel may also be called upon to draft formal documents such as trust deeds.

Case preparation

2.50   Under the third heading of case preparation come many of the factors already discussed affecting the working life of the litigation solicitor (see above, paras **2.27–2.35**). The advocate needs to be familiar with all the documents in the action, the evidence of the witnesses, the other side's arguments and the law bearing on the case. As the case proceeds, it is essential to keep track of its development, so that the appropriate steps are taken at the right time. Here again computerised litigation support can have a role. Preparation will usually involve consultations, meetings with the client and the solicitor at which the progress and state of the case will be discussed. Here there is direct contact with clients, and it is essential to know how to handle the great variety of human beings with whom advocates come into contact. The advocate will probably become involved in negotiation, whether seeking settlement with the other side in civil cases, plea negotiating in criminal ones, or seeking legal aid; a consultation may follow on from such negotiations, at which the advocate can have to help the client come to terms with getting rather less than she wanted from the case. In a criminal case, if in consultation the client confesses guilt to his advocate, the latter should not put forward any defence inconsistent with that admission, but is entitled to test the prosecution evidence, and plead defences such as insanity or self-defence.

Advocacy in court

2.51   As can now be seen, practice at the Bar involves a great deal more than just oral advocacy skills and knowledge of the law. Nonetheless these remain the characteristic aspects of an advocate in the public mind, and perhaps the chief attraction of the career from the point of view of a prospective intrant. The requirements of oral advocacy are familiar from, if somewhat too highly coloured in by, TV courtroom dramas. A visit to your local court will show you that most of the time the atmosphere in court is low-key, not to say dull for those not directly involved. A case has to be presented lucidly and persuasively, rather than aggressively and loudly. It is the judge and, where necessary, the jury who have to be convinced, not the audience on the public benches. Witnesses have to be examined, so that either a consistent story emerges if the witness is for counsel's client, or doubts are raised if the witness is on the other side. Objections to the leading of certain types of evidence or to the other side's line of questioning of witnesses have to be made promptly, so that it is essential to be able to concentrate and listen while other counsel are at work. Arguments on law have to be researched and thought through, so that the advocate is able to deal with the counter-arguments from the other side and the questions and interjections from the Bench which usually accompany a debate on the law. If the flow of an argument is interrupted by judicial questioning, the advocate has to be able to handle that and ensure that the presentation of the argument remains coherent. It is desirable therefore to be a good speaker, a quick thinker and a relatively unflappable personality for success at the Bar; having said that, there are those who have done well despite being possessed of none of these qualities! The Faculty of Advocates itself refers to the need for its members to 'carry the seven lamps of advocacy – honesty, courage, industry, wit, eloquence, judgment and fellowship'.

JUDGES

2.52 A brief word should be said about the judiciary in any discussion of lawyers in Scotland, since, with the exception of the District Court outside Glasgow, appointment as a judge is only open to the legally qualified. However, for most readers of this book, appointment as a judge will be a distant prospect indeed, although no doubt a worthy ambition. Only fairly senior and experienced lawyers are appointed. To become one of the judges in the Court of Session and the High Court of Justiciary, you must be one of the following:
(a) an advocate or principal Clerk of Session of not less than five years' standing;
(b) a Writer to the Signet for the space of ten years;
(c) a sheriff principal or sheriff who has held office for a continuous period of not less than five years;
(d) a solicitor who has had a right of audience in both the Court of Session and the High Court for a continuous period of not less than five years.
Under the Scotland Act 1998 the appointment is made by the Sovereign on the recommendation of the First Minister of the Scottish Parliament, who will have consulted the Lord President. Conditions (a) and (b) above were provided for in the 1707 Union, which continued to be the sole basis for judicial appointments in the higher courts in Scotland until the Law Reform Act of 1990, which added (c) and (d). Since 2001 a non-statutory Judicial Appointments Board has nominated candidates for both shrieval

and Court of Session vacancies to the First Minister, following advertisement and interviews. (See further http://www.judicialappointmentsscotland.gov.uk/.) In practice only advocates have ever been appointed as judges in the Court of Session and the High Court of Justiciary, and in modern times only Queen's Counsel. It is unlikely that the pattern will change until a cadre of solicitors with rights of audience in the higher courts and experience in exercising them has emerged. The first woman to become a permanent judge in the Court of Session was Hazel Aronson QC who upon appointment in July 1996 took the title Lady Cosgrove. She has since been followed by Lady Paton (1999) and Lady Smith (2001).

2.53 The Scottish judges appointed to the House of Lords have in modern times been almost invariably drawn from the ranks of the Court of Session bench. But it is not impossible for the appointment to be made directly from the Bar, notable examples being Lords Watson, Macmillan and Reid. Solicitors with rights of audience are now also eligible for appointment. The appointment is by the Sovereign on the recommendation of the Prime Minister, a process also applying to the appointment of the Lord President and the Lord Justice-Clerk (although with these offices only nominees of the First Minister may be so recommended). The first female Law Lord, Lady Hale (an English lawyer), was appointed in 2003. A new process involving a judicial appointments committee is likely to form part of the replacement of the House of Lords with a Supreme Court (see above, para **1.31**).

2.54 Sheriffs may be appointed from amongst persons who have been legally qualified for at least ten years. They may be either advocates or solicitors. A sheriff may be appointed on a part-time basis, the previous 'temporary sheriff' having fallen victim to the Human Rights Act 1998 (see *Starrs v Ruxton* 2000 JC 208). A solicitor who was first appointed a sheriff might then be eligible for appointment as a Court of Session judge after five years on the shrieval bench, without ever having had rights of audience in that court. Women have been appointed as sheriffs and sheriffs principal, the first female sheriff principal having been Dame Margaret Kidd QC in 1960, and the first female sheriff (or sheriff substitute, as the terminology then was) having been Isabel Sinclair QC in 1965. Appointment as a sheriff or sheriff principal is by the Sovereign on the recommendation of the First Minister following a process before the Judicial Appointments Board. The First Minister again must consult the Lord President.

2.55 Judges are immune from civil liability for their judicial conduct, 'otherwise,' as Stair remarked in his *Institutions* (IV, i, 5), 'no man but a beggar, or a fool, would be a judge'. But they are subject to removal for misconduct. By statute a judge in the House of Lords may be removed from office on address to both Houses of Parliament. The procedure by which a judge of the Court of Session and High Court is removed was settled by the Scotland Act 1998, which provides that removal is by the Sovereign acting on the recommendation of the First Minister following a motion to that effect by the Scottish Parliament. There must also have been a previous report from a tribunal chaired by a member of the Judicial Committee of the Privy Council, to the effect that the judge in question is unfit for office by reason of inability, neglect of duty or misbehaviour. This is somewhat akin to the procedure for dismissing sheriffs – a report to the Secretary of State for Scotland by the Lord President and the Lord Justice-Clerk followed by an order by the Secretary of State subject to annulment by Parliament. That has been used twice in recent times: in 1977, when Sheriff Peter Thomson was dismissed for political activities incompatible with judicial office, and in 1992, when Sheriff Ewen Stewart was dismissed as unfit for office on grounds of inability. The latter dismissal led to litigation only concluded in 1998 (*Stewart v Secretary of State for Scotland* 1998 SC (HL) 81).

2.56 Judges may choose to go of their own accord, but surprisingly few do so except for reasons of health. Generally they stay on to ensure an adequate pension. Retirement is compulsory at 70.

PART II

Entering the profession

How does one enter the Scottish legal profession? Basically there are two approaches: either starting by obtaining a Scots law degree at university (the LL.B), or starting by taking examinations set by the governing body of the branch of the profession – solicitor or advocate – which you wish to enter. Under either system you must pass examinations covering certain subjects: the compulsory courses. In both cases, the next step is a further course lasting one year, the Diploma in Legal Practice, which is taught mainly by practitioners but is based in the universities. Thereafter you proceed to practical training in a solicitors' office. In the case of solicitors this will normally involve a two-year period of service under a post-Diploma training contract with an employing solicitor (the traineeship). For advocates, there is also a training period in a solicitors' office which is on the same basis as a trainee solicitor save that it is for the slightly shorter period of 21 months. If you have obtained a first- or second-class honours degree in law from a Scottish university, this period is reduced to 12 months. You then enter a period of full-time pupillage with a practising junior advocate, which lasts for between 9 and 10 months. When the period of full practical training is complete, you are either enrolled as a solicitor or called as an advocate.

This section begins with an account of the compulsory courses and some discussion of how they relate to the legal system and legal practice as described in Part I. The norm for both branches of the profession is to start with the university law degree (probably 95% or more of entrants come to the profession through the route of the university law degree), so that route of qualification will be dealt with next in this section. Then we will turn to the alternative of entry by means of the examinations of the Law Society of Scotland and the Faculty of Advocates, before going on to consider the Diploma in Legal Practice and the requirements of professional training.

CHAPTER 3

Courses

INTRODUCTION

3.01 This chapter surveys the subjects which you have to pass, either at university or through the professional examinations, if you want to qualify as a Scots lawyer. There are syllabi of subjects in which passes are required by the Law Society of Scotland and the Faculty of Advocates before they will grant you admission. For most entrants to either branch of the profession these subjects will be studied and passed as part of an LL.B degree. But it is worth noting that there is variation in the approach of each of the law schools to enabling students to satisfy the professional requirements. You will have to discuss with your school director or adviser of studies the curriculum which you need to follow to gain the professional exemptions. The aim here is to give a general account of the ground which the profession expects you to cover, and to show how it relates to the practice of law in Scotland as described in Chapter 2.

COMPULSORY SUBJECTS FOR BOTH BRANCHES OF THE PROFESSION

3.02 First we will set out the required subjects of the Law Society and the Faculty of Advocates in parallel columns, which helps to demonstrate the substantial overlap which exists between them. When reform of the profession was under discussion in the late 1980s, this close similarity between the requirements of the two branches of the profession was the subject of favourable comment, because it is easier for a person who has qualified on one side to move over to the other. This was in contrast to the position of solicitors and barristers in England, who had very different educational requirements. The routes to qualification as solicitor or barrister in England remain quite distinct, and partly as a result are subject to some degree of supervision by central government in the shape of the Standing Committee on Legal Education within the Department of Constitutional Affairs in Whitehall (see http://www.dca.gov.uk/dept/legeduc/standconf.htm). Although something similar under the Secretary of State for Scotland was suggested in the run-up to the 1990 reforms of the legal profession, admission remains a matter of self-regulation for the Law Society of Scotland and the Faculty of Advocates. It seemed likely at the time of writing (April 2004) that the Faculty would cease to prescribe the content of degrees and instead insist upon prior qualification as a Scottish solicitor, requiring of intrants only the sitting of pre-entry examinations in evidence, procedure, Roman law and international private law. These new regulations may be promulgated in 2005.

3.03   The table below is substantially based on the syllabi published by the Law Society and the Faculty in April 2004:

Table 1

LAW SOCIETY OF SCOTLAND	FACULTY OF ADVOCATES
SCOTS PRIVATE LAW	SCOTTISH PRIVATE LAW
fundamental legal concepts	
family law	family law
obligations –	obligations, including –
contract	contract
delict	delict
unjustified enrichment	
property	property, including –
heritable	conveyancing
moveable	landlord and tenant
	acquisition
	transfer
	rights
	restrictions
trusts	trusts
succession	succession

LAW SOCIETY OF SCOTLAND	FACULTY OF ADVOCATES
	JURISPRUDENCE
SCOTS CRIMINAL LAW	SCOTTISH CRIMINAL LAW
SCOTS COMMERCIAL LAW	COMMERCIAL LAW AND BUSINESS INSTITUTIONS

financial services
insurance
diligence
negotiable instruments
moveable securities
guarantees
sale of goods
carriage of goods and passengers
insolvency
agency
partnership
companies

EVIDENCE	EVIDENCE
PUBLIC LAW AND THE LEGAL SYSTEM	CONSTITUTIONAL AND ADMINISTRATIVE LAW

CONVEYANCING
landownership
deeds
registers burdens
transfer
heritable securities
floating charges
leases
land transfer contracts

EUROPEAN COMMUNITY LAW	EUROPEAN LAW AND INSTITUTIONS
TAXATION	
	ROMAN LAW OF PROPERTY AND OBLIGATIONS
	INTERNATIONAL PRIVATE LAW

Public law, private law and commercial law

3.04   The first thing to notice about these lists is the way in which they distinguish three main categories of law, namely public law, private law and commercial law. The distinction between public law and private law was explained in Chapter 1 (para **1.39**). There are various reasons why commercial law is further distinguished from private law, although generally it too involves relations between private persons (in the sense that the law treats companies and other business organisations as persons for these purposes). One of these is historical in that for many centuries trade and commerce were governed and facilitated by the trans-national 'law merchant' (whence 'mercantile law', as commercial law is still sometimes known), a body of rules which remains at the heart of modern business law in many ways. In this sense the law merchant was not merely Scots law. In modern French and German law you still find that the Civil Code, covering the law governing private relationships, is quite distinct from the Commercial Code, which regulates business transactions. In Scotland, the distinction is still often reflected, not only in the professional syllabi, but also in the law schools which have one course called Scots law or private law, and another called commercial or business or mercantile law. Textbooks also often use this traditional division. In the early 1960s two classic works were published as a complementary pair: one on purely private law, *A Short Commentary on the Law of Scotland* (1962) by T B Smith, the other on *The Mercantile and Industrial Law of Scotland* (1964) by J J Gow. More recently, and at a more elementary level, LexisNexis UK in Scotland have produced *Scots Law: A Student Guide* by Nicole Busby and others (2nd edition, 2003) and *Scots Commercial Law* by Angelo Forte (1997); while W Green published in 2003 *Fundamentals of Scots Law* by several authors, covering basic private law, and *Commercial Law in Scotland* by Fraser Davidson and Laura Macgregor.

3.05   Another factor distinguishing commercial from general private law is the increasing amount of public regulation of commercial activity, itself much stimulated by the privatisation and commercialisation of many functions formerly discharged by the state: for example, telecommunications, the energy utilities such as gas and electricity, and (in England and Wales) water. Note too the important role of such public bodies as the Competition Commission and the Office of Fair Trading in regulating business activities.

Private law: obligations, property, family law

3.06   One further reason why the distinction between private and commercial law survives is because much of the material covered under the private law head is a necessary preliminary to a proper understanding of the more complex commercial subject matter. The law of contract and property, covered under private law, is of critical importance for business, much of which consists of making contracts to transfer items of property from one person to another. Contract and property are also the best illustrations of two fundamental legal concepts which inform much of private and commercial law: the *personal right or obligation* enforceable only against a particular person or persons (contract), and the *real right* good against the world (property). For these reasons it is also likely that much of private law will be covered in the first year of an LL.B programme, with commercial being held over to the second year. It is obvious that commercial law is fundamental to solicitors and advocates engaging in commercial work, and for that reason it is not surprising to find that the subject is compulsory along with contract and property. But the latter two are also important in private client work, as are family law, trusts and succession. The law of delict, on the other hand, is most significant in civil court work, as it deals with claims for damages and other remedies in respect of injuries of various kinds. Unjustified enrichment is probably also of greatest significance in court work, as it also involves the provision of remedies to deal with situations where one person has received a benefit – be it money, property, or services – in circumstances making it unjust to retain the benefit when it is reclaimed by the person at whose expense it was rendered. Both subjects are also part of the law of obligations or personal rights. Much of private law is also common law, found mainly in the decisions of the courts; only family law has a major statutory element. Commercial law, on the other hand, is mainly statutory, albeit with a very large body of case law explaining and illustrating the application of the legislation.

Conveyancing, evidence and tax

3.07   Three of the compulsory subjects can be seen as in some way ancillary to or necessarily based upon a knowledge of private and commercial law and tend to be taken in later years at university – conveyancing, evidence and tax. Conveyancing, the process of transferring property, is obviously closely connected with property law. It tends to be dominated by land transfer, because this is its most important element for solicitors. Evidence is obviously crucial for court lawyers, but the law's requirements need to be borne in mind by others, for example lawyers drafting documents which may be used as evidence in any later dispute. Taxation is of fundamental importance to a large number of situations in which lawyers become involved, whether merely as a factor to be taken into account, or as something to be minimised or avoided so far as the law allows. A taxation course will typically cover income tax, corporation tax, capital gains tax, value added tax (VAT), inheritance tax and stamp duty land tax. Income tax is likely to be of concern to all private clients, and corporation tax and VAT to corporate ones; inheritance tax affects succession and certain transfers of value carried out by a person within a given period of years before death; and stamp duty land tax and capital gains tax will impinge on most transactions of any size, particularly those involving land.

Public law: legal system, constitutional law and administrative law

3.08   Having completed the main subjects covered under the heading of private law along with the closely related conveyancing, evidence, tax, and commercial law, we now turn to public law. Public law is that body of law which affects the structure of the state and government, and the state's relationship with its citizens and other states. The most basic part of public law is an account of the legal system of Scotland, elements of which are touched upon in this book's description of the courts and other legal institutions, sources of law and the legal profession. Something like this has to be compulsory for the intending lawyer.

3.09   The central subject of public law is usually dealt with in the law schools in a course named constitutional law, so called because it deals with the structure of government, or the constitution, of the United Kingdom. The law is first concerned with defining the functions and powers of the different branches of government – the executive, the legislative and the judicial – and the relationships which exist between them. The creation of the Scottish Parliament and the phenomenon of devolution throughout the United Kingdom have introduced a further dimension to the subject here. Next it is concerned with the relationship between the state and the individual. In taking decisions which affect an individual, has the state exceeded the power which it has under law? Has it followed a fair procedure in reaching the decision? In answering these questions, the courts – the judicial branch of government – are always careful to point out that they are not concerned with the merits of the decision, but rather that proper procedures have been used. It is the executive function to take the decision, and parliament's to debate the merits; the court's role is to ensure that the legal proprieties are followed. This part of constitutional law is usually known as administrative law, and is often the subject of separate textbooks, focusing on the remedy of judicial review, a special procedure for use in such cases. Administrative law does not stretch, however, to other aspects of the relationship between the state and the individual. The state accords its citizens certain privileges by comparison with other people, so rules are needed to identify citizens, regulate immigration from other countries and provide for asylum and extradition. The state also enjoys coercive powers over citizens which are defined by law: for example, the law regulating the powers of the police and the armed forces. The law also enables the state to protect its own interests, for example, through the rules on official secrets, the Security Service, and the prevention of terrorism. But this is countered by the protection of citizens' general freedoms of speech and movement; hence laws are needed to balance the conflict of interests here, notably in respect of public meetings, protest and demonstrations. Written constitutions in other countries usually contain declarations of fundamental human rights and freedoms, but in Britain these have had to be spelt out from a whole host of specific legal rules and practices. But the Human Rights Act 1998, which incorporates the European Convention on Human Rights into domestic law, is encouraging a more principled approach.

3.10 Most of the great constitutional and administrative law cases have taken place in England, because most of the main organs of central government are based in London. So although constitutional law is essential background knowledge for most lawyers, it has been rare for purely constitutional questions to impinge on ordinary legal practice in Scotland. But the creation of a Scottish Parliament with legally limited powers of legislation has meant a change in this situation, particularly alongside the Human Rights Act 1998. Petitions for judicial review are already a significant part of the case load of the Court of Session, since even before the Scottish Parliament came into existence there were many governmental organisations in Scotland taking decisions which affect individuals in various ways. As a result, lawyers working in the public sector will often find a knowledge of constitutional and administrative law of critical importance.

Criminal law

3.11   Criminal law can be included under the heading of public law since this branch of law deals with when the state may inflict punishment on the citizen. This is the branch of the law with which the general public is most familiar and with which law in general is most often associated. Yet, as already indicated, the majority of practising lawyers do not work in the field of criminal law, and for this reason it might seem slightly surprising that it is a required subject for both branches of the profession. On the other hand, the beginning law student is hardly in a position to tell whether or not she wishes to specialise in or avoid criminal law, and it is unquestionably an extremely important part of the law, of which it is desirable that every lawyer should have at least a background knowledge.

European Community law

3.12   European Community law is the most recent addition to the list of compulsory subjects in public law, having been adopted by both the Law Society of Scotland and the Faculty of Advocates in 1989 to affect all entrants to the profession after 1 January 1991. Although the United Kingdom joined the European Community in 1973, it was only in the 1980s that the full impact of Community law across a wide range of fields likely to affect legal practice was fully realised. The course will familiarise students with the institutions, sources of law and law-making processes of the Community, the general principles of Community law and its relationship to the national laws of member states, and a number of specific topics of Community law: the free movement of goods, persons, services and capital, significant ancillary social law aspects thereof, the law on competition, state aids and internal taxation, and intellectual property. As this list shows, Community law is increasingly significant for private and commercial as well as public law.

Jurisprudence

3.13 Finally, and moving away from public law, jurisprudence, which is most simply defined as the philosophy of law, appears as a separate subject for the Faculty of Advocates but not for the Law Society of Scotland. Instead it is incorporated into Scots private law under the heading 'fundamental legal concepts'. This heading provides a useful starting point for considering the scope of Jurisprudence as a compulsory subject. Much of law is defined in terms of 'rights' and 'duties', 'obligation' and 'property'. Certain concepts run through several branches of the law: for example, causation is important in delict and criminal law, both of which say that only if someone causes injury to another will he be liable. Both also place liability ultimately on moral grounds of intention, fault and wrongfulness. Contract law is based on the concepts of 'promise' and 'agreement'. Property law rests on the basis of individual ownership. There is a large and sophisticated philosophical literature on such matters, for which law forms an excellent test case, and which in turn can help refine the concepts which are the tools of the lawyer's trade. Still greater questions may be whether there is or ought to be any relationship between law and morality, the justification for law, the perception of law in other cultures and belief-systems, and what distinguishes law from other systems of social and political control. Is law really a system of rules guiding the decisions of government, courts and lawyers, or are other factors brought into play? A variety of political, philosophical and economic ideas have been brought to bear on the law over the centuries, and the study of jurisprudence gives a valuable insight into the nature of law itself, as well as some of its elemental concepts.

SUBJECTS REQUIRED ONLY BY THE FACULTY OF ADVOCATES

Roman law of property and obligations

3.14 In one sense it is obvious why Roman law might be a compulsory subject for any Scots lawyer, given its historical significance in the Scottish system and the fact that it is still a formal source of law today, albeit a residual one (see above, para **1.50**). Moreover the requirements of the Faculty of Advocates are limited to the Roman law of property and obligations, the topics in which Roman law had its greatest influence on the content of Scots law. But Roman law was not originally an entry requirement of the Faculty on utilitarian grounds; instead, when it emerged in the seventeenth century, it was on the basis that knowledge and understanding of Roman law was the mark of an honourable and learned man worthy of admission to an honourable and learned society. A greater stress on 'useful' knowledge began to emerge only in the mid-eighteenth century, and that did not displace Roman law. It is only in relatively recent times that the place of Roman law amongst the compulsory subjects has come under question. The value of studying Roman law remains, however, whether or not it is directly relevant in practice at the bar or continues as a compulsory subject. It enables the student to see some of the basic concepts which have underpinned the western legal tradition for centuries and continue to do so, as well as their relationship with each other. Moreover it opens the way to the work of many great jurists, and is essential to the study of legal history and culture as well as comparative law.

International private law

3.15   What in the syllabus of the Faculty of Advocates is called international private law is sometimes also known as private international law. It is distinguished from public international law, the law affecting states in their relations with each other, because its concern is primarily with the private affairs of persons. The international element arises because these affairs may involve more than one legal system. This fact gives rise to other names for the subject: 'choice of laws', 'conflict of laws' or, more simply, 'conflicts'. The gist of IPL, as it is sometimes abbreviated, is that when cases arise involving a foreign element, there are rules answering three basic questions:
(1)   Does a Scottish court have power to deal with the foreign element?
(2)   To what extent should the court take account of or even apply foreign law?
(3)   Should the court and other authorities recognise and apply the judgments of foreign courts in contentious matters?

3.16   The subject is very important in Scotland because, in Scottish IPL, England and English law are foreign elements. The significance of this is that businesses commonly work on both sides of the border, while people own property in both countries and travel from one jurisdiction to the other is unrestricted. As the European Community develops towards internal economic coherence, similar effects are likely there as well, and have indeed begun to happen. A simple but sadly not uncommon example of an IPL problem concerns the custody of children following the divorce of a couple of different nationalities, one being a Scot. Suppose that a foreign court grants the divorce although the marriage took place in Scotland, and that it gives custody of the children to the non-Scottish parent. If the Scottish parent then snatches the child back to Scotland in defiance of the foreign court's order, and the foreign parent seeks to regain possession via the Scottish courts, what happens? The answer to such questions is to be found in IPL. Another example is provided by the bombing of the PanAm jet over Lockerbie in 1988. The criminal act, although initiated elsewhere, took effect in Scotland, so the Scottish criminal courts had jurisdiction (although by special arrangement the High Court tried the case in the Netherlands); but the airline's civil liability (if any) for negligently failing to detect the bomb, could be enforced in the USA because it was registered there. It was also better for the injured parties, whatever their nationalities, to sue in the USA, because the courts there generally award higher damages than elsewhere. The rules of IPL are thus part of what is known as 'forum shopping', that is, looking for the court in which it is most advantageous for the pursuer to sue. Because it is so concerned with what courts ought to do, it is not surprising that IPL is a compulsory subject for advocates; but given the general significance of the foreign dimension in Scottish economic and social activity, one might argue that it ought to be compulsory for solicitors as well. Certainly it would be professional negligence not to realise that a case with a foreign element could raise issues going beyond entirely domestic law.

NON-COMPULSORY SUBJECTS

3.17 The compulsory subjects do not exhaust the range of possible studies in law. Some of the other options are discussed in the next chapter (see paras **4.27–4.31**). One point which is likely to emerge from considering the professional syllabi is that the coverage is by and large related to those areas of law connected with the creation and administration of property and wealth (in a relative sense) in a framework of economic activity. It has been argued that the law which the two branches of the profession require entrants to know bears little relation to the needs and concerns of most people in Scotland. Thus the socially significant fields of employment law, housing (with special reference to public sector housing), local government (which probably affects more Scots directly on a daily basis than any decision taken in St Andrews House, Victoria Quay, or Whitehall), the law on health care provision, social security, social work and the housing of homeless persons receive little attention in the required courses. This is not to say that there are no courses available in these subjects, for most of the Scottish law schools do in fact offer the subjects at both Ordinary and Honours level. On the other hand, it could be argued that, so far as they go, the compulsory subjects reflect the reality and main concerns of private legal practice; indeed, that they fail to cover all the subjects which are of importance in such practice. Examples of such subjects which are given either no or scant attention within the compulsory group (although again university courses are usually available) would include building and construction law, agricultural law, environmental law, town and country planning, intellectual property and, in the case of solicitors, IPL. Nor is this lack made up in the Diploma.

3.18   It may be therefore that in seeking a rationale for the present group of compulsory subjects one should not draw the conclusion that the profession is engaged in a conspiracy to confine the training of lawyers to the subjects of relevance only to the property- and wealth-owning classes in society. Much that is included in the list is there as a result of the law's intellectual traditions, stretching back to the time of Justinian and beyond. This of course does not in itself justify the list of subjects as it presently stands. But it does suggest that the approach which has been taken to this issue is not a strictly utilitarian one, asking either what the lawyer needs to know in practice, or what law is significant in society and about which the lawyer ought to know. If there is too great an emphasis on knowledge – or perhaps the wrong kind of emphasis on knowledge – we may miss a point. It is doubtful whether the law student retains the detailed knowledge built up to pass various examinations through all subsequent studies and training so that on the morrow of admission to the profession a client can be effortlessly advised on any aspect of law covered in the compulsory subjects. Even if such a wonderful feat of memory were humanly possible, it might not be useful, since the law moves on and is not likely to be exactly as it was when the relevant course was taken. The aims of requiring entrants to the profession to take and pass law courses must include knowledge of the concepts, scope and general thrust of the law, but arguably also extend to the capacity to master detail, to handle problems in accordance with legal doctrine, and to find and understand legal materials. The particular subjects taken to demonstrate these abilities may matter rather less.

CHAPTER 4

The university stage

DEVELOPMENT OF GRADUATE ENTRY INTO THE PROFESSION

4.01   There has been university law teaching in Scotland for as long as the country has had universities. St Andrews, Glasgow and Aberdeen are the oldest, having been founded in 1410, 1451 and 1496 respectively. The law taught in the fifteenth-century universities was not Scots law, however, but rather the 'learned laws' – the Roman or Civil Law, and the Canon Law. The main aim of late medieval universities was the education of prospective churchmen, and so there was little direct concern with purely secular affairs. The sixteenth century saw, not only the foundation of Edinburgh University in 1583, but also the division of the Church known as the Reformation, whereby large parts of Christendom split away from the Roman church. This accelerated a trend towards the secularisation of universities throughout Europe, but in Scotland, although the Reformation took place in 1560, it was not until the early eighteenth century that Scots law as such became part of the universities' law curriculum. Before this time, therefore, Scots lawyers learned their law mainly in practice, by associating themselves with already-established practitioners who passed on their wisdom and experience. In the case of advocates, however, this period of apprenticeship was usually preceded by a period studying Roman law at one of the great European universities; typically in France up to the early seventeenth century, more often in the Netherlands thereafter.

4.02   University teaching of Scots law seems to have developed in Scotland along lines first laid down in private courses run by advocates in

Edinburgh at the turn of the seventeenth century. An Edinburgh law school was founded in 1707 and a Glasgow one in 1714. William Forbes, professor at Glasgow from 1714 to 1745, initiated the teaching of Scots law there, while in Edinburgh Alexander Bayne was appointed as the first professor of Scots law in 1722. The funding of the Edinburgh professorship was incidentally provided from a tax on beer, and it has, most unfairly to all its subsequent incumbents, been described as 'the drouth's chair'. Aberdeen began to teach Scots law in the nineteenth century, while Dundee and Strathclyde came on the scene in the twentieth. The early years of the twenty-first century added Abertay, Glasgow Caledonian, Napier and Robert Gordon's to the list of universities offering degrees in Scots law, and there may be more to come (see below, para **4.04**).

4.03   By the mid-twentieth century law was typically a second degree taken on a part-time basis, with classes held in the early morning and evening around a working day in a legal office. The present pattern, in which law can be and usually is taken as a first degree in a programme of full-time study, was only established in 1960. Nevertheless, and despite the growth of graduate entry to the profession, a law degree is still not compulsory, and it is important to understand that academic legal education grew in a context of practical training. But both branches of the modern profession prefer graduate entry, and, as noted earlier, the vast majority of people entering the profession today do so after taking a university law degree.

4.04   In the case of advocates, generally a person applying for admission to the Faculty of Advocates must hold a degree in law from a Scottish university. For solicitors also it is usually necessary for the applicant to hold a degree in law granted by a university, but there is a contrast with the advocates' regulations in that the universities recognised by the Law Society of Scotland for this purpose are specifically named in the Society's Admission Regulations, rather than generically identified as Scottish universities. The nine universities named in the Law Society regulations – Aberdeen, Abertay, Dundee, Edinburgh, Glasgow, Glasgow Caledonian, Napier, Robert Gordon's, and Strathclyde – are, at the time of writing (April 2004), the only Scottish universities accredited by the Law Society to provide a law degree satisfying professional requirements. Heriot-Watt and St Andrews do not give law degrees (although law subjects are offered as part of other programmes at Heriot-Watt). Abertay, Glasgow Caledonian, Napier, Paisley, Stirling and Robert Gordon's also offer BA degrees in law, legal studies and law and administration which do not satisfy professional requirements.

GAINING ENTRY TO UNIVERSITY

4.05 Applicants for admission to law schools are usually divided up into three broad groups: school-leavers, graduates (those who already hold a degree in another discipline) and mature candidates (that is, those aged 21 or over when they begin their university studies and who do not already possess a degree). What follows is intended to cover all three categories, with differentiation made clear where appropriate. In every case it should be borne in mind that the position varies in detail from university to university, and accordingly you should not rest content with reading what is written here but seek further information via university prospectuses and websites, and through inquiries at schools and admission liaison offices. Most universities also hold 'open days' and participate in careers fairs and similar events. In seeking further information, the best thing to do is either to write or telephone these offices, and make yourself available for a fact-finding interview. You should also take a tour of the premises, and see what resources are available to students there. How big is the law library? What is the computer provision like? Are the lecture theatres reasonably comfortable and well-equipped? For addresses, telephone numbers and websites, see Appendix 1.

The UCAS application

4.06 Application for admission to universities is carried out through the Universities and Colleges Admissions Service (UCAS) system (website http://www.ucas.ac.uk/). Application forms are obtainable from UCAS (see Appendix 1 for the address), or from schools and colleges. The closing date for applications each year is 15 January. Late applications are only considered at the discretion of the universities concerned. The significance of this, particularly if you are someone thinking of going into law as a second degree or as a change of career, is that you must start planning and applying a full year ahead of the time at which you hope to start the degree. While there is always a chance that a late application will be successful, it is a slim one.

4.07   The UCAS form is a complex document, and it is probably as well to seek advice on its completion from teachers or careers advisers. You will be able to nominate up to six institutions to which you wish copies of the form to be sent, and to state with each one which course you wish to pursue there. There is no need to indicate any order of preference. You will get information about the courses on offer at each university from *University and College Entrance: The Official Guide* and the *UCAS/ Universities Scotland Entrance Guide to Higher Education in Scotland* (both available from UCAS). Remember that only nine of the Scottish universities offered LL.B degrees in 2004, but check these guides for the up-to-date position. You do not have to limit your choice on the application form to law courses. It is perfectly legitimate to keep your options open until the universities have made their decisions on whether or not to offer you places on the courses you have put in the form. On the other hand, it may be wise not to overdo this, scattering law among a number of other choices such as history, business studies or medicine, as this can cause some selectors to doubt motivation.

Qualifications

4.08   The form provides you with some space to set out your academic record to date and the examinations (if any) which you are proposing to take later on in the academic year. As you will see from the *UCAS/ Universities Scotland Entrance Guide to Higher Education in Scotland*, entry qualifications for law are usually of a high standard, although many of the law schools also operate 'widening access' schemes for students coming from parental and/or school backgrounds with little or no previous connection to higher education (see further para **4.10**). The main recognised qualifications are:

(a)   SQA (Advanced Highers, Highers and Standard grades);
(b)   GCE (A, AS and O levels) examinations;
(c)   a previous degree;
(d)   Access and similar qualifications for mature students.

Mature students may of course also present SQA, GCE or Open University course qualifications, but the HND in legal studies and other modules are not generally recognised as entrance qualifications for LL.B degrees. (However, see further below, paras **5.04–5.06**.) The purpose of defining mature students is to permit the relaxation of entrance qualifications for such candidates; if however you are 21 or over and already possessed of a university degree, then you are not in need of a reduction in qualification levels, and your application will rest on the basis of your existing degree.

4.09 It is generally not a good idea to present a mixed bag of different types of qualification – for example, combining Highers with A levels – nor should you rely on qualifications which are more than a few – say five – years old. One reason for having entry qualifications is that they show your capacity to deal with study and assessment, which changes over time. Performances made some time ago are therefore not good indicators of how you are likely to get on in the future at university. Similarly, if you are a mature student, you may have already taken professional examinations such as those for the Institute of Bankers in Scotland or in the police service, but because these are closely related to specific employment requirements they are not usually seen as broadly-based enough to count as formal entrance qualifications for university. Some SQA and GCE subjects may similarly not be recognised by law schools on the ground of lack of broad academic content. This does not mean that professional qualifications are irrelevant, however. There are two possibilities. Your success in professional exams may be a reason for the selector choosing you ahead of other candidates without the formal requirements provided that you take further, traditional qualifications such as Highers or Access courses and pass at an appropriate level. Alternatively the university to which you are applying may have special admission procedures for mature candidates in your position; it is worth enquiring whether this is the case.

Widening access

4.10 Widening access to higher education is currently a priority within the wider national policy objective of social inclusion. In 2003 the Scottish Executive commissioned the report *Minority and Social Diversity in Legal Education* (http://www.scotland.gov.uk/library5/justice/masd-00.asp) which addressed concerns about the ethnic and social class composition of entrants to the legal profession in Scotland. There are several 'widening access' projects run across Scotland, a few of which are linked to law schools. The Greater Opportunity for Access and Learning with Schools (GOALS) programme in Glasgow (http://www.goals.ac.uk/) gives pupils the opportunity to discover and realise the benefits of higher education. The Lothians Equal Access Programme for Schools (LEAPS) (http://www.leapsonline.org/) aims to increase participation in higher education among students from non-traditional backgrounds. At Edinburgh University the Pathways to the Professions scheme has the support of professional bodies and provides information, guidance and programmes to school students interested in studying law or medicine (http://www.rals.ed.ac.uk/widening/pathways.html).

Offers

4.11 Demand for places in law schools usually outstrips supply, and accordingly the offer of a place is generally based on examination grades (although note the 'widening access' programmes referred to at para **4.10** above). You may well need a high proportion of As in your exam passes. The offer of a place may be unconditional, because you have already met the requirements of the law school's 'going rate', or conditional: that is to say, dependent on your achieving certain grades (usually high) in the examinations which you are about to take. Scottish school leavers generally apply when in sixth year, their first attempt at Highers safely behind them. If you have the grades which law schools require, then you can proceed to a course of Advanced Highers or A levels, or even take a 'gap year' before university entry, since an offer, if made, is likely to be unconditional. You can also apply for 'deferred entry', that is to say, entering the law school two years from the time of application rather than in the following year. If you opt for a year off between school and university, ensure that you use the time in a reasonably disciplined and constructive manner; it can be difficult to regain the appetite for study and exams! If you have not quite made the grade, then you may find it difficult to gain a place at all, and an offer, if made, is likely to be conditional on performance in fresh Highers (rather than re-takes). A-level candidates are usually applying before they have taken their final examinations, so only conditional offers can be made, unless Highers which achieve the 'going rate' have already been taken. This can sometimes put candidates from outside Scotland at a disadvantage, inasmuch as most places tend to be taken up by candidates receiving unconditional offers based on Highers.

What courses should I take?

4.12 Applicants or potential applicants are often concerned about what are the appropriate courses to take before seeking entry to the law degree. There is a popular perception that law is more suitable for those with an inclination towards or background in the arts, humanities and social sciences. While subjects and courses in these fields will provide a perfectly good basis for moving on to law, there is equally nothing about law that makes a scientific or mathematical background inappropriate. Indeed the greatest of all Scots lawyers, the institutional writer Lord Stair, was a scientist, although perhaps modern scientists would find it difficult to recognise his scientific writings as science at all since, despite the earlier work of Copernicus, Kepler, Galileo and Newton, Stair adhered to a Ptolemaic concept of the universe. Lord President Cooper wrote papers about astronomy, while in his *Introductory Essays on Scots Law* Professor W A Wilson included an invaluable account of how the intensity of noise is measured, a matter very important in environmental law and the law of health and safety at work. Other lawyers have been distinguished mathematicians: for example, Lord Mackay of Clashfern, the first Scots lawyer to be Lord Chancellor of Great Britain, and, among English lawyers, Lord Denning. A grasp of basic mathematics is also helpful in approaching Professor Wilson's article on noise mentioned above. Computer skills are increasingly useful in legal studies and legal practice. The logical mind of the scientist and the mathematician, not to mention the philosopher, can be a considerable advantage in legal reasoning. The best advice would seem to be to follow the courses and subjects which interest you most. If 'relevance' worries you – and it should not – then you should consider that almost anything can be relevant to law. For a text-based discipline such as law in which communication skills also play a major part, English is always important; languages are an increasingly necessary skill as international frontiers dissolve; history, geography, economics, business and modern studies all sharpen your appreciation of the world in which the law has to function and develop; an understanding of science and technology is invaluable in coming to grips with legal problems in many fields ranging from family and criminal law to intellectual property. Lawyers need to be numerate, not only to calculate fees, but to compose and read accounts, understand financial documents and work out tax liabilities. In general, therefore, law students and the lawyers that they will become need flexible and fairly well-stocked minds, or at the least minds which are receptive and able to get to grips quickly with new material and ideas when necessary.

4.13 It might seem that one useful subject which could be taken before applying to a law school is law itself. Unfortunately there are no SQA Advanced Highers, Highers or Standard grades in law, and the subject is not generally taught in Scottish schools. There are however GCE A-levels in law and constitutional law. You should be cautious about these, however, as the syllabi are based on English rather than Scots law. Indeed, in some Scottish law schools neither was recognised as an entrance qualification at all until recently. As already noted, the HND in legal studies is also not generally recognised as an entrance qualification for a university law degree.

4.14 A popular misconception is that you need Latin before you can do law. This is not the case; most law students and lawyers get by very well with minimal or no knowledge of Latin. It is true that lawyers use Latin from time to time, and so Latin, like most other subjects, can be useful. Generally these usages are of words or phrases, the meaning of which is well-known to lawyers in general even when they know no other Latin. They are used as a form of shorthand, because the Latin can express some concept or legal idea more economically than English. A list of these is included as Appendix 4, and this illustrates the point just made. Another way in which Latin comes up in law is its use in 'maxims', that is, sentences embodying some basic legal principle. The Latinity occurs because very often these maxims originate in some Roman or Civilian text. The reason for their continued use is because, once again, the Latin is often neater than any English translation. Latinity which goes beyond the ability to recognise well-established phrases and maxims is still of value and often essential in two contexts, one academic, the other practical. The first is where as part of your studies you engage in advanced work in Roman law and general legal history at honours or post-graduate level, when you will have to grapple with Latin texts; but such study is not required of every law student. Secondly, until the nineteenth century most conveyancing documents were in Latin (usually very bad Latin), and these often still have practical significance today, making the Latinate lawyer a useful person to have around. However, most lawyers now recognise that the use of Latin is generally a way of obscuring meaning for lay people, and will seek to avoid it where possible. All conveyancing is in English, although it is a moot point whether the quality and comprehensibility of much of the language used is any advance on the old conveyancers' Latin. If you find your law teachers or lawyers using Latin which you do not understand, you should feel free to ask for a translation and explanation. As a teacher myself, I learned my lesson when the phrase '*stare decisis*' which I had used in a lecture came back in exam scripts as 'starry deceases'! A final word would be that knowledge of Latin, like that of any other language, extends your knowledge and understanding in a variety of valuable ways as well as making much important legal culture more accessible to you; if your talents and interests lie in this direction, then *hoc age*!

Personal statement on the application form

4.15 Returning to the UCAS form, the next important section is the one in which you are allowed to write about yourself as someone other than a taker of exams. Although exams and attendant grades are likely to be the most important factor determining the success or otherwise of your application, this section of the form also needs care and attention. Most candidates use it to describe extra-curricular activities and interests, factors which have led to the choice of law as a university subject, career aspirations (which need not be entry to the legal profession – see further Chapter 13 below), and experiences which might be relevant to your studies or show a special aptitude for them. All these are things well worth bringing to the selector's attention, and they may help tip the balance in your favour if matters come to a choice between you and other applicants when purely academic factors are equal.

4.16 There are three groups of applicants for whom this personal section may be particularly important: mature applicants, those who already hold a degree, and those who suffer from disabilities or health problems.

4.17 *Mature applicants* may find this personal section a useful place in which to flesh out the bare bones of their CVs. If there is not enough space for you to say all you want, you should not hesitate to write directly to the universities to which you are applying with more details. Especially where at the time of application the candidate has yet to take any of the recognised examinations, or has not taken any recently, this is probably the best chance of catching the eye of the selector, and being asked to come for interview or even being made an offer. Aside from the factors already mentioned above, you can use this opportunity to give a more rounded picture of yourself, the steps of inquiry you have already taken – for example, into what is involved in a legal career – your employment career, any experience relevant to law (for example, as a client, a juror or in your employment), any further education taken, any signs of aptitude for law, and why you want to change direction at this stage.

4.18 For *graduate applicants* the advice is much the same as for mature ones, especially if you have been in employment since you took your first degree. If you are coming straight on to the law degree from your first one, it may also be worth explaining why you did not start with a law degree (which could be for the basic reasons that your entry qualifications were not good enough at the time, or because you had not thought of it then). You should certainly mention courses in your first degree that might be relevant to law or were indeed law courses.

4.19   *Physical disabilities and health problems* which you know affect your studies or which might do so are worth mentioning in the personal section of the UCAS form. This is not because these things affect your chances of getting in, either favourably or adversely, but because once you are admitted the form is usually the basis of the university's file on you. Universities have obligations under the Disability Discrimination Act 1996, and there are a variety of support services available for students. Knowledge in advance that particular types of support are or may be required helps ensure that they are given where needed. It also enables the university to be alert to, and deal with, any difficulties which you may encounter, for example, with dyslexia, hearing difficulties, or wheelchair access to buildings.

Who should my referee be?

4.20   The last section of the UCAS form is for a referee's report. For school leavers, this will usually be provided by a head or careers teacher; for recent graduates, a tutor or adviser/director of studies may be the best bet. Older graduates and mature applicants may have more difficulty in identifying an appropriate referee. A good guiding principle is to choose someone with a university or academic background who has some reasonably well-informed knowledge of your own academic and intellectual abilities. This reference is not quite the same thing as a reference for a job, and the matters which are important for an employer may not be quite so significant for a university selector. So this is a matter requiring some thought on the part of the applicant and the person approached to be a referee. It is also important to remember that the reference can help mark out your application from others in a very competitive entry field, so choose your referee with care.

FUNDING

4.21 University is an increasingly complex and expensive business for the student and those who support him or her. You can apply to the Student Awards Agency for Scotland (SAAS) for support towards tuition fees and living costs. See Appendix 1 for the address of SAAS; its website is http://www.student-support-saas.gov.uk/. The requirements which you must meet to have tuition fees paid are:

(a) ordinary residence in the United Kingdom *for the last three years*;
(b) ordinary residence in Scotland *at the time of the application* (ordinary residence means the place you live in as your home);
(c) your course is eligible for support (a first undergraduate degree in law will be); and
(d) no previous help from public funds for tuition fees on another full-time higher education course.

If, as will be the case with a Scots law degree, your course is at a Scottish university, SAAS will pay your annual tuition fees directly to your institution. In 2003–04 these were £1,125 (a figure well below the cost of the programme per student, incidentally). Graduate entrants, who will normally have already received support from public funds in respect of their first degree, cannot be supported in this way (see further below, para 4.23). If your tuition fees have been paid in this way, you will be liable to make payments to the Graduate Endowment once awarded a degree. The payment is in recognition of the higher education benefits you have received, and the income generated goes towards future student support. The amount payable if you had started in higher education in academic year 2003–04 was £2,030, a total that will increase by the rate of inflation for those entering higher education in later years. See para 4.22 for the repayment mechanism. You will not be liable for the Graduate Endowment, however, if you are classed as a mature student at the start of your course. Students in general may also claim allowances in respect of spouses and dependent children, something which is most likely to be of importance to mature students.

4.22 In addition to tuition fees, all students have to meet *accommodation and living expenses*, and the cost of buying texts (not insubstantial in law) and other materials (eg pen and paper, laptop). *Student loans* are the main way in which support towards such living costs can be obtained from public funds. If you want such a loan, apply to the SAAS on the same form as the one by which you apply for a contribution towards meeting your tuition costs (if any). The amount which you will be entitled to receive depends to some extent upon the contribution which you, your parents or your spouse are expected to make. SAAS will confirm the amount of the loan that you are entitled to and invite you to say how much of it you want. The loan will however be paid to you by the Student Loans Company (address in Appendix 1, website http://www.slc.co.uk/index.html). Loans and the Graduate Endowment will be repaid through the Inland Revenue, meaning that repayments will be collected by your employer alongside tax and national insurance. Special arrangements will apply to you if you are self-employed or are not a UK taxpayer. Payments will begin automatically once your income reaches an appropriate level (£10,000 gross per year at April 2004), and the amount repaid will be 9% of your income above this. The level of your repayment will rise directly in line with your income. If for any reason your income falls below the threshold, you will not have to make repayments.

'Young students' bursaries

4.23   As well as having their tuition fees met in full, students who are 'young students' (either under 25 on the first day of their course; or unmarried; or who have supported themselves from their own earnings or benefits for three years prior to the start of their course; or whose parents are dead) can claim for the 'young students' bursary', depending on the level of their family income. The maximum they can get at the time of writing (April 2004) is £2,100 regardless of where the student lives during term-time. This reduces to nil at a family income of £27,200. The bursary does not need to be repaid. An income-assessed loan is also available over and above the bursary.

Graduate entrants

4.24   If you are a graduate going into a law degree, you are not entitled to a public contribution towards your tuition costs. On the other hand you are eligible for a student loan. Otherwise, however, you will be self-funding, having to cover the tuition fees in particular, and at many universities these are much higher than for first degree students. Checking the exact level should be a priority for any graduate contemplating entry. Taking law as a 'second first degree' will involve a substantial personal financial commitment. There are a variety of ways of raising the money apart from parental or other family support, bank loans, and casual employment.

There are a number of educational trusts and charities which give varying levels of support to second degree students. Directories of these can often be found in public libraries. A charity which has provided extensive support for second first degree law students of Scottish extraction is the Carnegie Trust, which is based in Dunfermline (see http://www.carnegie-trust.org/grant6.htm). Other charitable endowments which may be helpful to second degree law students are the Clark Foundation for Legal Education, the WS Society Educational Scholarship, and the Pritchard Educational Trust (administered by the Law Society of Scotland). The Clark Foundation may give financial assistance to those not able to obtain grants for degree-level study (see further http://www.todsmurray.com/recruitment/clark-foundation.htm, email address clarkfoundation@todsmurray.com). The WS Scholarship is more directed towards financing the study of and research into law or the practice of law with special reference to Community law; first preference is given to members of the WS Society, followed by qualified assistants and trainees, but all applications will be considered. The Pritchard Trust, however, aims to help those pursuing the academic qualifications necessary for a career in law. For further information on funding and charities, see Appendix 3.

UNIVERSITY EXAMINATIONS AND PROFESSIONAL EXEMPTION

4.25   Once you are admitted to the law degree, you are embarked upon a course of full-time study with courses taking place during the day. The Strathclyde Law School runs a part-time law degree with evening classes, but completion can take up to six years, compared with two to four years full-time. If you already hold a degree, then generally it will be possible to complete your full-time law degree in two years. For all other full-time students, the period of study will be either three or four years. The Ordinary degree takes three years and the Honours four. The academic difference between the two is that in the latter during third and fourth years (in some cases in fourth year only) you take courses which are taught at a higher level (SHE Level 4 on the Scottish Qualifications Credit Framework), usually with smaller class sizes, while in the Ordinary degree your courses are generally taught at a somewhat lower level (SHE Levels 1, 2 and 3 on the SQCF)[1]. Whether you have one or the other makes little difference to your eligibility to enter the legal profession, save that in the case of an advocate possession of a first- or second-class Honours degree shortens your period of training in a solicitor's office from 21 to 12 months. Generally possession of an Honours degree may be more attractive to employers, especially if you go outside Scotland, where the concept of an 'Ordinary' degree – is it some sort of compensation for failure in Honours? – is, sadly, not always well understood. What is crucial if you want to go into the Scottish legal profession is that the courses you take satisfy the requirements for entry into, first, the Diploma in Legal Practice and, second, the profession itself. It is worth noting that each law school has its own way of enabling its students to fulfil these requirements which will not necessarily correspond head-for-head with these lists, but all are currently accepted as covering the ground to the profession's satisfaction.

1   For the Scottish Qualifications Credit Framework as it applies to university courses, see http://www.scqf.org.uk/.

4.26   The benefit of ensuring that your degree course covers the professionally-required subjects is that you will not need to do any more exams post-Diploma to enter the profession. The admission regulations of both the Law Society and the School of Advocates provide for a subject-for-subject exemption from their own exams in respect of degree passes. But some students choose not to use their law degrees as a basis for entry into the profession, only later changing their minds. Another quite common scenario is the student who chooses to omit from the degree some of the subjects required only by the Faculty of Advocates and not by the Law Society or the Diploma – for example, Roman law and international private law – but who later seeks admission as an advocate. In both situations the law graduate is allowed to take the relevant professional examinations and so make further progress towards entering his or her chosen branch of the profession. A further alternative is to return to the university law school and take the relevant courses and examinations on a non-graduating basis, which has the advantage over the professional examination that there is formal instruction preceding the exam.

Curriculum

4.27   The present range of compulsory subjects does put some restrictions on the curricular choice available to the law student wishing to use the LL.B as a platform for entry into the profession. A good deal of the degree will be taken up with satisfying the professional requirements, and the amount of time available to explore other options available in the law schools may be rather limited unless you take Honours – and even then you may have to cram all the professional subjects into your first two years of study. The range of other options potentially available is very wide, and a number have already been mentioned. Others which may be found include courses in yet more branches of the law. Public international law governs such matters as international relations between states, war and the exploitation of the seabed outside territorial waters, and seems ever more important as people and governments struggle rather unsuccessfully to cope with 'the new world order'. International law cannot become a source of domestic law without an enabling statute (hence, for example, the European Communities Act 1972 and the Human Rights Act 1998, giving effect to the EC Treaty and the European Convention on Human Rights). This can sometimes obscure a little the reality of international law; but in Scotland the High Court of Justiciary examined international law directly to deal with cases arising from protests against the location of Trident missiles in the Firth of Clyde (see *John v Donnelly* 1999 SCCR 802 and *Lord Advocate's Reference No 1 of 2000* 2001 JC 143).

4.28 New courses spring up all the time: Media Law, Medical Law and Information Technology Law are examples of more recent entrants to law school curricula. Comparative law, in which different legal systems, and their approaches to legal problems, are compared in order to determine the relationships between them as well as, perhaps, which has the best solution, has revived because it involves the study of other legal systems, a matter of increasing importance in Europe in particular. Some subjects use the methods of other disciplines to throw fresh light on the law and its development, such as criminology, penology and sociology of law. Empirical study of what the courts and other legal institutions actually do from day to day, as opposed to the examination of the doctrinal material which they produce, is at least a necessary balance to the more traditional rule-based approach. Note also the economic analysis of law, under which legal rules are tested by the standards of economic efficiency.

4.29 Forensic medicine deserves a word or two more than others because this is a subject of particular importance to court lawyers. Essentially the subject covers those aspects of medicine and psychiatry relevant to law. The most familiar instance is probably provided by the forensic scientists who analyse the cause and time of death in the murder cases confronting TV policemen such as Taggart and Morse. Indeed in some TV series, such as *Silent Witness* and *Dangerfield*, the forensic scientist became the detective hero in his or her own right, as did the forensic psychologist in *Cracker*. But medical evidence can also be crucial in delict and other civil cases, while the law is also frequently concerned with the mental state of individuals in order to determine both civil and criminal matters. The forensic scientist is often an expert witness in such cases, and the course provides an invaluable basis for the lawyer who is going to have to work with such evidence. It has been suggested that there ought to be other such courses in fields of technical and scientific knowledge such as engineering, architecture, computers and biotechnology, but these have yet to develop.

4.30   Reference to the gains to be made by looking at law with the techniques of other disciplines throws up the possibility of exploring the intellectual resources of the university outside the law school. It is not uncommon for law students to take courses in such subjects as politics, economics and history, the content of which have much relevance to legal studies. Managing partners in law firms often say that knowledge and understanding of the problems of business and management, such as might be gained in business studies courses, could be helpful both from the point of view of appreciating the problems of business clients, and for tackling the administration of the law office which is of necessity also a business. For this reason many solicitors now undertake relevant postgraduate business administration courses such as the MBA. Perhaps most significant of all as legal horizons expand to Europe is modern languages. French and German are likely to remain the most popular choices, with Italian and Spanish coming next among the languages of the European Union. In some universities there may be courses in some of these languages specially geared to the needs of law students. Looking to the wider world, Japanese should be borne in mind, especially given the current level of Japanese investment in Britain, while, looking perhaps more to the future, there is also Russian and Chinese. Coming back home, there is of course Gaelic, not to mention the languages of the various ethnic minorities, any one of which may be the first or only language of a lawyer's clients.

Joint or mixed Honours degrees

4.31   Some students may decide to take degrees which combine law fully with some other discipline and give rise to what is known as either a joint or mixed Honours degree. Although possible with all the outside subjects already mentioned, and others, joint Honours is most common in two fields, law with a modern European language and law with either business studies or accounting. With the latter two, the aim of the student has usually been to go on to a business or accounting career, in both of which knowledge and understanding of law is extremely valuable. But as noted in the previous paragraph, the business and accounting elements can be equally useful in a legal career, while the attraction to a solicitor employer of an Honours language graduate also qualified in law is obvious. Advocates too may need languages at an advanced level to take advantage of the increasing opportunities to appear in the courts of the European Union. While joint Honours can therefore prove very rewarding in several senses, you should be warned that the exigencies of reaching Honours standards in two disciplines while at the same time completing the compulsory subjects for entry to the profession can be extremely demanding. While many students embark on the programmes, few survive to the end. Those who make it usually do very well, perhaps because you have to be strong academically to get so far. The small number of joint honours graduates in law is to be regretted, since the degrees are certainly worth having both from a personal point of view and from the point of view of the legal profession as a whole; but they may only become common if the range of the compulsory subjects is in some way reduced.

SOCRATES

4.32   As noted in the brief discussion of the subject in Chapter 3 (para **3.12**), a key concept of European Community law is the free movement of persons and services throughout the Community. With regard to students and universities this has been promoted by the Community's SOCRATES programme (sometimes also known as ERASMUS), which enables students to spend time studying at a university in another member state and have that time counted towards their degrees at their home universities. Universities throughout Europe have entered a host of agreements and networks through which they exchange students for periods ranging from a few weeks to a full academic year. The Scottish law schools have participated in these schemes, and every year each receives numbers of law students from various parts of the Community and sends out some of its own. The programme offers a splendid opportunity to study the law of another country in that country, normally, although not invariably, in its own language. Quite apart from the social and intellectual advantages which the experience will confer, it will also be attractive to employers. Students studying abroad under a SOCRATES exchange will receive a 'top-up' grant which covers the extra costs which may be incurred because the cost of living in the host country is higher than in the United Kingdom. You continue to receive any maintenance award which you may have from the SAAS or your LEA and remain eligible for a student loan. No fees are payable to the host university, but home fees remain payable, however, in effect keeping your place warm for you. More information can be found on the following websites: http://europa.eu.int/comm/education/programmes/ socrates/erasmus/what_en.html (the European Union site), and http:// www.erasmus.ac.uk/index.html (the United Kingdom one). You may also find it useful to check your own university's websites on international exchanges.

4.33   It will generally also be possible to study Community law in the host university; if the curriculum there covers the topics described earlier (see above, para **3.12**), the course will probably satisfy the professional requirements. You should check this with the Law Society of Scotland or the Faculty of Advocates, as appropriate, as soon as you know what the curriculum of the host university's course is.

Graduation

4.34   The upshot of successful completion of your university studies in law is the award of the degree of Bachelor of Laws, in abbreviated form the LL.B. Note the plural 'Laws', which is an inheritance from the days when universities taught only the two learned laws, the Civil and the Canon. The Latin form, *baccalaureus utriusque juris*, meaning 'bachelor of both laws', is a reminder of the origins of university study of law. The double 'L' of LL.B follows the Latin convention for abbreviating a plural word by repeating its initial letter, so the degree should never be rendered 'L.L.B.' or 'Ll.B'. 'LLB' is just permissible. The award takes place at a colourful graduation ceremony which is a most satisfying and enjoyable occasion for the graduand who thus becomes a graduate.

CHAPTER 5

Alternatives to the law degree

ENTERING THE PROFESSION: ALTERNATIVES TO STARTING WITH A LAW DEGREE

5.01 As the historical material noted earlier makes clear, the qualification of a degree in Scots law was grafted on to the older system of training by apprenticeship. In both branches of the profession it remains at least theoretically possible to qualify without having first taken a law degree. But there are still a number of academic and other hurdles to be jumped.

ADVOCATES

5.02 The first stage for anyone seeking admission as an advocate is to petition the Court of Session for admission. A petition currently costs £106. The court will then remit you to the Faculty of Advocates to matriculate you as an intrant[1]. To become an intrant to the Faculty of Advocates and embark upon the path to calling without recourse to a university degree in Scots law, you need an exemption from the Dean of Faculty under regulation 8 of the regulations for intrants, who will decide after consultation with his Council. Only in exceptional circumstances will the exemption be granted, but regard may be had to such objective evidence of the applicant's intellectual ability as the applicant may produce. In general, that means holding the qualifications necessary to enter upon the curriculum for a degree in law at a Scottish university (see above, para **4.08**). Any application for an exemption must be accompanied by a fee of

£25. Having been exempted, you then pay matriculation fees (currently £150), and must go on to pass the Faculty examinations. If your non-law degree included law passes, you may get appropriate exemptions. There is a formidable list of examinations, which is set out in Chapter 3 (para **3.03**). All take the form of a written paper, but an oral examination may be held. A fee of £25 is charged for each examination taken, and there are no express limits upon how often you may attempt each one. But if the Faculty's examiners are satisfied, having regard to an intrant's previous performance in Faculty examinations, that he or she should not be permitted to sit any further examinations, or that permission should only be given subject to conditions, the Dean of Faculty may exclude that intrant absolutely or conditionally from further examination. Absolute exclusion from examinations entails removal from the roll of intrants, although this requires further procedure before the Dean and the examiners. There are three diets [sets] of examinations each year, in February, May and October. The standard of the examinations is the same as for university law degree examinations. So academically there is no real difference here from the position under the degree route. If you have the qualifications necessary to do the law degree, you are probably academically better off doing it rather than the Faculty's examinations, especially as the Faculty provides no formal courses of instruction to prepare candidates for examination. Indeed, many intrants sitting Faculty examinations take the relevant university courses on a non-graduating basis. They do, however, have the advantage of the right to study in what is the best law library in Scotland, and one of the best in the world, namely the Advocates' Library. Countering the academic benefits of a degree course, if in going to university you would have to pay the fees from your own pocket, it is worth noting that the fees for matriculating and being examined in the Faculty are considerably less. After completing the examination requirements, you are then admitted to pupillage, as to which see paras **7.19–7.26** below.

1   Note that the admissions procedure as described from this point on was under review at the time of writing (April 2004). It is likely that the Faculty will cease to prescribe the content of degrees and will instead insist upon prior qualification as a Scottish solicitor, requiring of intrants only the sitting of pre-entry examinations in evidence, procedure, Roman law and international private law. The new regulations may be promulgated in 2005.

SOLICITORS

Pre-Diploma training contract with a solicitor

5.03 The first step is to enter into a pre-Diploma training contract with an employing solicitor. This means (1) possession of the necessary academic qualifications; and (2) finding a solicitor who is willing to employ you on this basis.

Necessary academic qualifications

5.04 During the pre-Diploma training you must take and pass seven of the Law Society's examinations in the compulsory subjects (see above, para **3.03**). To be eligible for these examinations, you must already hold certain academic qualifications. These are of a somewhat lower standard than those required by university law schools and the Faculty of Advocates. There are six possible types of qualification: SQA passes, GCE passes, the HND in legal studies, a university degree other than one in law (otherwise you would not need to be using this avenue of qualification), membership of a professional accountancy body, and a commission as an officer in one of the British armed services if the commission was obtained following study at a Royal Navy, Army or Royal Air Force college. For full details of the recognised qualifications, you should refer to the admission regulations, but it seems worthwhile to deal in a little more detail here with SQA passes and the HND in legal studies, as these are the qualifications which are held most often by people seeking entry to the profession in this way.

SQA qualifications needed

5.05 If you are offering SQA qualifications, you need five passes, obtained at no more than two sittings, at either Higher or Standard grade. These must include:
(1) Higher English at B or better;
(2) one other Higher in mathematics or an approved science or an approved language other than English; and
(3) Standard grade passes must include mathematics, an approved science or language in whichever group has not been studied to Higher level, and must be at grade 3 or above.

Finally, you must obtain 8 points on the Law Society's scale from your passes as a whole. Only Highers count for this purpose; an A is given 3 points, a B 2, and a C 1. It follows from this that you need a minimum of three Highers to obtain the preliminary entrance certificate.

The HND in legal studies

5.06   The HND in legal studies is fully recognised by the Law Society as a qualification. It must be a Scottish HND offered by a college of further education approved by the Council of the Law Society. However, it is not a sufficient qualification on its own; candidates must offer alongside it a Higher pass in English at Grade B or better.

Mature candidates

5.07   Like the universities, the Law Society relaxes some of its academic requirements in respect of mature applicants for entry. If you are at least 21 years of age, you can apply to the Council for relaxation of the entrance requirements. The Council must still be satisfied that you are a fit and proper person to be a solicitor, and there must be evidence of academic attainment (that is, there must be *some* qualifications). A further relevant factor may be experience of legal work, for example as a secretary or an unqualified assistant in a law office. Initial inquiries should be made at the Law Society.

Finding a solicitor who will employ you

5.08   Finding a solicitor who will employ you in a pre-Diploma training contract can be a difficult matter unless you are already employed by a solicitor (the obvious examples are again the secretary or unqualified assistant), or are on good terms already with a member of the profession. You should check that the employing solicitor or his firm satisfy certain conditions. Before a solicitors' firm can take on a trainee, at least one of the partners or the directors must have been in continuous practice for at least three years immediately before the training contract begins. In the case of sole practitioners (firms with only one partner – check the firm's notepaper and see how many names appear on it), or where the employing solicitor is working for a local authority or some other organisation, the solicitor must have been in three years' continuous practice immediately prior to the employment of the trainee. It is also important to remember that some solicitors are not allowed to take on trainees without the consent in writing of the Council of the Law Society, and you should not be afraid to ask the prospective employer whether he has been disqualified as a trainer. You can always check with the Law Society in any event. Similarly there are limits on the number of pre- and post-Diploma trainees a firm may have at any one time. Sole practitioners are only entitled to have one, while other firms may employ up to twice the number of partners in the firm or twice the number of the directors in the incorporated practice. The numbers who may be employed by local authorities and any other solicitors practising in Scotland (for example, in-house lawyers in large companies or banks) are determined in a similar way: twice the number of solicitors employed by the solicitor's employer unless he or she is the only one, in which case only one trainee may be taken on. Again, therefore, it is worth making inquiries of your prospective employer or of the Law Society concerning the number of trainees in the organisation; if the employer has unwittingly exceeded, or by employing you is about to exceed, the permitted number, the written consent of Council should be sought to cover the position. So you should check:

(1) How long have the principals been in practice?
(2) How many principals are there?
(3) Does the Law Society of Scotland allow this employer to take on trainees?
(4) How many trainees does the firm have?
(5) How many trainees may it have?

Registration of contract with Law Society of Scotland

5.09 Despite all these potential problems, people do obtain pre-Diploma training contracts. Each year, typically, two or three people qualify for entry to the profession along this route, and obviously there is a much larger number in the midst of the process at any given time. What happens if you are one of the lucky ones? First, remember to send your training contract to the Law Society as soon as possible. The admission regulations provide that pre-Diploma contracts must be registered with the Society within three months of their commencement. This will cost you a small sum of money (£25 in April 2004). If you do not send your contract in within the three-month period, the penalty is that your training period of three years can be treated as not commencing until the contract is actually produced. So none of the period during which you have been working and receiving training without registering your contract will count towards the three years you need; frustrating both for you and your employer. So make sure that this is done; the onus is on you.

Content of pre-Diploma training

5.10 The contract will comprise three years of full-time training with your employing solicitor. Part-time training is allowed, but the total time spent working under such a contract must equate to three years of full-time training. The contract obliges the employing solicitor to provide training in the following areas of legal work:
(1) conveyancing,
(2) litigation, and
(3) either trusts and executries or the legal work of a public authority (which depends on the nature of your employing solicitor's practice).

Assignation of training contract

5.11 Not all employing solicitors will be able to fulfil these obligations as to the content of the pre-Diploma training contract. Once again, this is a matter worth raising when negotiating the contract, since the solicitor will have to provide the Law Society with a letter confirming that training in the three prescribed areas can be offered by the firm. But it does not follow that, if the firm is unable to offer all of the prescribed areas of practice, you will lose your chance of starting training with it. It is perfectly possible for the pre-Diploma trainee to transfer from the first to another employing solicitor approved by the Council of the Law Society, to enable completion of training in the three prescribed areas of practice. Such transfers are known as *assignations*. If arrangements are made based on early discussion among all concerned, a great deal of trouble can be saved. It is no good entering your contract without being aware of what training can actually be provided by the employing solicitor. The worst way of finding out is through the failure of the employing solicitor to provide the training during the contract. You can also assign your contract to another employing solicitor in order to extend the range of your training generally (again a matter which should be discussed first with your current employing solicitor if you wish to avoid or minimise difficulty in the matter). Finally, you may assign for other reasons than those already mentioned, but only if Council considers such reasons reasonable. Examples might be where relations between the trainee and the employing solicitor have broken down, or where the trainee's domestic circumstances require a move to another area. Here, obviously, the Law Society must be approached first. A final point about any assignation is that, like the original training contract, it must be registered with the Law Society.

Secondment

5.12   Another possible way of dealing with the situation where a trainer cannot provide training in a prescribed area of practice is *secondment* of the trainee to another employer who can provide work in that area. This is a less formal process than assignation, and might well be negotiated between the two employers concerned; but the approval of the Law Society must be obtained before such an arrangement goes ahead.

Law Society examinations

5.13   The pre-Diploma trainee is eligible to sit the Law Society's examinations, which are generally held in two diets each year. Before the trainee can move on to the Diploma stage of qualification, these examinations must be passed. A list is provided in Chapter 3 (para **3.03**). The examinations are of university standard but, like the Faculty of Advocates, the Law Society provides no formal courses of instruction, and preparation is a matter for the candidate. Combining private study with full-time employment as a trainee is a formidable task. The admission regulations allow a pre-Diploma trainee to attend classes in law at a university or elsewhere during office hours, but the consent of the employing solicitor must be obtained first. This is another matter which should be settled before the contract is made. A number of other points need to be borne in mind. If you do want to attend university or other classes, formal application will have to be made to the institution concerned, and fees will have to be paid. If you are lucky, your employer may meet these, but in my experience this is the exception rather than the rule. If you live at a distance from a university, making regular attendance impractical, it is nonetheless worth inquiring whether there are materials which might be sent to you and if there is a law teacher willing to act as an occasional coach or tutor for you. Bear in mind that a fee is appropriate for both these services, and ask at the outset what the charge will be.

5.14   You have four years in which to pass all the Society's examinations once you have taken your first one. This means that you can still take the examinations even though your pre-Diploma training contract has expired (although note that Law Society examinations cannot be taken *before* you have entered the contract). To be still sitting the examinations after three years of pre-Diploma training is not a very satisfactory situation, however, and you should try to work out a schedule of examinations which, all being well, will enable you to proceed smoothly from the completion of the contract on to the commencement of the Diploma. Subject to the four-year rule mentioned above, you are allowed four attempts to pass each examination. You should not necessarily feel that failure in an examination means that you are incapable of practising as a solicitor, but repeated failures can have a damaging effect on morale and motivation. If they start to occur relatively early in your progress through the examinations, it may be worth re-thinking your career plans, and it is certainly something that you should discuss with your employing solicitor. Here again the Council of the Law Society has a dispensing power, in that it may allow you to exceed the four-year period and waive the restriction to four attempts at any one paper. The support of your employing solicitor who knows the quality of your work in the office will certainly be helpful in persuading Council to exercise this discretion in your favour.

5.15   After all this talk of failure in the Law Society's examinations, it is worth saying that the majority of intrants taking the papers pass them despite occasional setbacks, and proceed without too much difficulty on to the next stage, the Diploma in Legal Practice.

CHAPTER 6

The Diploma in Legal Practice

INTRODUCTION

6.01 The Diploma in Legal Practice was introduced in 1980 and is a necessary step in qualification for both branches of the Scottish legal profession. It does not matter whether one starts by taking a university law degree or by taking the examinations of the Law Society or the Faculty of Advocates. Those who emerge from these courses of study and training must next submit themselves to the Diploma, which, as already noted, is a programme mounted in the Scottish law schools but taught principally by practitioners. The aim of the Diploma is to provide a bridge from university classes in law to legal practice, showing how the law studied during the degree is applied by and forms the approach of the practitioner. The diplomate thus enters the legal office rather better prepared for both the formalities and the rough and tumble of professional life. Although the Diploma has not been short of critics since its inception, it seems to be generally accepted that the modern diplomate is readier for the realities of practice than the mere graduate entrant of yesteryear, and to that extent at least it must be regarded as a successful and integral part of legal training in Scotland. Indeed, it has been held up as a model to follow in other jurisdictions within the United Kingdom. However, it has undergone some modification, and a new-look Diploma came into full operation in October 2000.

EXEMPTION FROM THE DIPLOMA

6.02   Those who have come through the pre-Diploma training contract sometimes argue that the Diploma should not be necessary for them, given that they have already undergone a three-year period of in-office training coupled with the academic study required to pass the Law Society examinations. Further, the practical difficulties for such people in taking the Diploma can be very great. Although for some the Diploma is funded by postgraduate vocational grants from the Student Awards Agency for Scotland (SAAS) covering part of the fees and means-tested maintenance, and for which those who have come through the pre-Diploma training contract are eligible (see further below, para **6.05**), the fact that it is a full-time course means giving up regular paid employment for the year the course lasts. As the Diploma is only available in the university towns of Aberdeen, Dundee, Edinburgh and Glasgow (Glasgow and Strathclyde Universities offer a joint programme at the Glasgow Graduate School of Law), there can be problems of travel and accommodation for those who have lived and worked in other places. As a consequence, requests for exemption from the Diploma requirement are sometimes made by such candidates for admission. The Law Society's admission regulations do provide for such an exemption where the Council is satisfied that it is justified by exceptional circumstances. It is clear, however, that merely having done the pre-Diploma training contract is not an exceptional circumstance; nor, generally, are consequential financial, travel or accommodation problems. There are specific exemptions for lawyers qualified in other jurisdictions (see below, para **6.03**). The Dean of the Faculty of Advocates in consultation with his Council also has discretion to exempt in exceptional circumstances an applicant from the Diploma requirement imposed by the Faculty, but the circumstances must include other relevant professional experience. It is most likely to be applied in the case of lawyers qualified previously in other jurisdictions and now entering the Faculty. So it seems that most prospective entrants to the Scottish legal profession, whether or not they are coming through the degree route of qualification, must take the Diploma into account in making their plans.

6.03   Some people are exempted from the Diploma as of right under the two sets of admission regulations:
(a)   a solicitor of three years' standing who wishes to become an advocate;
(b)   an advocate who wishes to become a solicitor;
(c)   an English/Welsh or Northern Irish solicitor seeking to become a solicitor in Scotland;

(d) an English/Welsh or Northern Irish barrister with five years of recent active practice seeking to become a solicitor in Scotland;

(e) an English/Welsh or Northern Irish barrister seeking to become an advocate in Scotland;

(f) colonial solicitors to whom the Colonial Solicitors Act 1900 applies seeking to become solicitors in Scotland; and

(g) EC qualified lawyers seeking to become Scottish solicitors or advocates who have passed the eligibility and aptitude tests for such candidates.

See further on points (a) and (b) paras **8.07–8.08**, and on points (c)–(g) paras **8.14–8.17**.

ADMISSION

6.04 Admission to the Diploma follows on applications made before the end of February in the year in which you wish to commence the programme. LL.B graduates need not go directly from their degree studies on to the Diploma, nor need they take the Diploma at the university in which the degree was obtained. Admission is competitive, and success depends on academic merit, primarily as indicated by performance in degree and professional examinations. In some, but not all, of the universities, it is not necessary to have all the professional passes from the degree before you start the Diploma, but the general expectation (and the norm) is that you will do so.

FUNDING

6.05 As already noted, there is an SAAS grant scheme for Diploma students, which has so far survived several Scottish Executive reviews. Several further words of warning must be uttered here. First, under the arrangements prevailing in 2003–04, there were grants for only 300 students, although over 500 students currently take the Diploma each year. There is accordingly competition for grants (the award of a grant is currently judged on academic merit), and a number of students will have to go without. All students who have applied for a place on the Diploma are considered for a grant by the Diploma Co-ordinating Committee in the summer preceding entry to the course, and successful students are then sent a grant application form for submission to the SAAS. By contrast with the degree, the position is not alleviated by the student loan scheme, as student loans are not available to Diploma students. Those who do not get grants will have to work out other ways of financing their studies, which include the possibility of 'Career Development Loans' (see further http://www.lifelonglearning.co.uk/cdl/). The scheme applies to one-year postgraduate courses such as the Diploma, but cannot be used for the LL.B degree. The Clark Foundation for Legal Education and the Pritchard Educational Trust, mentioned earlier (para **4.24**), are other possible sources of support. See further Appendix 3.

CONTENT

6.06   The following courses in the legal practice area are taken during the Diploma year:
(1)   conveyancing;
(2)   company/commercial law or public administration (the choice largely depends on whether you intend to enter private practice or the public sector);
(3)   criminal court practice;
(4)   civil court practice; and
(5)   private client.
In these courses an emphasis will be given to office skills as well as the substance of the law and practice. In addition there are specific skills courses:
(1)   professional ethics and conduct;
(2)   practice management skills;
(3)   financial services and related skills.

6.07   The rough balance is that about a quarter of your time will be spent on court practice, another third on conveyancing and private client, and the remainder will be divided up more or less equally between the other subjects. The relation between the Diploma subjects and the areas of practice described in Chapter 2 is fairly obvious. It should also be noted that they cover a wider range of subject matter than the three prescribed areas of practice in the pre-Diploma training contract, providing one explanation of why the Diploma is regarded as essential even for those who began qualification under that route. It is also the case – and this is a benefit extending to all who take the Diploma – that its courses enable a more systematic coverage of the work lawyers have to do than is possible in an office, where what can be learned is largely dependent on the contingency of what clients it has and the work which those clients want done for them.

DURATION

6.08   The Diploma course involves approximately 30 weeks of teaching and assessment time, beginning in September and finishing by the following May, with a Christmas break. Diplomates would be expected to be ready to commence their office training (see Chapter 7) by the 1 June after completion of the course. It is likely, however, that firms will continue to recruit trainees later in the summer. Note that during the training contract trainees must undertake an approved course of further study (the Professional Competence Course, or PCC), likely to be of about two weeks in duration (see further below, para **7.10**).

EXEMPTION FROM DIPLOMA COURSES

6.09   Although exemption from the Diploma is extremely rare, as already noted, it is rather more common to gain exemption from particular courses in the Diploma. For example, students with accountancy or banking qualifications may gain exemption from at least part of financial services and related skills. Interesting questions in respect of conveyancing may arise in future with regard to qualified conveyancers who seek to move on to a full solicitor's qualification.

STYLE OF DIPLOMA TEACHING

6.10   The emphasis of the Diploma is on office and other professional skills, and the characteristic feature of Diploma teaching is that it is mainly done by legal practitioners, who are therefore only part-time teachers. Full-time academics only become involved in Diploma teaching if they also have substantial practical experience which is of an on-going nature. The teaching techniques used vary from traditional lectures and seminars to case studies, practical exercises, mooting and mock trials, working through the whole process of civil and criminal cases, and computer-based studies. Students engaging in advocacy exercises may be videoed to permit playbacks and critiques of their performances. Diploma assessments also reflect this practical approach; the emphasis is on examination by the completion of tasks and class performances (written and others) as well as the more traditional written papers. Failure in these assessments is by no means unknown, and possession of the LL.B does not confer a divine right to the Diploma. Should you be unlucky enough to fail a Diploma course or courses, you have the opportunity to re-take either the examinations or the courses in question over the next year. But some who fail at this stage abandon the specifically legal career in favour

CHAPTER 7

Professional training

PRACTICAL POST-DIPLOMA TRAINING: SOLICITORS

7.01 The Diploma having been completed, the next stage in qualifying as a solicitor is the post-Diploma training contract. This is a two-year period of full-time training with an employing solicitor. In this period also the Test of Professional Competence must be passed and the Professional Competence Course completed. The training period must be started within two years from the date of 1 January first occurring after you obtain the Diploma; that is, if you are awarded the Diploma in July 2004 you have until 31 December 2006 to start your traineeship. The Council of the Law Society can extend this period but may impose such conditions as it thinks fit when such an extension is made. An example of a situation in which an extension might be granted would be where an applicant had undertaken a period of postgraduate study in law or had been in employment related to law. Normally, however, most trainees go straight on from the Diploma to the traineeship.

Applying for a training place

7.02 There are several points to be made about obtaining a training place. First, over the last few years, there have typically been around about 400 training places available annually with Scottish firms (note the mismatch with the number of Diploma places: para **6.05**). There is no formal universal application system like that for entering university or the

Diploma. Most people start applying during or just before the final year of degree studies. Expect a long haul. You have to find out for yourself which firms, local authorities and other employers are able and willing to take on post-Diploma trainees at the time you happen to want a traineeship. While some traineeships are advertised in the press – for example, those in the Crown Office – by and large you find out about the availability of traineeships in one of three ways. One is to contact potential employers yourself; a second is to respond to the programmes which many firms have for attracting trainees; and the third is through a register of training places maintained by some of the universities.

7.03   The traditional method of application is to write to all the solicitors in the town or area where you want to practice; in effect a pot luck system. You can find out about the private firms by using the various law directories: *The Scottish Law Directory* [the White Book], *The Blue Book: The Directory of the Law Society of Scotland, Chambers Guide to the Legal Profession,* and *The Legal 500.* Look also at *Yellow Pages* and the lists of firms and solicitors on the Law Society website (http://www.lawscot.org.uk). Many of the larger firms now run their own websites which may tell you something about the firm and the training opportunities which it offers. There is also information about public sector and some commercial employers in a few of these directories, most of which should be in your law library. Sometimes these sources also give information about the kind of work done in particular firms, which is helpful if you want to gain experience in particular areas of practice. Talk to your teachers in the law school as well. But you should remember that traineeships ought to give you good general coverage of legal practice, and that over-concentration on one area at the training stage can limit your options later on. Your letter to employers should spell out:

(a)   your qualifications, focusing primarily on those relevant to becoming a solicitor (degree or Law Society examinations, and the Diploma);

(b)   any useful skills not apparent from your academic qualifications (eg languages, driving licence);

(c)   when you expect to start the traineeship, and

(d)   the names of two referees.

Be prepared, however, for a disappointing response. Most applicants have great difficulty in obtaining training places. With any luck you will get some interviews; but you will also get answers saying that all the firm's training places for the period in question are filled, or that training applications will only be considered six months hence, as well as, in some cases, no reply at all or a note saying that the firm has decided not to offer training places this year.

7.04 Many firms, in particular the larger ones, now have a more systematic approach to the recruitment of trainees, however. Some run programmes of vacation employment for law students at the degree stage, which enable both sides to learn more about each other at an early stage. Many have websites, as already mentioned, and produce brochures and other publicity material about themselves, making them available to prospective recruits through the law schools and careers offices. Some hold receptions, seminars or 'open days' in their offices for law and Diploma students. All these things are designed to give students more and better information about prospective employers, and should be exploited as fully and as early as possible. Often the end result is an application form to be taken away and filled in after you have had some time to consider what you have seen. This at least means that you know when the firm is considering applications, ignorance of which is probably the most frustrating thing for those seeking training places.

Things to check about the trainer

7.05 In taking up a training place, there are things to check about your employer. A checklist was provided in an earlier chapter for pre-Diploma trainees (para **5.08**), and the same list of points can be applied to post-Diploma training contracts. Has the employing solicitor been in continuous practice for the last three years? Is the employing solicitor allowed to take on trainees at all? How many trainees is the employing solicitor allowed to take on, and how many are there presently employed?

Entrance certificate

7.06 One formality must be satisfied before you start, the entrance certificate from the Law Society, without which you cannot begin your traineeship. An application form is obtainable from the Diploma unit in your law school. You have to submit the names of two referees who can satisfy the Council that you are a fit and proper person to be a solicitor, one an academic from your university, the other a person 'of standing in the community' who knows you personally – perhaps a school teacher, a minister or a doctor. You also have to show that you hold the formal qualifications of degree or Law Society exam passes (with a completed period of pre-Diploma training where appropriate), and the Diploma. A very important element in satisfying the Law Society that you are a fit and proper person is the disclosure of any criminal conviction (however trivial) which you may have. Such a conviction will not necessarily debar you from becoming a solicitor, but it is nonetheless important to disclose it. It can be even more embarrassing if the conviction emerges later on. An application for a standard disclosure is also required, and an application form is available from the Society or the university Diploma unit. Standard disclosures are provided by Disclosure Scotland, a service introduced in 2002 and designed to enhance public safety by providing potential employers and the voluntary sector with criminal history information on individuals applying for posts. Disclosure Scotland issues certificates – known as 'disclosures' – which give details of an individual's criminal convictions or state that they have none. This process can take some time. The aim of the service is to enhance public safety and to help employers and voluntary organisations in Scotland to make safer recruitment decisions (see further the Disclosure Scotland website, http://www.disclosurescotland.co.uk/). The Law Society is particularly concerned if the offence was one of dishonesty.

Registration of contract with Law Society

7.07   Having started the training period, your next task is to register the contract with the Law Society. You have three months from the date of commencement of your contract to do this; the penalty for failure is that the period during which you fail to register will not count towards the two-year period required under the admissions regulations. The onus, as in the case of the pre-Diploma training contract, is on the trainee, so do not leave this to the firm to handle. Registration will cost you a small sum of money (£25 in April 2004). The purpose of the registration is so that the Society has records for all trainees and can monitor their progress in accordance with the regulations.

Content of training

7.08   Unlike the pre-Diploma training contract, the admissions regulations do not specify particular areas of practice in which you must be trained at the post-Diploma stage. The precise content of training will vary from firm to firm, and from organisation to organisation, in accordance with the nature of its business. The majority of trainees are now to be found in large corporate practices, and the former staples of the traineeship – conveyancing, court work and executry – do not figure largely in the workload of such firms. The variety of work may instead be restricted to the different types of purely commercial practice. Criminal experience is something you will have to go and look for. In any training you should be exposed to clients both private and corporate, instructed in the art of letter-writing, and given some sense of how the office administration functions.

Test of Professional Competence (TPC)

7.09 Under the Test of Professional Competence, trainees are required to keep logbooks of work undertaken in particular areas during the training period. Each of a number of different areas of practice has a logbook in a form approved by the Law Society[1]. The logbook lists the activities a trainee might encounter in each area of practice, and the trainee is supposed to check each of these off when encountered. There is no upper or lower limit on the number of logbooks a trainee must maintain during the traineeship, nor is it intended that every activity listed be ticked off. More than one logbook at a time may be maintained. Logbooks must be renewed every quarter. The trainer must also conduct a quarterly trainee performance review, based on the logbooks, and assessing with grades the trainee's development of the skills listed in a Law Society document entitled 'Professional Competence'[2]. The review is then submitted to the Law Society for monitoring, and if there is any cause for concern on either side, the Society will intervene. The Law Society may then, or at any other time, require sight of the completed logbooks, and it is the trainee's responsibility to keep them maintained and available. Eight reviews must be completed during the traineeship. In deciding whether to grant a practising certificate to the trainee (see below, para **7.15**), the Law Society will take into account the completed reviews and (if necessary) logbooks, as well as the trainer's confirmation of fitness.

1   They are: agriculture, banking law, commercial leasing, company law, competition and regulation, construction and engineering, conveyancing (commercial), conveyancing (domestic), corporate finance, employment law, family law, housing law, intellectual property, liquor licensing, litigation (civil), litigation (criminal), local government conveyancing, local government law, pensions law, planning law, private finance initiative, social security, trusts & asset management and

wills & executries. The forms can be accessed on the Law Society website, http://www.lawscot.org.uk.

2   A copy of this document is also available on the Law Society website. The skills are professional conduct and ethics, communication skills, time and work management, dealing with clients, legal research, drafting, negotiation skills, commercial awareness and office procedures.

Professional Competence Course (PCC)

7.10   During your training period, you also have to undertake a Professional Competence Course (PCC). The Law Society accredits a number of providers to put on courses for any trainee: in April 2004 they included law schools (Aberdeen, Edinburgh and GGSL), professional bodies (the WS Society and the Glasgow Bar Association) and a law firm (Maclay Murray & Spens). In addition three law firms are accredited to provide in-house PCCs for their own trainees only (Dundas & Wilson, McGrigors and Shepherd & Wedderburn). The course consists of 36 hours of core modules (on personal organisation and time management, practical ethics, IT and the legal office, client care, financial and commercial awareness, drafting, writing, negotiation and interviewing) and 18 hours of elective modules as offered by the course providers. The modules may be taken all together, in which case the course will last about two weeks, or at different times with different providers. The course must be completed between the six- and the 18-month stages of the traineeship. While trainers must pay the salary of their trainees on the course, the Law Society only encourages them to pay the course fees (£1,000 to £1,200 plus VAT in April 2004) and not to deduct the period of the course from holiday entitlements. The Law Society has a fund to assist trainees with accommodation and travelling costs if they are unable to attend a locally delivered PCC. Further details about the course are available on the Law Society's website, http://www.lawscot.org.uk.

Service elsewhere under a training contract

7.11   Post-Diploma training contracts can only be assigned (transferred) to another employing solicitor where the Council so approves. The general policy is to ensure that there is genuine oversight by a trainer of the trainee's progress throughout the training period. But the admissions regulations do allow a trainee, subject to the prior approval of the employer and the Council, to extend the range of the training by undertaking legal work under appropriate supervision within Scotland on secondment, or in any other part of the United Kingdom or in the European Union (in the case of service outside Scotland, for no more than six months altogether). If the trainer has a place of business outside Scotland, the trainee may serve there during the training contract, but for no more than six months altogether; there is no need here for the approval of Council.

Effect of absence from work

7.12 Service with a trainer will generally be full-time, although part-time completion of the two-year period is possible. Service must be continuous; you cannot do, say, one year now, have a couple of years off, and then finish the traineeship with one more year. But short periods of absence – for example, for illness – may be allowed, provided that the employer is prepared to certify the trainee's fitness to become or continue as a solicitor. Such short periods of absence should not exceed an aggregate of six months altogether. If the trainee is absent for an aggregate of three months in any period of six months without reasonable cause, the period of the training contract may be extended, assigned or even terminated by the Council. Council also has the power to do this where the employer is continuously absent for an aggregate of three months in any six, as well as when it is of the reasonable opinion that the training contract ought to be terminated, assigned or extended. If the contract is terminated, the trainee is entitled to enter a further training contract with another employing solicitor, subject to such conditions as Council may impose: for example, that completed service under the previous contract be taken into account in calculating the two-year period.

Salaries

7.13 Trainee salaries are differentiated according to whether you are in your first or second year. Each year the Law Society sets a recommended rate for each year. Firms may pay more, or less. In 2003–04 the first year recommendation was £11,500, while for second year it was £15,000. It is only fair to say that, although these rates are lower than many first-year salaries for graduates, many firms think that they are too high, and it may even be that they prevent some firms offering traineeships at all. Every employee in a firm has to earn his or her salary, in the sense that their work generates enough fee income to cover the cost of employing them. There is a popular view in the profession that first year trainees do not do this, and that it is only in the second year that the trainee becomes a net earner for the firm. While the counter-arguments, that law firms have to pay training salaries which will induce graduates to choose law as opposed to any other graduate-entry profession, and that first year trainees perform necessary tasks which may release others to more remunerative work, are always worth making, it behoves trainees to remember that they have to earn their keep and show that they are indeed worthy of their hire. Every firm is taking the risk of the unknown quantity when a trainee joins the firm, but is committed for two years whether or not the risk turns out to be a good one. It is in that context that employer grumbles about 'high' trainee salaries should be understood.

Dismissal of trainee

7.14   It has been known, very occasionally, for employers to sack trainees. Strictly speaking, the employer can only do this if the trainee has been guilty of serious breach of contract, but the whole unpleasant scenario is unlikely to arise if, when problems develop, the matter is brought before the Law Society. The powers of Council already discussed, to extend, assign and terminate training contracts, can usually be brought into play to resolve the situation in a manner satisfactory to both sides.

Discharge of training contract

7.15   The focus here on problems and difficulties should not mislead; the great majority of training contracts proceed satisfactorily to their intended conclusion. The conclusion usually works itself out in two stages. At the end of the first year of post-Diploma training the trainee may submit to the Council a declaration by the employer certifying that during the year the trainee has fulfilled his or her obligations under the contract and is a fit and proper person to be admitted as a solicitor in Scotland. The trainee is then admitted as a solicitor with a qualified Certificate of Fitness. The significance of the qualified Certificate is usually that it enables you to appear in court. The second stage of admission comes at the end of the second year when the trainee submits another declaration by the employer certifying that in his opinion the trainee continues to be a fit and proper person to be a solicitor in Scotland. This has the effect of discharging the training contract, and enabling the trainee to have a full practising certificate. The responsibility for deciding to issue the trainee with a full Certificate of Fitness rests with the Law Society, however, and in discharging this duty the Society will consider the completion of the TPC (above, para **7.09**) as well as the employer's confirmation of fitness. No contract may be discharged unless the trainee has completed both the PCC and the TPC.

7.16 The admission regulations provide that, in considering whether an intrant is a fit and proper person to be a solicitor, the employer is to have regard not only to the moral character of the intrant but also to aptitude for and application to his or her duties along with conduct generally. It is, as it ought to be, a serious matter for most employers, because in the event that the trainee becomes an incompetent or dishonest solicitor, all other solicitors will have literally to pay for that incompetence or dishonesty, either through the Guarantee Fund or the premiums for the professional indemnity policy. So a discharge cannot be taken for granted on either side. Generally speaking, however, a refusal to discharge should not be sprung on a trainee but should have been preceded by warnings and indications of a need for improvement during the traineeship. If you are confronted with a problem over discharge of your training contract, you should contact the Law Society. Where an employer refuses to give a declaration of fitness, the Council may waive the requirement if, after enquiry, it seems reasonable to do so; but it can impose further conditions upon the intrant: for example, a further period of training in another firm which is then prepared to certify fitness.

PRACTICAL TRAINING: ADVOCATES

7.17 It has already been pointed out (para **5.02**) that the first step in entering the Faculty of Advocates is a petition to the Court of Session, which will then remit you to the Dean and Faculty for trial of your qualifications and a report. Your law degree and Diploma will satisfy the academic requirements to become an intrant; you may also have to take the Faculty exams in any of the Bar's compulsory subjects which you have not passed at university.

Period in a solicitor's office

7.18 As also already noted at the beginning of this chapter, there are two stages in the practical training of an advocate: first the period in a solicitor's office, lasting 21 months (reduced to 12 months if you hold a first- or second-class Honours degree in law from a Scottish university); and, second, nine to ten months of pupillage with a member of the junior bar. The 21-month period in a solicitor's office follows much the same course as that for a solicitor's traineeship, including the possibility of a European *stage* for up to one-third of the time; indeed the Faculty of Advocates advises you to enter a post-Diploma training contract so that you can, if you wish, switch to the solicitors' branch of the profession. Nearly all intrants today will have undertaken the full solicitors' traineeship and indeed practised as a solicitor for a further period. This may also solve a problem which can otherwise arise, namely the office which is reluctant to take on a trainee for a period of less than two years because it is only in the second year that the firm begins to recoup the investment which is represented by the trainee's salary (see above, para **7.14**). As may be deduced from this statement, the period in the solicitor's office is salaried, an important contrast with the following stage of pupillage. Finally on the training in the solicitor's office, the Faculty indicates that it is not desirable for it to be confined to litigation work[1].

1   At the time of writing (April 2004), the Faculty was considering whether to make qualification as a solicitor a compulsory step before admission to the Bar.

Pupillage

7.19   The period of pupillage is the distinctive feature of an advocate's practical training. There are some terminological points to be made at the outset of any description of pupillage. Although the Faculty's regulations for intrants use the word 'pupillage', during this period intrants are usually known as 'devils', and their activities as 'devilling'. The regulations reflect this usage to the extent that the member of the junior Bar to whom the intrant is attached during pupillage is there designed as 'the Devilmaster'. The word 'devil' in this context is derived from an old usage in the printing trade, where the printer's errand-boy was known as a devil. It seems to have found its way into Scotland in the nineteenth century from a usage at the English Bar describing apprentice barristers. Originally the Scottish devil was said 'to have the run of the master's papers', and that is still not a bad description of a principal feature of devilling, which is the right of access to all papers which the devilmaster receives from instructing persons in the course of practice.

7.20   How do you find a devilmaster? The advocate concerned must have been admitted to the Bar for at least seven years and be practising before the Court of Session. In other words, you cannot devil with an advocate who is insufficiently experienced, or not in practice, or whose practice does not include work in the Court of Session. An advocate with a mainly criminal practice in the High Court of Justiciary or the sheriff court is unlikely to take on devils, although all devils must spend some time with a 'criminal' devilmaster, learning about the criminal courts. It may be that you will have some ideas of your own about who your devilmaster should be, especially if you are switching to the Bar from practice as a solicitor, in which you have had the opportunity to get to know suitable advocates. The Clerk of Faculty will however be the prime mover in placing you with a suitable devilmaster. Some quality control on the training you will receive results from this and the fact that no advocate may take a devil without the prior consent of the Dean of Faculty. Generally, however, the test for whether an advocate may take on devils is sufficient experience and seniority. The flexibility inherent in this system can work to the advantage of the prospective devil, however, in that it may be possible if you are aiming at particular areas of work to have yourself attached to an advocate with a good practice in those fields, and thereby pursue your own career development. It is now also normal to divide your pupillage between different devilmasters, and thereby gain a wider spread of experience than would be possible with just one; commonly devils have one civil and one criminal devilmaster. Further, devilmasters whose practice does not offer devils appropriate experience of written work are required to approach other counsel to seek assistance for their devils in this respect.

Content of pupillage

7.21   Pupillage must commence on the first Monday in October in any year, and an intrant intending so to begin must give notice to the Clerk of Faculty by the preceding 30 June (this may change to 31 May). At the outset the intrant must take and pass an examination in evidence, pleading, practice and professional conduct, reputedly the most difficult of all to pass (although few fail), and from which no university pass can exempt you. In the Faculty's *Guide to the Professional Conduct of Advocates* it is said (paras 13.2–13.3) that (a) 'it is the duty of a devilmaster, so far as he is able, to ensure that, on completion of his devilling period, the devil is fit to exercise the office of advocate', and (b) 'the duties of a devilmaster include the duty of teaching the devil the rules and customs of the Bar, and ensuring that he has read and understands this Guide'. These rather vague statements are fleshed out by a scheme for the content of devilling under which the devil should receive instruction in court and other appearances, the paper work of an advocate, consultation with clients, negotiation, the Faculty's Code of Conduct, and the way in which the Faculty, courts, library and Faculty services work. Further details may be found in the Devil's Handbook, available from the Clerk of Faculty. What does all this mean in practice? As already noted, the devil is given access to the papers which the master receives in the course of practice. Normally the master will allocate particular sets of instructions to the devil to work on. The devil will be expected to draft summonses, written pleadings and opinions as well as carrying out legal research for the master. The correction of these drafts by the master is often a salutary experience for the devil. In addition the devil will attend the master's consultations, usually having read the papers in advance, and be present when the master is pleading in a court or tribunal, or working at a public inquiry. The devil is entitled to study in the Advocates' Library, subject to the regulation of the Keeper of the Library and to the rights of the members of the Bar. With the growth in the numbers of the practising Bar, accommodation in the library is at something of a premium during court hours.

7.22   In 1995, the Faculty of Advocates introduced an entirely new approach to the training of intending advocates. Having investigated how advocates are trained in other parts of the world, particularly the United States and Australia, the Faculty decided that all devils should undergo practical training in the skills associated with being an advocate. The foundation course takes place at the commencement of devilling. Over about five weeks, devils learn the skills of oral advocacy (including how to examine a witness and address a judge or a jury), drafting court documents and writing opinions and notes, consulting with clients, and many other tasks. Further courses take place throughout the devilling period, and all the courses involve 'learning by doing', with devils practising their skills in workshops under the watchful eye of senior members of the Bar who have been trained to teach advocacy. Extensive use is made of video too. The Faculty also runs an extensive continuing education programme for devils and practising members (many of whom have now also taken training courses).

Funding pupillage: 'the idle year'

7.23 The devil receives no payment from the devilmaster during the period of pupillage, nor may the devilmaster request or accept a fee for acting as such. The absence of payment is supposed to facilitate the independence of the Bar by severing your connections with your previous profession or trade; in the nineteenth century it was perhaps the main feature of what was then called 'the idle year'. It is this, coupled with the various matriculation and entry fees (see paras **5.02** and **7.27**), which means that there are relatively few intrants coming to the Bar immediately after graduation from university. Instead most are individuals who have gained valuable experience in practice as solicitors for some years, and whose savings and support from spouses/partners enable them to face a year without regular income. However, the Faculty has established the Lord Reid Scholarship and a variable number of other Faculty scholarships of lesser value, which provide funds to one or more intrants at the start of pupillage, to help meet the problems of financial need where it arises. Information about these scholarships is available from the Clerk of Faculty, and on the Faculty website at http://www.advocates.org.uk/web/tra/scholarship.htm.

Conclusion of pupillage

7.24 The intrant may be admitted as an advocate no earlier than the last Friday before the court rises for vacation in July in the year following commencement of pupillage; that is devilling will typically last between 9 and 10 months. For intrants who practised as solicitors for more than five years, admission is on the first Friday in June. At the conclusion of the period of devilling the devilmaster must complete a report confirming that the devil has displayed sufficient diligence, competence and trustworthiness during the pupillage to be suitable to be admitted as a member of Faculty. Where there has been more than one devilmaster, it is the principal devilmaster who prepares this report. The report is now tied in with the Faculty scheme on the content of devilling. The devilmaster may refuse to complete a report and, if so, the question of the devil's admission to the Faculty is referred to a review committee which in turn reports to the Dean of Faculty. Only if the committee's report is in favourable terms can the devil go on to seek admission.

7.25   What happens if there is an unfavourable report? It may be possible for the devil to continue with a pupillage. But every intrant is subject to the discipline of the Dean, and if an intrant's conduct is such as to manifest unfitness to exercise the public office of advocate, the Dean may, after consultation with his Council, the Lord President and the Lord Justice-Clerk, order the intrant's name to be removed from the roll. A procedure must be followed before this happens: the intrant must be given written notice of the grounds of removal, and an opportunity to appear in person before Dean and Council.

7.26   As an extension of the existing certification process, the Faculty is introducing a scheme for assessment of devils' competence in oral and written advocacy. During pupillage, all devils are assessed by senior members of the Bar in four practical exercises. Those intrants found to be competent will be allowed to proceed towards admission to the Faculty. Those found to be working towards competence will be assessed again towards the end of pupillage, and if found to be competent then, they will be admitted. If a devil is found to be not competent at that stage, a report will be submitted to the Dean, and the devil may be required to give up devilling and be removed from the roll of intrants.

THE FINAL FORMALITIES

7.27   At long last the great day dawns when all the examinations have been passed and the years and months of training come to an end and you become qualified to practice law as either a solicitor or an advocate. Both branches of the profession hold pleasant ceremonies to mark the occasion, at which it is possible for the newly-qualified to bask in the congratulations and admiration of family and friends. For the solicitor there is the enrolment ceremony, usually held at Parliament House, at which the names of all those whose names have now been added to the roll of solicitors are called over, and the President of the Law Society presents Certificates of Enrolment, before an address suitable to the occasion is delivered by some distinguished person. For the advocate there are two ceremonies, held one after the other. The first starts at a meeting of the Faculty held in the Advocates' Library and chaired by the Dean. The Dean requests the Clerk of Faculty to state whether any objections have been made to the admission. No objections having been received, the candidate is admitted to the Faculty and led by the Dean to a sitting court. The proceedings of the court are interrupted by the Dean, who requests the presiding Lord

Ordinary to administer to the new advocates the declaration of allegiance to the Sovereign, or the declaration *de fideli administratione* for those unable to affirm allegiance. The new advocate then dons wig and gown. This second ceremony reflects the principle that the advocate is an officer of the court and so can only be admitted as such by the court. The ceremony is preceded by the advocate's paying entry money (£850 in April 2004) to the Faculty, or agreeing to pay four instalments of £250 over a three-year period.

CHAPTER 8

Continuing legal education

INTRODUCTION

8.01 This short chapter discusses the various forms of legal education available outside the undergraduate degree, the Diploma and professional training, and what may be required in moving from one branch of the profession to another. It also considers how you can use your Scottish legal qualifications in order to enter the legal professions of jurisdictions other than Scotland, and the extent to which foreign qualifications are of use in entering the Scottish profession.

POSTGRADUATE STUDY

8.02 Postgraduate study is an increasingly popular option amongst law graduates. Most making this choice do so at the conclusion of the LL.B degree rather than later, and it can be difficult to return to student life after more than a year or two in the profession or some other employment. There are two main types of postgraduate degree, the taught LL.M or Master of Laws degree, and the Ph.D or Doctor of Philosophy, a degree obtained by the completion and writing up as a thesis of a piece of research. The LL.M takes one year, while doctoral research is usually funded for a three-year period. As the last comment may suggest, funding is a crucial issue for postgraduate students, and if you contemplate such study at all, you should couple investigation of the academic possibilities with the financial ones. Your law school advisers should be able to give you guidance on this; possible sources include the SAAS, the school itself through bursaries and scholarships, and charities such as the Clark Foundation for Legal Education and the WS Society Educational Scholarship (see above para **4.24**).

8.03 Why undertake postgraduate study? For most students undertaking the LL.M, the course provides an opportunity to specialise in a particular field of law, thereby developing his or her knowledge and understanding of it, and enhancing one's chances of entering legal practice or some other employment in that area. Doctoral research also offers an opportunity to specialise, but the student's aim is to advance knowledge in the topic researched by uncovering new material, fitting together known material in a new way, and developing fresh perspectives on the whole subject. Many of the students entering doctoral research are thinking of an academic career, but others have their eyes firmly fixed on developing knowledge that will be of value in the professional world. In some cases, doctoral research will be funded by interested outside bodies, such as the Arts and Humanities Research Board (AHRB), soon to be a Research Council, or the Economic and Social Research Council (ESRC).

8.04 Another attraction of postgraduate study is the opportunity it offers to sample pastures new, whether within the United Kingdom or without. America is an attractive destination for many, while Europe offers several possibilities, particularly in the context of European Community law. So far as the LL.M is concerned, your choice of university will also depend on the courses offered, and your qualifications. For doctoral students, there are further complications. Your research is under the supervision of a law school member, and it is important that this person should be a competent researcher in the field concerned as well as a sympathetic guide through the intricacies of postgraduate life. It is also very important that the university has the library and other resources to enable the proposed programme of research to be carried out effectively. These again are matters on which guidance will be obtainable within your undergraduate law school, and you should make every use of it you can.

POST-QUALIFYING LEGAL EDUCATION

8.05 Once you have qualified as either a solicitor or an advocate, there are some further formal requirements with regard to continuing education and training. The main instance of this is that, when you become a principal in a solicitors' firm for the first time, you must within 12 months attend a practice management course run by the Law Society of Scotland. This is a course of practical training in the management of solicitors' practices. The reason why this requirement was introduced in 1989 was that people trained as lawyers are not necessarily automatically equipped by their education to be effective managers of a business.

8.06   Further, the Law Society of Scotland requires its members to undertake 20 hours per year of continuing professional development (CPD), to ensure that they keep up-to-date on developments in law and practice. At least five of these hours must be devoted to practice management issues, broadly defined. Courses are provided by the Society itself, the university law schools, and by commercial organisations. You will probably receive a regular flow of circulars advertising these courses, and if you wish to go on one you should not be backward in asking your employer for permission to do so as well as expenses (it is rare for the course fees to be low). Provided that the course is relevant to your work, attendance will probably be beneficial for both you and the employer. Although the practice of an advocate is sometimes said to require of necessity that the advocate keep up to date with developments in law and practice, the Faculty of Advocates requires its members to undertake 10 hours of compulsory CPD each year.

MOVING FROM ONE BRANCH OF THE PROFESSION TO THE OTHER

8.07   It is comparatively easy to move from one branch of the profession to the other, and it is now common for those becoming advocates to have first qualified as solicitors. The name of a solicitor wishing to become an advocate must be removed from the roll of solicitors. The solicitor who has been actively engaged in practice in Scotland for at least three years prior to petitioning for admission will be exempted from the Diploma requirement, but will have to undergo pupillage and take the Faculty of Advocates' examination in evidence, practice and procedure. In addition, the intrant will have to pass any of the subjects required by the Faculty in which a pass has not already been obtained *en route* to becoming a solicitor. These are quite likely to include Roman law and international private law.

8.08 The advocate wishing to become a solicitor is exempt from the requirements of pre-Diploma training, passing the examinations of the Law Society of Scotland, and the Diploma, but must undertake six months of training before applying for admission as a solicitor. Of course, if the advocate had previously qualified as a solicitor, this requirement is likely to be waived.

GOING TO ENGLAND

8.09 There are two possible scenarios if you decide to use Scottish qualifications to try and enter the English legal profession. If you go south at the conclusion of either your LL.B degree or your Diploma, you will have to undertake at least two more years of study. First, whether you intend to be a solicitor or a barrister, you have to take the Common Professional Examination (CPE). This is based on the 'seven foundations of legal knowledge', as follows:

(1) criminal law
(2) equity and trusts
(3) law of the European Union
(4) obligations I (contract)
(5) obligations II (tort)
(6) property law
(7) public law (constitutional and administrative law and human rights)
(8) legal research.

With your Scots law degree, you may get exemptions from constitutional law, contract and tort, but that still leaves a number of other papers to sit. Preparation is by means of a course lasting one year and taken in an institution of higher education. If you want to be a solicitor, this will then be followed by a one-year Legal Practice Course (LPC) which is the English equivalent of the Diploma, and a Professional Skills Course (PSC), equivalent to the TPC and PCC in Scotland. If you want to be a barrister, you take the one-year Bar Vocational Course (BVC). In both courses the emphasis is on legal skills rather than legal knowledge. Finally, a would-be barrister has one year of unpaid pupillage with another member of the Bar, while the would-be solicitor must complete a two-year training contract (formerly known as 'articles') with a solicitors' firm in England. For further information on qualification in England, see the websites of the Law Society of England and Wales (http://www.lawsociety.org.uk/) and the Bar Council (http://www.barcouncil.org.uk/ and http://www.legaleducation.org.uk/Main/).

8.10   An alternative route to qualification in England is to become fully qualified in Scotland and then seek admission in England. A system for doing this has been in place since 1991. Under it, any person who has qualified as a solicitor in Scotland may become a solicitor in England by passing an examination in the English law of property set by the Law Society of England and Wales. The exam covers property, litigation, professional conduct and accounts, and principles of common law. There is a similar system for qualifying as a solicitor in Northern Ireland. You should contact the Bar Council for information on how to re-qualify as an English barrister. Consult the websites mentioned in the previous paragraph (**8.09**) for further details.

GOING TO EC MEMBER STATES

8.11   Following a Council Directive in December 1988, the member states of the European Community have all enacted systems under which lawyers qualified in one member state may by passing an aptitude test in the law of another member state become qualified to practise law in that other member state. Further details should be sought from the professional governing bodies of the other member state concerned.

THE REST OF THE WORLD

8.12   So far as qualifying in any part of the world other than the United Kingdom or the European Community is concerned, it may well be necessary to undertake the full programme of education and training which the profession requires in the relevant country. Usually there will be some concessions if you have been qualified and in practice for some years, but even this is not certain.

COMING TO SCOTLAND FROM ANOTHER JURISDICTION

8.13   If you have qualified as a lawyer in a jurisdiction other than Scotland and wish to become qualified here, the requirements as to further education and training will vary according to whether you come from another part of the United Kingdom, another member state of the European Community, or some other part of the world.

(a) Lawyers qualified in another part of the United Kingdom

8.14 For English and Northern Irish solicitors wishing to become Scottish solicitors, the Intra-UK Transfer Test set by the Law Society of Scotland has to be passed. At present this consists of two 2-hour papers in conveyancing, trusts & succession and Scots criminal law, evidence and civil and criminal procedure). In addition, if you qualified in your home jurisdiction after 1 January 1992 you must pass a paper in European Community law. English and Northern Irish barristers who have completed a full period of pupillage in England or Northern Ireland and wish to become advocates in Scotland must pass an aptitude test set by the Faculty of Advocates. This consists of:

(1) a written examination paper in Scots legal system, constitutional and administrative law;

(2) a written examination paper covering two of: (1) trusts and succession; (2) property and conveyancing;(3) bankruptcy and diligence; the choice to be made by the candidate;

(3) an oral examination on criminal law and one of either: (1) contract and quasi contract or (2) delict and quasi delict; the choice to be made by the candidate; and

(4) the Faculty examination in evidence, pleading, practice and professional conduct.

As already noted (see above, para 6.03), those becoming Scottish solicitors or advocates by these routes are exempted from the Diploma, the TPC and the PCC, nor need they undergo professional training.

(b) Lawyers qualified in another member state of the European Community

8.15 A lawyer qualified in another member state of the European Community wishing to become a Scottish solicitor must pass an aptitude test. This normally includes four written examinations as follows (duration of paper in brackets):

(1) the law of property, including trusts & succession, and family law (3 hours);

(2) Scottish legal system, including evidence and civil & criminal procedure (3 hours);

(3) European Community law and institutions (2 hours);

(4) Professional conduct and the accounts rules (2 hours).

Further, under the Establishment Directive 1998 (98/5/EC), nationals of an EU member state who are also qualified in an EU jurisdiction may register with the Law Society of Scotland and practise in Scotland under their home title for a period of three years. Thereafter, providing that they can satisfy the Society that they have for that period 'regularly and effectively' practised Scots law, they may be admitted as Scottish solicitors. To become an advocate the lawyer must pass the same aptitude test as is required for English and Northern Irish barristers (see above, para **8.14**).

8.16   Again, as already noted (see above, para **6.03**), those becoming Scottish solicitors or advocates by these routes are exempt from the Diploma, the TPC and the PCC, nor need they undergo professional training.

(c)   Lawyers qualified in a jurisdiction other than in the United Kingdom or the European Community

8.17   Generally speaking, lawyers qualified in a jurisdiction outside the United Kingdom and the European Community will need to undertake the full programme of education, examinations and training in order to become either a Scottish solicitor or an advocate. There are some concessions in respect of solicitors, however. An intrant to whom the Colonial Solicitors Act 1900 applies is exempt from the Diploma (but not from the TPC or PCC), and need only undertake one year of training. Under the Overseas Solicitors (Admission) Order 1964 (SI 1964/1848), as several times amended, the 1900 Act applies to solicitors admitted in Australia (excluding Western Australia), New Zealand, Hong Kong, much of Canada and the West Indies, Zimbabwe, Sri Lanka, Bombay and Malawi. But the Law Society of Scotland still requires 'colonial' solicitors to pass its examinations or gain exemption therefrom. Lawyers from other jurisdictions will also have to pass the examinations or gain exemption, and in addition take the Diploma, pass the TPC, take the PCC, and complete one year of post-Diploma training before applying for admission. The Council of the Law Society has a general dispensing power, however, with regard to all these rules. At the time of writing (April 2004), the Society was in the process of devising an alternative route to qualification for non-United Kingdom or EU solicitors, which will involve a transfer test akin to that for United Kingdom and EU lawyers (see above, paras **8.14–8.16**).

PART III

Studying Scots law

Karl Llewellyn, a great American jurist of the mid-twentieth century, wrote a classic introductory work for law students called *The Bramble Bush* in which he described the first year of law school as follows:

'It aims, in the old phrase, to get you to "thinking like a lawyer". The hardest job of the first year is to lop off your common sense, to knock your ethics into temporary anesthesia. Your view of social policy, your sense of justice – to knock these out of you along with woozy thinking, along with ideas all fuzzed along their edges. You are to acquire ability to think precisely, to analyze coldly, to work within a body of materials that is given, to see, and see only, and manipulate, the machinery of the law. It is not easy thus to turn human beings into lawyers.' (p 116)

The aim of this part of the book is to describe something of how you go about this process, which, as you will see if you turn to the end of the section, is not quite so drastic as Llewellyn makes it sound. Essentially it deals with the mechanics of the process, rather than the process itself, which is the function of the first year. It describes teaching and study techniques, to give you some idea of what to expect and of what can be expected of you in the law school. The section also gives an introduction to researching the law and developing a critical stance towards it.

A few preliminaries before the descriptions begin. Little that is said here about how to study law should be regarded as mandatory or prescriptive. Everyone has their own study techniques, and you will develop yours as you go along. The chapters contain mostly suggestions which you may or may not find helpful as pointers to the methods that suit you when you set about your work. This is probably true of even the things which I think you should avoid doing. Again, while it is always a good idea to talk to your fellow students about these matters, you should not be too disconcerted if others seem much more confident and assured about what they are doing than you feel you are. As lawyers quickly learn, first impressions may or may not be lasting, but they are often highly misleading. Finally, do not over-organise the process of study; my experience is that you only end up in a state when you can't adhere to your own timetable. A methodical approach and the development of time-management skills are highly desirable, especially for prospective lawyers, but should not become ends in themselves, at the expense of substantive knowledge and understanding.

CHAPTER 9

Lectures, tutorials and seminars

INTRODUCTION

9.01 As with most other non-science subjects, university law teaching revolves round the traditional format of lectures, tutorials and seminars, all of which are described below. 'Clinical' teaching based on real problems such as you find in medicine is not found as part of the formal course in law schools, although learning by clinical work can certainly happen during your years as a law student (see further below, para **9.25**) and will of course take place during the period of professional training. There is a tendency in some quarters to challenge the value of the traditional academic approach to studying law and to propose a more 'skills-based' approach, focusing on matters such as client-counselling, advocacy, negotiation, and communication skills in the widest sense as well as knowledge and understanding of legal rules and concepts. Unquestionably all these are good things. But, as I hope to show, the traditional approach can be seen as also developing desirable skills as well as knowledge and understanding, and while it is by no means immune from criticism, it should retain an important place in legal training.

LECTURES

9.02 Lectures consist essentially of oral exposition of some topic by a lecturer, usually lasting for just under an hour. Most lecture courses will have two or three per week. In the early Scottish law schools, the lecturer dictated notes to the students based upon the elementary textbooks, and this survived as a method of teaching for a long time: see for example the description by Sir Nicholas Fairbairn QC, MP, of his experience as a law student at Edinburgh in the 1950s, contained in his autobiography *A Life is Too Short* (1986). Indeed there are stories of how law students used to read out the textbook along with the lecturer, while in *Caird v Sime* (1887) 14 R (HL) 37 a Glasgow professor of Moral Philosophy successfully sued former students who were selling printed copies of his lectures, and had thereby saved current class members the inconvenience of attendance! Thus was justified the famous definition of a lecture as a process whereby the lecturer's notes passed into the student's notes without passing through the minds of either. But more extemporary methods, first introduced with enormous success to the law schools in the eighteenth century by Professor John Millar of Glasgow, are now standard.

9.03   A lecture may but need not be a monologue. Another approach common in American law schools and not unknown in Scotland is the 'Socratic' technique, which consists of the lecturer calling on a member of the audience and asking him or her questions on material prepared by the whole class in advance. (See, for a dramatic account of varying methods at the Harvard Law School, Scott Turow, *One L* (1977), pp 29–55.) In this country, more often the lecturer may invite questions or some other form of audience participation, or members of the audience can interrupt (although it is generally courteous to signal a desire to do this by raising a hand and then waiting to be called). If you have a question during a lecture, however, think whether it is worth interrupting the flow of the lecture to ask it. Is it the sort of point you can check later elsewhere, for example, by asking a classmate, looking up the course textbook, going to the library, or raising in a tutorial? Also, few lecturers object to discussion and questions of more detailed points after the lecture is over; it is good to find that the audience was listening!

9.04   Lecturers rarely rely on their powers of oratory alone. Most use some form of support or other. Handouts giving lecture structures, references to cases, statutes and readings, and sometimes more or less detailed summaries, are common in law teaching. Visual aids may range from the good old blackboard (white board in dynamic modern institutions) through flipcharts to the wonders of audio-visual technology – overheads, Powerpoint slides, videos and Internet links. There are also the textbooks of which there are now a good number directed towards the student market (see Appendix 5). In subjects where a statute is the main source of the law, the lecturer may want you to have copies of it in the lecture theatre; but extracts may be included in the handout or displayed on an overhead. There are commercial publications of statutes relevant to students: the most useful to students are the Avizandum Statutes series, on family law (by Jane Mair), on obligations (by Laura Macgregor) and on commercial and consumer law (by Jenny Hamilton). (W Green also publish conveyancing, criminal law and family law collections of statutes as well as the comprehensive looseleaf *Parliament House Book*, but these are aimed more at the practitioner market.) Whether or not you use such collections in lectures, it is essential to have full texts of statutes available for private study. You may also be allowed to use such full texts in the examinations on the subject.

9.05 What are the purposes of a lecture? A basic aim is undoubtedly the communication of information. A student can gather more information in a one-hour lecture than would be possible for most in one hour's reading. In law, an important feature will be that the lecture can be up-to-date, referring for example to cases decided or proceeding on the very day it is given, whereas it is a rare textbook that is not out-of-date by the time it appears, in consequence of the inevitable time lag between writing and publication. But most important of all is that the lecture is an opportunity for the student to hear a legal mind at work, fitting the different sources of the law together; relating them to the real world, both in terms of problems that have arisen and have yet to arise, or which the law fails to address; and showing how legal reasoning leads to the conclusions which have been adopted in the cases on the subject. Here is someone who has already developed some of the skills you hope to acquire; how does he or she go about the law? Usually too the lecturer is a specialist, enthusiastic about the subject, and the interest and commitment which follows from this can be infectious.

9.06 What should you be doing during a lecture? The normal activity would be listening and taking written notes of what is said. Given that lectures are not dictation exercises, your notes will not be verbatim transcriptions unless you are a shorthand writer. In any event, transcription is an infringement of the lecturer's copyright. The aim has to be the creation of a record of the lecture which is adequate for later reference back, most especially when you are revising for examinations. What happens in the lecture theatre may therefore be only the first stage in a process. Some authorities suggest that listening, with the occasional note of the principal heads of the discourse, should be the main activity. But I have always found that trying to take more or less continuous notes was helpful to concentration, especially when the subject matter of a lecture was new to me. Few can concentrate on what one person is saying over a period as long as an hour without the mind wandering or switching off altogether, and the discipline of taking notes keeps you focused on the lecture. There is also a 'skills' argument in favour of this approach, inasmuch as in legal practice, and especially in meetings and in court, it is often necessary to take fast and accurate notes of what is said by someone else – a client, a witness, or opposing counsel – to enable you to refer or respond to it later. The argument against continuous note-taking is that you cease to think about what it is that you are listening to. My own answer is that, given that you are not transcribing, the effort of thinking how to summarise the points being made in the lecture is as good a way as any of engaging with its themes. But in the end this is up to you, more than almost anything else discussed in this chapter.

9.07 If you take more than minimal notes, you will have to develop an abbreviation system. This might be subject-specific – 'O & A' for offer and acceptance in Contract Law, or 'd/c' and 's/c' for duty of care and standard of care in delict, for example. Initials can often be used with statutes – 's' for 'section', 'SoGA' for the Sale of Goods Act, 'UCTA' for the Unfair Contract Terms Act – or Latin phrases – 'JQT' for *jus quaesitum tertio*, *pf* for *prima facie*, *bf* for *bona fide* – or even the names of cases – 'D v S' for *Donoghue v Stevenson* 1932 SC (HL) 31. With the last, however, the commonest abbreviation is to use one or part of one of the names of the parties – *Donoghue* in the previous example, or *Cantiere* for *Cantiere San Rocco SA v Clyde Shipbuilding and Engineering Co Ltd* 1923 SC (HL) 105. There are also a number of well-established abbreviations which can be used across a range of subjects, however. Examples include 'P' for pursuer, 'D' or perhaps 'Dfdr' for defender, 'Co' for company, 'Tr' for trustee, 'Exr' for executor, and 'Liqr' for liquidator. Look at the way these and other common terms are abbreviated in case citations in the textbooks as a starting point.

9.08 It is worth trying to structure your notes as you take them. A lecture handout is useful for this purpose. Alternatively, listen out for the lecturer's use of words indicating structure: eg first, second, etc; the main points are ...; moving on ...; lastly. Use simple layout techniques – starting fresh topics on new pages, using headings (perhaps centred on the line) and sub-headings, with underlinings, indentations and spaces between blocks of notes. Case and statute names should be underlined. If you look at the case summaries with which law reports begin, you will see that the actual decision is usually prefixed with '*Held*', and this is a useful convention to adopt in note-taking. You may wish to leave space in which to add further notes later on.

9.09   If you have time, it can be worthwhile to read up on the lecturer's subject in advance, although to do this most usefully you probably need a syllabus of what each lecture will cover. A quick survey of the relevant bit of the course text can help make clear what is important or difficult in the subsequent lecture. Making a fair copy of notes after the lecture is probably not a worthwhile exercise if it is merely copying out the notes taken in the lecture, but it can be useful to try and draw them together with other notes that you take in advance, in tutorials or in the library.

9.10   Lecture notes should be made on paper that is easily filed afterwards. Developing a filing system for notes is sensible, since you want to be able to find your way about them later on. The accumulation of paper over a year can of course be large. One solution to this is the battery-powered laptop or palmtop computer with a hard disk onto which notes can be typed in the lecture and preserved electronically. If you do this, however, remember to back up files to floppy disks, CDs or removable hard disks. One other technological device for recording lectures is the audio recorder (not to mention the camcorder, I suppose), but for this the lecturer's permission is necessary as a matter of law as well as courtesy since, as already noted, the lecturer has copyright in the actual words used in the lecture.

TUTORIALS

9.11   Tutorials are meetings of smaller groups of students with a tutor, usually but not always a member of the law school staff. Like lectures, they normally last for just under the hour. In most courses you will have one of these meetings once a week or fortnight. By contrast with the typical lecture, the aim is group discussion of a topic, led by the tutor. The topic will be one which has already been, or is being, covered in the lecture course. The form of the discussion depends on the tutor and the class. Some tutors like the Socratic dialogue; others prefer the students to ask the questions and to propose the answers. Whatever, the expectation is that the student will participate, and you will gain far more from the tutorial if you do so. It is, of course, also an opportunity for you to raise the points you have not understood in the lectures and have not been able to answer for yourself.

9.12   A useful way of getting discussion going in a tutorial is for the tutor or course organiser to set a hypothetical set of facts as a problem which can be answered on the basis of the legal topic to be covered. In many courses you will find that there is a programme of such problems issued at the start. The problem will probably include some reading material; if it does not, follow some of the suggestions made later on in this book (see below, paras **10.09, 11.04–11.18**). Preparation is essential, otherwise much of the point of the tutorial will be lost. This is very much geared to making you 'think like a lawyer'. Often the problem will be stated so that the exercise is to advise one of the characters in it. Then you have to ask what it is that that person is likely to want in this situation, and how the law is going to help or hinder the achievement of that goal. Are there cases or statutes for or against the character? If they seem to be against, can any other interpretation be placed upon them? If they are for, are there any pitfalls of other possible interpretations which need to be guarded against? Do you need to know more facts than are given in the problem before you can say one way or the other? In this way, you begin to learn how to handle the law and the reasoning that supports the law. The benefit can sometimes be increased by dividing the tutorial into the two sides of a litigation based on the facts.

9.13   It is definitely worth jotting down the views you take in a preliminary way before you go into the tutorial, along with the authorities you think support your conclusions. These both focus your mind and give you something on which to base further notes taken during the tutorial. Given a tutorial's informal nature, note-taking is less easy than in a lecture, and listening and talking are far more important. In tutorials the seeds of the oral skills of questioning and arguing are being sown. But it is good practice for a tutor to try and draw the threads of discussion together in some sort of conclusion at the end of the tutorial, and this may be the moment when a note should be taken.

9.14   Tutorials can take other forms: the discussion of a more general question about the values or social utility of a particular group of rules, for example. You may be asked to prepare more formal essays in advance of a tutorial. The same general approach of advance preparation is required. What is your view, and with what arguments and facts do you support it? How would you meet opposing views? Again, you may be asked to draft legal documents in response to some set of hypothetical requirements, where not only do you have to go through the identification of the legal issues involved but you have to find the precise form of words which will cope satisfactorily with them.

9.15 An increasingly important type of tutorial teaching is that using computer expert systems (computer-assisted learning, or CAL). Here the computer replaces the tutor (one reason why, in an era of dwindling resources, you are increasingly likely to encounter this form of teaching). The method works best with the problem-solving type of tutorial exercise. The screen displays a question which you answer from the material in front of you, sometimes selecting from a range of possible answers, sometimes by choosing yes/no or true/false, but sometimes also with the input of data or key words by you. The computer's next question depends on the answer given at the preceding stage, and the process continues until finally the computer provides you with the answer to the problem. Examples with which I am familiar include systems on the following: can people marry? Is a delictual claim for damages time barred? Has a contract been made? Has a contract been broken and, if so, what can the aggrieved party do about it? Is a transaction subject to inheritance tax, and if so, for how much?

9.16 The educational advantage of such systems is the demonstration of the logical structure of legal rules. Also the computer tells you when you are wrong, whereas in a conventional tutorial you may find it difficult to get individual feedback. The ability to use expert systems is also an increasingly significant part of legal practice. The main limitation is that at present, being pre-programmed, a computer program cannot respond as flexibly as a human tutor, nor can it deal well with the more subjective issues raised in law – value judgments, socio-political issues, and so on. So it may be some time before computers totally displace people in tutorials. It is a good idea to do a CAL tutorial along with a partner with whom you can discuss the answers you give the machine, as this keeps the element of discussion and debate which is such a crucial part of the more traditional tutorial.

9.17 Other instances of technological teaching include the use of videos, perhaps showing a teacher expounding the solution to a problem made available in the class or library. Inter-active videos exist, however, where the student is asked questions or set tasks and the display depends on the student's response to this. The best example I have seen was a video on evidence, where the student had to be ready to object to opposing counsel's questions or the witness's statements; once an objection was made, the judge on the video then gave a ruling. This was both instructive and fun, and it is to be hoped that resources may be found one day to enable similar developments in Scotland.

SEMINARS

9.18 Seminars are more likely to be encountered in Honours than in Ordinary classes. They are closer to tutorials than lectures. They are usually made up of small groups led by a teacher but expected to contribute to a discussion in which all take part. Often they will last longer than tutorials, but if so then there may be only one a week in a course.

9.19 Many of the comments made about preparation and participation in tutorials apply with equal force to seminars. The difference between a tutorial and a seminar is that the students are expected to have read up the subject matter of the latter in much greater depth than would be the case in the former, and to have developed more critical views about it. In other words, the format is supposed to encourage a greater intellectual independence in the student. Having been exposed to the sources to a greater extent, and being better equipped to handle them than a beginner, the student is in a better position to form views about what they mean, and about their value, and so to challenge the views of the teacher.

9.20 Like tutorials, seminars may have reading lists issued to students in advance. A number of basic points ought to be remembered in preparing these. The course teacher will probably choose controversial material and will certainly be looking for discussion about it. The questions which the teacher has in mind may be on the reading list. So you need to be forming views about it as you prepare. (See further below, paras **10.21–10.30**, **10.37–10.50**, on this.) In addition there may be material referred to in the reading which is not on the reading list. If there is time, why not go and look it up? There may be something there of value. On the other hand, it may not be necessary to look at everything on the list, especially if a group of you can distribute the work among you before the seminar. You will need to have read it all before the exams, but discussion in the seminar will flow so long as each item on the reading list has been covered by at least a few in the class.

9.21 There may be an expectation that one or more members of the seminar will prepare papers in advance to set discussion rolling. The first advice is to keep it short. It takes an hour to read 5,000 words aloud at a reasonable speed, so a 15-minute presentation should be 1,250 words, or four to five word-processed A4 pages. Do not describe the material researched (facts, case holdings, statutory provisions), since everyone else should have read it or most of it. Instead, raise issues and questions for the seminar to discuss.

9.22 Taking notes during the seminar presents the same difficulties as in tutorials, but given proper advance preparation detailed notes of the discussion should be unnecessary. Again the good seminar leader will try and pull things together to some extent at the end, but remember that the purpose of the seminar is to set you thinking for yourself and not to provide you with the cut-and-dried off-the-peg solution of another person.

SKILLS TEACHING

9.23 A brief word may now be said again about skills teaching. The traditional teaching methods just described ought to teach, not only legal doctrine, but also how to research and handle it, the skills of problem-solving, legal debate in both written and oral form, some legal drafting, and computer literacy. This may not be everything a lawyer needs but it does take you some way down the road. The Diploma, with its emphasis on learning by doing and the completion of tasks, develops these and highlights many other skills.

9.24 In addition, many informal opportunities exist within the law schools for the development of lawyerly skills. Mooting and client-counselling competitions and, to a lesser extent, mock trials are very popular in Scotland. Not only are there competitions within the various schools but there are now also Scottish, UK and international ones. Scottish teams have won in the worldwide competitions. Mooting is competitive debating before a judge on some legal issue, in which the skills of forensic argument can be developed. Client-counselling tests your ability to handle a client face-to-face. The client is played by an actor who presents several kinds of difficulty for the adviser; you are marked by various criteria on how well you respond to this and on how you handle the problem on which the client sought advice. Mock trials, which involve the examination of witnesses and evidence as well as legal argument, obviously need the involvement of many more people to be successful, but can be rewarding. None of this kind of thing is required by law schools, except to a limited extent in the Diploma, but you ought to try and participate if you can. In America, even modest success in such activities – quarter-finalist in the Senior Moot, for example – is regarded as a definite enhancement of the CV, and it should be here too. Setting such considerations on one side, they are also fun and a break from the class routine.

9.25   It is possible to play client-counselling for real. Many of the Scottish law schools provide limited facilities at which legal advice is offered to the public. An example is Edinburgh's Legal Dispensary. Most of the clients' problems lie in the consumer, welfare, housing and employment areas. Similarly your local Students Association probably runs advice centres for students and others, whose problems might have a legal angle. There are many other advice-giving organisations who appreciate any legal assistance they can get. One can learn a lot about the world as well as the

CHAPTER 10

Private study

INTRODUCTION

10.01   In the early years of university, formal teaching contact will probably extend to something between 12 and 20 hours per week. Later on, in Honours, the contact may drop to perhaps half that. This again reflects the goal of making the student increasingly independent intellectually and in effect able to instruct him – or herself – which, after all, is what the practising lawyer has to do with new law or the law forgotten since university days which suddenly becomes relevant to a client's needs. There is accordingly a big difference between school and university in terms of the amount of time the disposal of which is left to your discretion; and this increases as you move through the system. Similarly mature students sometimes find it difficult to adjust to an environment where study is much less directed and teaching more impersonal than they have previously experienced. The expectation is that you will use the time outside class hours for private study, and this section will try to explain what is expected of you and how to go about it. It may also be helpful to the person following the route of professional examinations into the legal profession and unable to take university courses.

10.02   In general it may be helpful to think of yourself as having a job to do. For most people this still means an eight-hour day – the classic 9 to 5, with an hour or so for lunch. This is at least a basis for calculating how much time during the day you ought to be devoting to study over and above class attendance. But it is probably better not to think of private study in terms of time but rather in terms of tasks to be accomplished – a tutorial to be prepared, an essay to be written, puzzles and difficulties to be resolved – and give each job the time it needs. This after all is the approach you need in the practice of law, which is definitely not a 9 to 5 matter. The university is open until late at night, and you can work at home or in your university residence, provided you have the books and access to an online computer.

10.03   Another thing to remember is that you are not alone, and that it is perfectly legitimate to seek help and support from your fellow students. In American law schools, the students commonly set up formal study groups to go about the process of study collectively[1]. There is nothing to prevent you and others doing this if you want, although in this country such groups tend to be much more informal and fluid in membership than in America.

1   See Turow, *One L* (1977), pp 57–61.

10.04   A useful book to acquire at the outset is a legal dictionary or glossary. Part of learning the law is learning the language of the law. Although often the words used in the law are ordinary English ones, their legal meaning is generally narrower and more precise. There are also words which are nowadays used only in the law, many having their own idiosyncratic pronunciation. If you get early into the habit of checking these words in your dictionary or glossary, it will considerably speed your advance into thinking like a lawyer. Two useful dictionary/glossary works are *Green's Glossary of Scottish Legal Terms* by S O'Rourke (4th edn, 2004) and *Scottish Legal Terms and Expressions* by J A Beaton (1982); there is also a glossary in *The Laws of Scotland: Stair Memorial Encyclopaedia*, separately published as *Glossary: Scottish and European Union Legal Terms and Latin Phrases* (2nd edn, 2003).

THE LAW LIBRARY

10.05   The first specific things you will have to do on arrival in the law school are find the law library in your institution, register as a reader, and familiarise yourself with its layout. There will almost certainly be a guided tour for new students before term starts, and a library exercise is likely to be among the first tutorials, so you are not on your own in this. But it is worth wandering around on your own, browsing along the shelves, and looking out for certain key features. These include:

- a statement of the opening hours and general regulations;
- the location of the service desk, staffed by librarians whose job it is to deal with readers' inquiries, and where borrowing formalities are completed;
- the location of the catalogues, both manual and computerised; note how to search these by names of authors, titles of works, or subject;
- the divisions of the library – the location of the case reports, statutory material, foreign and Community law, textbooks and other monographs, journals and periodicals; note also the subject sections, and the ordering of books on the shelves by annual volumes (sometimes more than one a year) in the case of legal source material and journals, by alphabetical use of authors' surnames in the case of books;
- the reserve section (which may be behind the service desk); here are held the most frequently consulted works, for which you have therefore to make a request and which you can probably only have out for a limited time to ensure maximum availability to all readers;
- the recent accessions shelf, where newly-acquired books are displayed, and the new periodicals rack, where the current issues of journals and other periodical publications (including the case reports) are held; and
- any other facilities such as photocopiers and computers for use in word-processing and in researching legal databases on CD-Roms and the Internet.

10.06 The library is often described as the lawyer's equivalent of the scientist's laboratory, so essential is it to the study and practice of law. You should come to regard it as your place of work throughout your studying career. Later on, we will look at how to use its resources to find the law, but the first step is to learn how to supplement and follow up what is provided in lectures and tutorials.

10.07 If you have the means, you may want to start your own library. Textbooks will certainly be recommended for purchase, and some examples of likely recommendations are given in Appendix 5. This may be especially helpful to those setting about the professional examinations without the benefit of formal courses of instruction. As already noted, collections of relevant statutory material are also available (see para **9.05**). You may also find casebooks, collections of extracts from leading cases with commentary and questions, useful for work away from the library or in class. See Appendix 5 for lists of these. There are special student rates available for most of the leading Scottish periodical publications, and early investment will stand you in good stead later on, as well as accruing in monetary value.

THE INTERNET

10.08   The primary source material of the law – legislation and court decisions – is increasingly available in full text on the Internet, especially the material first published from the 1990s onwards. Most law schools have now established their own websites and intranets which, as well as giving information about courses and staff, also provide links to other sites containing legally-relevant material. Many legal databases are also accessible by way of the Internet or a service such as ATHENS, provided your law school has taken out a subscription. Some of the most important of these websites and databases are noted in Chapter 11 and Appendix 7. There will probably be suites of computers linked to the Internet in your law library or in microlabs in the law school; but if you have a computer at home from which you can also access the Internet, then it becomes possible to have a very substantial law library in your own study space, without having to worry too much about other users taking away the volume you happen to want at the time. The limitations are the lack of older material (which is slowly being overcome) and the cost of the phone calls needed to make your Internet links (which again may be overcome by subscribing to certain Internet service providers, in particular broadband services).

HOW TO START YOUR PRIVATE STUDY

10.09   A useful way to start structuring your private study is by concentrating on following up lectures and preparing for tutorials in the library. You have to start reading cases and statutes sometime, and a good place to start is with the ones highlighted in the lecture. That does not mean reading every case or statutory provision cited, but rather picking out the ones on which the lecturer spent time or seemed especially interested by. You may even have cases for reading suggested to you by the lecturer.

Finding a case

10.10   Cases are referred to by the names of the litigating parties – pursuer against (rarely *versus*, despite the use of the abbreviation *v*) defender. The name is followed by a citation to the series of law reports in which the case is reported. This citation starts with a year, the initials of the series of law reports in which the report appears, and a page reference. There are four main series in Scotland, as follows, each producing annual volumes:

(1) *Session Cases*. The annual volume is divided into four parts, each paginated separately. The first part reports House of Lords cases and is cited as 'SC (HL)' (eg 1926 SC (HL) 51); the second (since 2000) reports Privy Council decisions and is cited as 'SC (PC)' (eg 2001 SC (PC) 1); the third part reports cases in the High Court of Justiciary and is cited as 'JC' (eg 1925 JC 58); and the final part reports cases in the Court of Session and is cited as 'SC' (eg 1911 SC 353). The series begins in 1907. Session Cases from 1930 are now available online to subscribers at http://www.justis.com/database/electronic_session_cases.html. At the time of writing (April 2004) the series is expected to be made available on both LexisNexis and Westlaw in the course of 2004 (see paras **11.09–11.10**).

(2) *Scots Law Times*. The annual volume of reports (as distinct from another annual volume of articles and other items cited as 'SLT (News)') is divided into two main sections, each paginated separately. The first reports House of Lords and Court of Session cases and is cited as 'SLT' (eg 1954 SLT 342). The second reports sheriff court cases and is cited as 'SLT (Sh Ct)' (eg 1971 SLT (Sh Ct) 49). There are other much shorter sections each reporting the decisions of other Scottish courts, identified in abbreviated form after the 'SLT' (eg 1989 SLT (Lyon Ct) 2, 1989 SLT (Lands Tr) 44). The series begins in 1893, and is now also available in its entirety on an annually updated CD-Rom, and from 1930 on Westlaw (see below, para **11.10**).

(3) *Scottish Civil Law Reports*. An annual volume, cited 'SCLR' (eg 1990 SCLR 335), and covering all civil courts in Scotland. The series begins in 1987. A commentary is appended to each report. The series is available in full via LexisNexis UK's Scots Law Direct service (http://wilson.butterworths.co.uk/stair/), as well as on LexisNexis (see para **11.10**).

(4) *Scottish Criminal Law Reports*. An annual volume, cited 'SCCR' (eg 1989 SCCR 119), covering all criminal courts in Scotland. A commentary is appended to each report. The series begins in 1981. This series is

also available in full via LexisNexis UK's Scots Law Direct service http://wilson.butterworths.co.uk/stair/), as well as on LexisNexis (see para **11.10**).

10.11   In addition, you need to be aware that from 1821 to 1906, the annual Session Cases volumes were known by the name of their editors, and the convention is to cite these volumes by the initial of the editor concerned, as follows:

S = Shaw (1821–1838)

D = Dunlop (1838–1862)

M = Macpherson (1863–1873)

R = Rettie (1873–1898)

F = Fraser (1898–1906)

A reference to a case in any of these series will start with the year in round brackets, the number of the volume in the series, the editor's initial (number and initial will normally be on the volume spines) and a page reference; for example, (1883) 11 R 193. House of Lords cases began to be reported in these volumes from 1850 and the '(HL)' citation convention is used here too, coming after the editor's initial thus: (1878) 5 R (HL) 105. Justiciary cases began to be reported in them in 1874, and reference to these is by the insertion of '(J)' after the editor's initial, as in (1881) 8 R (J) 41.

10.12   With the volume number and the editor's initial, you have all the information you need to find the volume you need, so that the year in the above citations is unnecessary information. The principle in Scotland is that when the year is used but not necessary for citation purposes it is placed in round brackets; if the year is essential to the citation, it is unadorned. You can also see the principle in operation with volumes of the *SLT* from 1893 to 1908, although just to confuse, between 1909 and the early 1920s the publishers started to publish two volumes a year, dropped the single volume number and instead spoke each year of a volume 1 and a volume 2. Thus the year became essential to enable the researcher to find the correct *SLT*, and in accordance with the principles of citation it lost its round brackets. (See further below, para **10.17**, for English customs in this important matter.) This remains the case, although each year now sees once again the publication of two volumes.

10.13   From 1707 to 1865 Scottish cases in the House of Lords were reported in private series, also cited by abbreviations of the chief editors' names as follows:

Rob/Robert	Robertson (1707–1727)
Pat	Paton (1726–1821)
Sh App	Shaw (1821–1826)
W & Sh	Wilson & Shaw (1825–1835)
Sh & Macl	Shaw & Maclean (1835–1838)
Macl & R	Maclean & Robinson (1839)
Rob/Robin	Robinson (1840–1841)
Bell	Bell (1842–1850)
Macq	Macqueen (1851–1865)

Citation follows the conventions of year, volume number, abbreviated form of editor's name and page.

10.14 Similarly there were private Justiciary reports from 1819 to 1916, cited as follows:

P Shaw	Patrick Shaw (1819–1831)
Syme	Syme (1826–1829)
Swin	Swinton (1835–1841)
Broun	Broun (1842–1845)
Arkley	Arkley (1846–1848)
J Shaw	John Shaw (1848–1851)
Irv	Irvine (1851–1868)
Coup	Couper (1868–1885)
White	White (1885–1893)
Adam	Adam (1893–1916)

The same conventions apply as hitherto.

10.15 The last major set of Scottish reports about which you need to know is *Morison's Dictionary*, a 22-volume monster covering all cases reported before 1811 and paginated continuously throughout all 22 volumes. This is abbreviated as 'Mor' or 'M'. If the latter is used, you can tell that it is not Macpherson's reports from the date, his work covering 1862–73 rather than the eighteenth and earlier centuries.

10.16   In 1999 Scottish Courts Administration launched a website – http://www.scotcourts.gov.uk – making Court of Session, High Court of Justiciary and some sheriff court decisions available on the Internet on the day they are issued. Initially, cases from late-1998 onwards were posted on the site. The site is searchable by the names of parties, key words and so on, and is an excellent way of checking out the very latest decisions. House of Lords cases since 14 November 1996 appear each Thursday during court terms at http://www.publications.parliament.uk/pa/ld199697/ ldjudgmt/ldjudgmt.htm. A printed guide to the latest cases is *Green's Weekly Digest* (GWD), which, as its name suggests, is a weekly publication in which appear summaries of recent cases grouped under subject headings and given a continuous numbering throughout the year. Cases here are cited by the year of publication, the abbreviation GWD, the number of the issue, and the number of the case: eg 1998 GWD 3-136. An online Scottish case digest can be found in the Lexis Nexis UK service, Scots Law Direct (http://wilson.butterworths.co.uk/stair/).

10.17   For the full complexities of English law reports, you will have to look elsewhere[1]. The present official system is based round *The Weekly Law Reports* (WLR), which covers the main English courts in reports published weekly[2]. At the end of the year these bind up into three volumes. Citation is by year, volume number 1, 2 or 3, the abbreviation WLR and a page reference. Since the year is needed to find the correct volume, it appears in *square* brackets (like us, the English use round brackets where the year is unnecessary). The reports in volumes 2 and 3 are further published in other annual series of reports, divided up according to the division of the English High Court in which the case started – Queen's Bench (QB), Chancery (Ch) and Family (Fam). If a case gets to the House of Lords, however, the report appears in *Appeal Cases* (AC). Citation of all these is by year in square brackets, volume number if appropriate, abbreviation, and page number[3]. You should also know about the *All England Reports* (All ER), an unofficial series running on the same lines as WLR but now having four volumes per year. Some of the Scottish appeals to the House of Lords get into All ER, WLR and AC as well as the Scottish reports. As with their Scottish counterparts, the English courts have a website on which cases appear as they are decided: http://www.courtservice.gov.uk.

1   See eg Glanville Williams, *Learning the Law*, 12th edn, pp 35–47.
2   *WLR* from 1953 is also available to subscribers from Justis.com at http://www.justis.com/database/weekly_law_reports.html.
3   *The Law Reports* are likewise available in their entirety to subscribers from Justis.com at http://www.justis.com/database/the_law_reports.html.

10.18   European Court of Justice (ECJ) cases are reported in *European Court Reports* (ECR), which now runs to several volumes a year. Citation is by case number, name, year in square brackets, abbreviation and page number: eg Case 192/73, *Van Zuylen Frères v Hag* [1974] ECR 731. Since the institution of the Court of First Instance in 1989, ECR has been divided into two separately-paginated parts for each of the Community courts, indicated by a 'I' or 'II' before the page number. The numbers of European Court of Justice cases are also prefixed with a C (for *Cour*), thus: Case C-46/93, *Brasserie du Pêcheur SA v Germany* [1996] ECR I-1029. If the case is an appeal from the Court of First Instance, a P (for *Pourvoi* – see para **1.29**) is added, thus: Cases C-241 and 242/91P, *RTE v Commission* [1995] ECR I-743. The case number of Court of First Instance cases is prefixed with a T (for *Tribunal*), thus: Case T-51/89, *Tetra Pak Rausing SA v Commission* [1990] ECR II-309. An unofficial series is *Common Market Law Reports* (CMLR), for which the same citation principles are in use: eg Case C-10/89, *SA CNL-Sucal NV v Hag* [1990] 3 CMLR 571. The case number is determined by the order and year in which cases arrive at the court registry; hence the second *Hag* case above was the tenth case to be lodged at the registry in 1989. The website at which you will find recent ECJ decisions is http://curia.eu.int. The full text of cases can also be found through the online database EUR-Lex, which is accessible on the Internet at http://europa.eu.int/eur-lex. The ECJ should not be confused with the quite separate European Court of Human Rights, the decisions of which have been reported since 1979 in the annually numbered volumes of the *European Human Rights Reports*, cited, eg, (1998) 28 EHRR. Again there is a website on which the full texts of judgments are available: http://www.echr.coe.int/.

10.19   The rise of Internet and database versions of judicial decisions has given rise to the now near universal practice of *neutral citation* systems, which enable the electronically literate lawyer quickly to identify the year of a case, the jurisdiction and the court from which it comes, and its number in the sequence of cases coming from the court in question.

Thus the House of Lords is UKHL (eg *Burnett's Trustee v Grainger* [2004] UKHL 8) and the Privy Council is UKPC (eg *HM Advocate v R* [2002] UKPC D3). English and Welsh cases are cited as follows:

Court of Appeal

Court of Appeal (Civil Division)	[2004] EWCA Civ 1, 2, 3, etc
Court of Appeal (Criminal Division)	[2004] EWCA Crim 1, 2, 3, etc

High Court

Queen's Bench	[2004] EWHC *number* (QB)
Chancery	[2004] EWHC *number* (Ch)
Family Division	[2004] EWHC *number* (Fam)
Administrative Court	[2004] EWHC *number* (Admin)
Commercial Court	[2004] EWHC *number* (Comm)
Admiralty Court	[2004] EWHC *number* (Admlty)
Patents Court	[2004] EWHC *number* (Pat)
Technology and Construction Court	[2004] EWHC *number* (TCC)

But alas, the Scottish courts below the House of Lords and the Privy Council have yet to adopt such a system. However, they have taken up a further aspect of neutral citation, the numbering of paragraphs in judgments, as this is the best mode of precise referencing for pageless electronic versions. These paragraph numbers now also appear in the printed law reports, making their use in all modes of citation the quickest and most precise means of accessing those parts of a judgment you want particularly to read.

10.20   For explanation of other citation abbreviations, consult D Raistrick, *Index to Legal Citations and Abbreviations* (1981). If you cannot find the volume of reports for which you have a citation, it is perfectly possible that there is another report in one or more of the other series of reports. A quick way to check for other citations is in the table of cases in a good textbook (see further below, para **10.46**), but often a search in volumes contemporaneous with the one you were referred to originally will produce the desired result.

Reading cases

10.21   Now that you know how to find a reference in the main series of printed reports, go and have a look at the case you have chosen. For a description of what you can expect to find in a printed report, see para **1.45**. Read the whole case (not just the summary, or *headnote*, at the beginning), relating what you read to what was said in the lecture. The lecturer will have summarised the case; why were some points picked out and not others? What justified the lecturer's assertion that the case stood for such-and-such a rule? Is that rule actually stated in the case, and if so, why did the judge not just confine himself to saying it? With this exercise you can begin to see how the lecturer has used the case as a source for a legal proposition, and perhaps you may even end up doubting whether the proposition was correctly made.

10.22   At some point fairly early on in your law course you will have explained to you in detail how cases are used as sources of law, and only a brief sketch is given here to make it easier to explain what to look for in a case report. At its most basic, a case is a source for the rule which connects the result of the case with its facts. The rule is known as the *ratio decidendi*, the reason for the decision. Finding the rule is a matter of interpreting the case, and so its content can be a matter of debate. As time goes on and the case is used as a source of law in later cases, so a preferred interpretation may come to take root. Legal textbooks also play a vital role in fixing the rule for which a case will stand, or in drawing together all the cases on a particular point and proposing a general rule which holds them together.

10.23   A further factor in analysing a case is the status of the court which decided it in the hierarchy of courts described in paras **1.15–1.32**. Lower courts are bound to follow the rules laid down by higher ones, and appellate courts are generally bound by their own decisions. To illustrate from the Scottish civil courts, this means that a sheriff is bound by the sheriff principal of the sheriffdom, the Inner House and the House of Lords. A Lord Ordinary is bound by the Inner House and the House of Lords, while the two Divisions of the Inner House are bound by each other and the House of Lords. But it is also important to note when courts are *not* bound by previous decisions. Higher courts are not bound by lower courts, and so can overrule their previous decisions as wrong. Judges at first instance do not bind each other, so sheriffs and Lords Ordinary can treat each other's decisions as mistaken. The House of Lords has power to overrule its own previous decisions, while in the Court of Session otherwise binding cases can be referred to a sitting of the Whole Court to be overruled. Finally, a judge confronted with an apparently binding decision in an earlier case can always distinguish it by pointing to significant differences in the facts of the present case or limitations on the rule derived from the earlier case.

10.24   In reading a case, therefore, there are a number of basic points of which to take note. First you must start off with the name and citation of the case. Next there is the question of which court decided the case, which gives some indication of its relative weight as a source in future. It is much more likely to be definitive if decided by the House of Lords than if decided by a Lord Ordinary. Third, it is important to note what the facts are, and what the result was; that is, who won? The headnote is very helpful here, but it represents an editorial summary, and you should not skip over any other material about the facts in the report. Make sure you identify who is pursuer, defender, reclaimer, appellant or respondent. Judges often refer to the parties simply by those titles rather than their names, and it is easy to lose track of exactly who is who as a result.

10.25   The facts of cases are often very complex and it can be helpful in coming to grips with them to draw diagrams illustrating in some way the relationships between the various parties involved; for example, by connecting with a line between their initials parties who have a contract with each other. It is often easier to comprehend situations involving more than two persons in this visual form.

10.26   In many reported Scottish cases, the 'facts' may not yet have been proved, because what is being reported is a *debate on the relevancy on the Procedure Roll*. What is happening here is that one of the parties has argued that even if the other proves all his allegations of fact, or *averments*, there would still be no entitlement to a remedy as a matter of law. A famous example is *Donoghue v Stevenson* 1932 SC (HL) 31[1]. Mrs Donoghue averred that she had consumed some ice cream on which she had inadvertently poured ginger beer containing the decomposed remains of a snail, and had suffered illness as a result. The manufacturer Stevenson argued that, even if these facts were proved, Mrs Donoghue still had no remedy against him. The House of Lords rejected Stevenson's argument and allowed the case to proceed. The existence or otherwise of the dead snail in Mrs Donoghue's ginger beer will be forever uncertain, however, as the action was then settled out of court.

1   For an online version of the case, see Scottish Council for Law Reporting website at http://www.scottishlawreports.org.uk/resources/keycases/dvs/donoghue-v-stevenson-report.html. The site also has reports for a number of other well-known Scottish cases.

10.27   *Donoghue* also illustrates, however, that the detailed facts can be relatively unimportant. What is significant about *Donoghue* is not the snail or the ginger beer, but the propositions that a manufacturer of products has a legal duty towards the ultimate consumer for the safety of his product, and, at an even more general level, that when it is reasonably foreseeable that your careless conduct will injure someone else you owe that person a duty to take care, breach of which will make you liable in damages if it in fact causes injury. Thus on the first proposition *Donoghue* could be treated as a source of law in a later decision where a man contracted a singularly unpleasant form of dermatitis from certain chemicals negligently put in underpants by the manufacturers (*Grant v Australian Knitting Mills* [1936] AC 85). On the second *Donoghue* has been a source of law in a wide variety of cases, ranging from solicitors failing to draw clients' wills properly so that intended beneficiaries do not get their legacies to workmen in the street failing to provide adequate safeguards around their excavations for the protection of the public. Both propositions can be found in the judges' speeches in *Donoghue*. It is what the judges say in explaining their decisions, usually given in full in a law report, which is the most important material in determining what rule or rules a case can stand for. Accordingly it is on these that your reading of cases should concentrate most. A judgment will usually start with the facts or alleged facts of the case, before summarising the arguments of the two sides. The judicial statements where the rule in the case are most likely to be found will come after this, although the summary of the arguments may contain the first indications of what the rule will be. The judge will say why the arguments of one party are to be preferred and those of the other rejected. Perhaps it all turns on the meaning of a statute or a previous case. You should note the contentious authority and the judge's final view on its meaning, as well as the reasons which support the conclusion. Notice how this is not only a process of determining the rule of the present case but also of fixing the meaning of rules found in earlier sources of law.

10.28   In many appellate cases there will be more than one judgment. It is bad practice to pick one and read it only. For a start, the judges may not all agree in the result. It is important to know what the majority decision was in such cases, and the existence of dissents (because this may weaken the authority of the case in future). In analysing a majority or unanimous decision, you should be looking to see if the judges all reached the decision by the same route, or whether there were differences of view on the correct approach. This affects our interpretation of the rule which the case as a whole can stand for. Also, if the judges took different views about the meaning of a previous case, that may affect the future interpretation of that case. Analysis of dissents is also important because they indicate, first, a case where the interpretation or application of the law may be particularly difficult. It helps the student to an understanding of legal method and reasoning to compare the dissenters' reasoning with that of the majority, and to essay an analysis of which is to be preferred. Nor is this exercise wholly academic, since the dissent may become the basis for a later overruling, whether on appeal or in a subsequent case. There are many examples of famous dissents which became legal orthodoxy later on.

10.29   All this can mean a lot of time spent reading and noting up one case, and the questions arise, how many cases should you read in this way, and if not all, which ones? I think that you should not attempt to read all the cases which may be cited to you in class. You must be selective. The process of selection may be aided by course teachers' suggestions and tutorial reading lists. Beyond that, assistance can be derived from two ideas. One is that of the 'leading case', a phrase which you may hear or read. There are a number of decisions which are regarded as definitive in particular fields, *Donoghue v Stevenson* being one such. It is worth reading these, because although in all probability they will have already been exhaustively analysed and interpreted, they usually contain clear or classic statements of legal rules, often in the context of memorable facts. The other helpful idea is that of the 'latest case', especially when it is from an appellate court. With these you may have to do more work on interpretation, because by definition there is no subsequent analysis in further cases and the literature on the case may be limited. The advantage of reading the latest case is that it will probably review the previous authorities and bring out what are now their major points.

10.30   A final basis for reading cases may be simply to get the feel of how perfectly well-settled rules of law have been applied in different situations. Legal rules are often stated in very abstract forms, and are meaningless unless you know the circumstances to which they are typically relevant. This kind of social context will often be supplied by lecturers and tutors, but the cases are about real people in specific settings, and this can be helpful in seeing what the meaning of the rules actually is.

Finding statutes in the library

10.31   Citation systems for UK statutes are not as complex as for cases. Statutes are usually referred to by a short title indicating subject matter, the calendar year in which it was enacted, and the chapter number. The chapter number is determined by the chronology of the statute's enactment. The information about the year is usually enough to get you to the correct volume in the various series of statutory publications, which include, not only *Public General Statutes* and *Acts of the Scottish Parliament*, but also *Current Law Statutes*. There may however be more than one volume per year, and in modern times there usually is. The first volume normally has contents lists, one alphabetical by title, the other by chapter number, and from these you can find your way to the volume which contains the statute you want. For the text of statutes from 1988 on (as passed, but not as subsequently amended), it is quicker to consult Her Majesty's Stationery Office website, HMSOnline, at http://www.legislation.hmso.gov.uk/acts.htm. Bills currently before Parliament, whether commenced in the Commons or the Lords, can be found at http://www.parliament.uk/bills/bills.cfm, enabling you to track progress and amendment alongside the Parliamentary debates, which are also maintained at this site (http://www.parliament.uk/hansard/hansard.cfm). A complete list of public bills introduced in Parliament in the current session, together with information about their progress, can be found in the Weekly Information Bulletin (available at http://www.parliament.the-stationery-office.co.uk/pa/cm/cmwib.htm). There are similar systems for publishing the Acts of the Scottish Parliament both in print and in electronic form (see http://www.scotland-legislation.hmso.gov.uk/legislation/scotland/s-acts.htm); the Scottish Parliament website enables one to keep track of Bills in progress, at http://www.scottish.parliament.uk/bills/index.htm.

10.32   Complications can arise with finding UK statutes before 1940. Parliamentary sessions usually straddle two calendar years and until 1939 annual volumes covered the preceding session rather than the calendar year. As a result, knowing the calendar year of passage does not always send you to the right volume. Another complication is the practice, abandoned in 1963, of giving chapter numbers in accordance with regnal years[1]. There is a checklist of regnal years in the *Parliament House Book*. The Scottish Parliament system is simply to number the statutes for a calendar year in accordance with the chronological order in which they were passed (see para **1.11**).

1   For an explanation see D M Walker, *The Scottish Legal System*, 8th edn, pp 252–253, or Glanville Williams, *Learning the Law*, 12th edn, p 53.

10.33   Statutory instruments are published in annual bound volumes. There are several volumes each year. Citation is either by a short title and year, or by the abbreviation 'SI', year and number. So, for example, you can have either the Copyright and Related Rights 1996, or SI 1996 no 2967 (commonly written SI 1996/2967). Statutory instruments passed by the Westminster Parliament but referring solely to Scotland have not only their own numbers but also a separate number with the prefix 'S', thus, for example, the Maximum Number of Judges (Scotland) Order 1993, SI 1993/ 3154 (S. 303). Since 1999 such purely Scottish instruments have continued to be cited in this way, for example, The Scottish Parliament (Disqualification) Order 2003, SI 2003/409 (S. 4). However, statutory instruments relating to Scotland and passed by the Scottish Parliament are known as Scottish Statutory Instruments or SSI's, and have only one number, for example, The Maximum Number of Judges (Scotland) Order 1999, SSI 1999/158. Scottish statutory instruments have their own series of bound volumes. Statutory instruments are also readily accessible online, although only as passed and not as subsequently amended: UK ones since 1987 at http:// www.legislation.hmso.gov.uk/stat.htm, Scottish ones since 1999 at http:// www.scotland-legislation.hmso.gov.uk.legislation/scotland/s-stat.htm.

10.34   European Community legislation is found in the L series of the *Official Journal of the European Union* (abbreviation 'OJ'), which comes out in almost daily parts, but which in libraries is bound up, usually in several volumes, at the end of each year. (The C series gives official communications, information and notices, including draft legislation and, in an annex, European Parliamentary debates.) There are two main types of EC legislation, the Regulation and the Directive. The former is cited by number then year, thus: 40/94 (the Community Trade Mark Regulation). Directives are cited by year then number, thus: 89/104 (the First Council Directive to approximate the laws of the Member States relating to Trade Marks). From 1999, in both systems the year is given in full. To locate the legislation in the *Official Journal*, there is also a reference system by OJ issue number, date and page. For example, the Trade Marks Directive just referred to is OJ, L40, 11.2.89, p 1, or, more concisely, OJ 1989, L40/1; while the Community Trade Mark Regulation is OJ, L11, 14.1.94, p 1, or OJ 1994, L11/1. Community legislation can also be traced in sources such as the *Encyclopedia of European Community Law, European Communities Legislation Current Status* and the *Directory of Community Legislation* *in Force* (the official publication). The online Community law database EUR-Lex (see above, para **10.18**) gives the full text of Community legislation and details of UK implementation.

10.35 Legislation of the pre-1707 Scottish parliament is still in force. The most convenient texts are likely to be those found in a slim HMSO publication of 1966, *Acts of the Parliament of Scotland 1424–1707*. But if you want an historically authentic text, check the 12-volume 'Record Edition' published in the nineteenth century, *The Acts of the Parliaments of Scotland* (cited as *APS*). A new edition of this, to be published on CD-Rom, is in preparation at St Andrews University (see http://www.st-andrews.ac.uk/~scotparl/).

10.36 In courses where statutes are of fundamental importance – for example, family law, trusts, succession, commercial and company law, conveyancing and taxation – it is desirable to buy your own copies. As already noted, there are several commercial publications in which statutes are grouped together by subject for the convenience of students (see above, para **10.07**). But it is nonetheless vital to be able to find your way quickly to any piece of legislation in the official publications and on the Internet.

Reading statutory material

10.37 What do you look for when you are reading a statute? The main thing is obviously the meaning of the legislative words. Again, a large part of your initial courses in law will be devoted to the methods of determining what a statute means, and it is an exercise in which you will have to engage regularly as you proceed with your studies. You will learn about the variety of methods of approaching a statute: the literal approach, focusing on the meaning of the words used, or the purposive approach, which looks at the words in the light of the overall purpose of the statute. There are also a variety of rules about the extent to which material extraneous to the statute can be used in determining its meaning. The argument against allowing reference to the record of Parliamentary debates, Law and Royal Commission reports and other preparatory material has always been that it is the statutory words which constitute the law, but judges may now use *Hansard*, the Parliamentary record, and also increasingly refer to the formal documents which precede legislation as an aid to determining its meaning. Whatever the formal rules may be in court now, there can be no doubt of the assistance which preparatory material can give the student in coming to grips with statutes, and you should ensure that you are familiar with how to find them.

10.38   Here, however, we concentrate on the text of the statute alone, and mention a few things which you should look out for as a guide to understanding it. The short title of the statute, found at the beginning, gives at least a little guidance as to its subject matter, and can be amplified by the long title which in modern UK legislation follows immediately. EC legislation also has titles, but in addition there is a long preamble – the *recitals* – which can be very helpful in stating the policies which the legislation is trying to implement, and is part of the legislative text.

10.39   In the body of the text, there are a number of key sections which should always be looked out for. An obvious one is the territorial application of the statute: is it UK, Scottish, or English and Welsh? In a UK statute, you should keep an eye out for sections which declare that they do not apply to Scotland, or make special provision for Scotland, or provide a translation of the statute's technical terms into the language of Scots law.

10.40   Another point which is often overlooked by students as a mere technicality is the date the statute came into force as law. There may be a section which gives a date, but often it is left to the government to fix a date later. This is done by passing a statutory instrument called a Commencement Order. Sometimes statutes are brought into force bit by bit, and so there may be several Commencement Orders and different dates to remember. Parts of statutes can be on the books for years without ever coming into force: recent examples include Part IX of the Consumer Credit Act 1974, which came into force on 19 May 1985, and Schedule 7 of the Health and Safety at Work etc Act 1974, some of which is still not in force. The importance of this is that generally statutes are not retrospective, meaning that the rules they contain only apply from the date of commencement. Sometimes this can lead to very complex situations. For example there have been three Copyright Acts in the last hundred years, in 1911, 1956 and 1988. Each one has changed the law significantly, but it had to be decided how existing copyrights under the previous law were to be treated once the new Act came into force. All the Copyright Acts therefore contain complex 'transitional provisions' to deal with such copyrights. This means that you still have to know about the dates of the Acts, when they came into force, when a work claiming copyright was created, and what the relevant transitional provisions say in order to give proper advice on copyright law.

10.41 Another section or group of sections which you must consult at the beginning are those dealing with interpretation of words and phrases used in the Act. In effect, these sections form a dictionary which guide you away from more general meanings to precise ones, or provide you with a vocabulary for the purposes of the statute. You must be familiar with these before you embark on a reading of the statute as a whole; and even if you only want to look at one or two sections, you should still check to see whether there is anything relevant in the interpretation section. A helpful technique which has been adopted in some recent legislation is for the interpretation section to say to which other sections particular definitions are relevant. The Consumer Credit Act 1974, which has its own particularly difficult conceptual and definitional framework, provides a set of hypothetical examples to show how its system works.

10.42 After the main text of the Act there will often be additional material known as Schedules. These are just as much part of the Act as the main text and should not be ignored. It is in Schedules, for example, that you find the examples of how to use the concepts of the Consumer Credit Act 1974, and the transitional provisions of the Copyright, Designs and Patents Act 1988. So always at least check the headings of the Schedules, especially if you are updating on a new statute, because there will be one listing the statutory provisions now being repealed.

10.43 As you read a statute you may notice how it confers powers on persons such as government ministers to make subordinate legislation. (Another example encountered in this book is the power of the Law Society of Scotland to make regulations about admission and other matters, which is conferred by section 5 of the Solicitors (Scotland) Act 1980.) Your reading of the law in the area will not be complete until you have checked the use to which that power has been put. Subordinate legislation takes the form of the statutory instruments already discussed (above, para **10.33**). To take an example close to home in the law library, the law on photocopying in libraries depends heavily on the Copyright (Librarians and Archivists) (Copying of Copyright Material) Regulations 1989 (as amended by the Copyright and Related Rights Regulations 2003, Sch 1, para 26), as well as on sections 37–44 of the Copyright, Designs and Patents Act 1988 under which the 1989 Regulations were made (the 2003 Regulations, on the other hand, were made under the European Communities Act 1972).

Reading legal textbooks

10.44   Legal textbooks vary so much in approach and content that it is almost impossible to set down generalisations about how to approach them which will hold good across the whole range. The more elementary a textbook is, the easier it becomes to sit down and read its chapters and sections as a whole. Perhaps this is the main advantage of such books in that they enable you to get a bird's-eye view of the whole of a subject without descending into what Stair called 'the nauseating burden of citation' (*Institutions*, Dedication to the King). More detailed texts are on the whole designed to be used as works of reference rather than to be read as literature, and you should not be in the least put off if you find them heavy going. Instead you should learn how to handle them as works of reference so that you can find your way about them quickly and easily.

10.45   There are a number of aids to using legal textbooks and works of reference. Some of these you will find in any reference work: for example, a table of contents, usually at the beginning of the book, and an index, usually at the end, both of which point you to the places in the book at which subjects are dealt with. Indexes are especially important, because they are normally more detailed than tables of contents. If when you refer to the index you cannot find the subject you want, try another related heading, and see if the subject is dealt with there. To speed this process, it is usually worthwhile to explore the indices of books which you are going to use regularly, to familiarise yourself with the system which they employ.

10.46   Indices and tables of contents are ways of getting into textbooks by subject. But often the point you want to check is how the book deals with a particular source, be it case or statute. Again, sometimes all you can remember about a subject is the name of a case or statute. Law texts meet these needs of readers by providing tables of cases and legislative materials, again usually at the beginning of the book. In these appear all the cases and statutes cited in the book, with a reference to page or paragraph numbers to enable you to move straight to the place where the source is discussed. The cases are usually grouped in alphabetical order, but the statutes may be chronologically arranged. The most useful tables provide you with all the citations of the cases (see above, para **10.20**), and references to the sections of the statute which have been referred to in the book.

10.47   Legal textbooks are also one of the basic ways of finding out what the legal authorities are on a given subject. The conventional textbook only rarely refers to or discusses statutes and cases in the text itself. Rather, it summarises what the author believes the effect of the authority to be, and the source is identified in a footnote at the bottom of the page. Sometimes footnotes are placed at the end of paragraphs, but only in badly thought-out presentations will they be put at the end of the chapter or the book. That is because it is necessary for the lawyer's eye to move constantly between text and note, checking the author's authorities and comparing the text's interpretation with one's own. Equally, if you are looking up the book to check what the author says about a case or a statute, you will start from the tables of cases and statutes, move to the footnotes on the pages given for the reference, and from there to the text.

10.48   There are of course books and other works written about the law which are meant to be read as opposed to referred to. Although the monograph literature on law has considerably increased, it is the periodical literature which the beginning law student is most likely to encounter. There is a large number of legal journals, ranging from the weekly to those which appear only once or twice a year. Journals contain articles in which the writers – often academic lawyers – discuss legal issues. These are usually more overtly argumentative and controversial than textbooks, suggesting new interpretations of the sources, analysing the effect of new law, or showing the inadequacies of the existing law in dealing with particular problems.

10.49   Reading discursive work is a rather different process from consulting works of reference. It is not merely a matter of noting information, although that is important, especially where new law is being analysed, but of absorbing an argument and assessing its merits. The obvious way of doing this is to read the whole of the work in question with care and attention, but there are some tricks of the trade worth keeping in mind. The writer will often summarise the argument of the work at its beginning and again at the end; so it is worth checking in both places to see if this has happened. If so, it may make it easier to follow the piece as a whole. It is increasingly common for journals to provide a brief abstract at the beginning of an article, which is helpful where it occurs. Check also for the structure of the work; has the writer provided headings and sub-headings to help make the divisions of the argument clear? On a skim through, do there seem to be regular references to a few sources, be it case, statute or something else? Once you know the subject a little, it is always worth glancing through the author's footnotes as a preliminary, since these can reveal the emphasis in the work and, sometimes, the author's scholarly allegiances – that is, if there is an issue on which opinions are generally divided, the author's approval of one camp and disapproval of another often emerges most clearly in the references.

10.50   When you are reading, do not try to take screeds of notes. Instead, compare what is being said with what you already know, have read elsewhere, or have already been told. Look for the passages where the author is stating disagreement with someone else, be it a court, Parliament or some other writer. This will often be the heart of the article. Look out for key words which show where the author is being controversial or unorthodox. The rather pompous phrase 'It is submitted ...' quite often leads into passages of this sort. On the other hand, assess the author's argument. Does the interpretation of the law seem right? Are there contentions which are not backed up by references and are therefore presumably based on the author's assumptions rather than research? Are other assumptions possible? Do the sources cited support what the author says? Are any sources of which you know not considered? In this way you begin to develop a critical approach to what you read. Your notes should reflect your understanding of what the author says, preferably in your own words, and some critical assessment of the argument, rather than being simply a summary of what has been written.

10.51   At this point we are beginning to move away from the assumption with which we began, that you are just starting your study of law, and move to another, that you are beginning to know something about the law and to be able to handle materials critically with that knowledge. It is an appropriate point to leave the studying that supplements teaching by others, and move to the studying in which you teach yourself and find the law without being guided to it. That is the subject of the next chapter.

CHAPTER 11

Researching the law

INTRODUCTION

11.01 A common complaint of legal practitioners is that students do not learn how to use the law library, but merely learn how to follow up references given them by their teachers. If this is so, it is despite the expectation of law teachers that students carry out independent research for essay and project work. In practice, of course, being able to find out what the law is from a starting point of little or no knowledge is an essential skill. In this chapter, therefore, we will see how to use the library to find out about the law for yourself.

11.02 Three points should be made at the outset. First, more detailed coverage of specific points can be found in other works such as Dawn Mackey's *How to Use a Scottish Law Library* (1992), Peter Clinch's *Using a Law Library: A Student's Guide to Legal Research Skills* (2nd edn, 2001; this contains chapters specifically on Scots law by David Hart), *How to Use a Law Library* by P A Thomas and J Knowles (4th edn, 2001), and *Legal Research Skills for Scots Lawyers* by Karen Fullerton and Megan MacGregor (1999). You should make yourself familiar with at least one of the works mentioned, preferably up-to-date and including Scottish material. Second, what follows focuses mainly on research in Scots and English law. Some reading on researching comparative law, European Community, Roman and international law is also suggested. Finally, in university study, problems and essays come to you with their subject matter identified in advance. In practice, you have first to decide which areas of law are relevant. Doing this well is the result of knowledge and experience, and this chapter does not attempt to short-circuit the process. That is a function of your legal studies and training.

11.03   The approach adopted here is task-based. This means that I try to explain the process of legal research first in terms of answering problems, and second in terms of writing essays.

RESEARCHING THE ANSWER TO A PROBLEM

11.04   As already noted, it is assumed that you know the general subject matter of the problem. How do you go about finding the relevant law?

Start with a textbook or encyclopaedia

11.05   The best starting point is as up-to-date a textbook as possible in the area of law concerned, or the relevant article or articles in the *Stair Memorial Encyclopaedia*, also available online through the LexisNexis UK Scots Law Direct service (http://wilson.butterworths.co.uk/stair/), with hyperlinks to other legislative and case material in the site (ASPs, SSIs, *Scottish Civil Law Reports* and *Scottish Criminal Case Reports*). For England, use *Halsbury's Laws of England* (also accessible on-line – see further Clinch, *How to Use a Law Library*, pp 133–137). The question of which textbook depends on the field of law concerned. Often there are several, and it is worth consulting them all. It is useful to know whether there is a consensus view or not. Because you will need authority, you are best with the detailed practitioners' works which will be most fully referenced with cases, statutes and other sources, but the more elementary student texts can still be useful in getting your mind oriented to the basic principles of the law and giving you the leading authorities. A list of these can be found in Appendix 5.

11.06   This piece of research should give you the main authorities in statute and case law, along with views as to what they mean. But, quite apart from the fact that you now have to read these authorities for yourself, you still have basic groundwork to do. Check the date of the textbook (usually on or near the title page). Generally the author's preface will say (near the end) something like, 'I have tried to state the law as at [such-and-such a date]', and this will be some time before you opened that page. Inevitably therefore you have to update what the author says. This is the bit where many students fall down unless they have had guidance from their teachers, but for obvious reasons it is extremely important to be able to give the law as it is today, not as it was when the text writer finished work.

Updating

11.07 There are two basic approaches to updating. The traditional one is manual, using printed sources and guides; the second is electronic, using computers and has only failed to replace the manual in so far as the electronic does not reach so far back into the past. You will thus probably have to combine the two approaches most of the time in really detailed research, although computer-based approaches will tend to suffice on current topics. For this reason, we will start with searching for legal information electronically, and then show how that can be supplemented by the manual systems.

Electronic updating

11.08 As we saw in Chapter 10, much legal source material has become available by way of online electronic databases, CD-Roms and the Internet. Here we will focus mainly on material available via various commercial online databases to which your law school should have subscriptions, making them easily available to their students. With a few mouse clicks at the relevant icons and hyperlinks on your screen, and the occasional need to type a few search terms, it is possible to search all this material very quickly while sitting at your desk or workstation, and avoid the sometimes laborious treks around the library shelves which manual searching often involves. You can search for cases and legislation by their names or a significant portion of their names if you cannot remember the whole thing. The search may reveal not only what the texts are, but also their content, as well as where and to what effect they have been used subsequently. In addition, you can search the material by devices other than case and statute names; for example, you can find all the references to particular legal concepts or key words, or how often a legal text (perhaps the one you began your research with) has been cited in the courts. The other great beauty of electronic research, apart from ease, convenience and speed, is that you do not have to rely on legal subject headings in doing your search. Suppose for example that you want to do research on cows in

Scots law. 'Cow' is not one of the headings used in *Current Law* or other paper digests and indices (see further below, para **11.12**). Probably you should try 'animals' to begin with in such sources. But a search on one legal database using the word 'cow' threw up the perhaps surprising number of 89 cases when carried out for the first edition of this book in 1993[1]. But although interesting, 89 was probably too many references to be useful unless you wanted to write a treatise on the subject of cows and the law. But if your concern was with liability for cows in shops, you could combine 'cow' with 'shop' in your search, and immediately you were down to one case. This was *Cameron v Hamilton's Auction Marts Ltd* 1955 SLT (Sh Ct) 74, which every law student ought to read to learn what remarkable beasts cows can be. The only problem with 'key-word' searching of this kind is that the computer will search only for the words 'cow' and 'shop'. It may therefore miss 'heifer' and 'supermarket' cases, while you will certainly not get anything about 'bulls' and 'outlets retailing chinaware'. So there is still a place for conceptual searching, and you should also think of any synonyms for the search words with which you start.

1   The search described here was conducted on the old Lexis system; alas, the same search on the present LexisNexis and Westlaw systems does not produce anything like the same pedagogically satisfying results.

11.09   The longest-established database is now called LexisNexis. Use the 'Professional' rather than the 'Executive' version. Among much other material from Britain, the European Community, America, and the Commonwealth, it contains full texts of all unreported Scottish House of Lords and Court of Session cases from the mid-1980s onwards. It also has judgments reported in the *Session Cases* from 1950–1993, and in *Scottish Civil Law Reports* 1986–1993 and *Scottish Criminal Case Reports* 1981–1993. All these are found on the file called 'Scottish Reported and Unreported Cases', which is under the UK CASES button. *Session Cases* from 1930 are expected to be made available in 2004. English cases are also available here, under 'England and Wales Reported and Unreported Cases'; reported ones from 1865, unreported ones from 1980. Under the button UK LEGISLATION you will find 'Statutes and Statutory Instruments of Scotland', which gives the full amended text of all Acts of the Scottish Parliament and Scottish statutory instruments since 1 July 1999 which are still in force; it also provides the text of those not yet in force, and lists those no longer in force, with a note explaining why the enactment no longer applies. There is also a file 'Statutes and Statutory Instruments of England and Wales', under which is collected all legislation passed by the

Westminster Parliament that relates to England and Wales and is currently in force. There is an unfortunate gap here, inasmuch as the file contains no material passed at Westminster and applying solely to Scotland. LexisNexis now has a very straightforward user interface, and information icons coloured red and online help links should enable you to answer most of the likely questions about content and searching.

11.10   Another very useful database is called Westlaw. Like LexisNexis, this has extensive worldwide coverage, but we will concentrate here on the United Kingdom resources. Its 'Scots Law' database gives full text of cases reported in the *Scots Law Times* since 1930. *Session Cases* from 1930 are expected to be made available in 2004. The database also enables you to access 'UK Statutes', which gives you the full text of all legislation since 1267 (for England and Wales) and 1706 (Scotland and the United Kingdom) currently in force and in its consolidated form, along with legislative history material. 'UK Statutory Instruments' has all statutory instruments since 1948. In addition the 'United Kingdom Case Law Locator' enables you to search for reported and unreported cases not only in Scotland but also in England and Wales, from 1865 (thus including the Scottish reports from that date listed at paras **10.11** and **10.14**, as well as *Session Cases, Scots Law Times, Scottish Civil Law Reports* and *Scottish Criminal Case Reports*). This is not, however, a full text facility: instead, it provides a summary of the case, lists the reports where it appears in full as well as the other cases and legislation cited in the decision, and citations to the case in subsequent cases. Like LexisNexis, Westlaw's user interface is not difficult to grasp; and there are help links and information buttons, this time coloured green.

11.11   Taken together with the other resources available on the Internet, some of which were referred to in Chapter 10 (notably legislation and judicial decisions), the LexisNexis and Westlaw databases are probably now the easiest, most effective, and least expensive way of obtaining up-to-date information about the doings of the courts, legislatures and governments of Scotland, England and Wales, and indeed, using the appropriate files, the European Community and the rest of the world. Many of the websites referred to in Chapter 10 also provide access to databases searchable in the same way as LexisNexis and Westlaw, that is, through the use of names of parties, key-words and so on (see above, para **11.08**). A useful site which forms a portal to many of the free databases and other websites produced by courts and legislatures in the United Kingdom is the British and Irish Legal Information Institute (BAILII) (http://www.bailii.org.uk).

Manual updating

11.12   Manual updating is carried out through various reference works, the location of which in the library you should find out as soon as possible. The main reference work covering the whole of the United Kingdom is *Current Law*. This comes out in monthly parts, which are bound up in annual volumes called *Current Law Year Book*. It is divided up by the countries of the UK, and each country's section is divided by subject matter arranged alphabetically. Here you find summaries of new cases (with references to the reports), and of new legislation, including statutory instruments. The full text of each statute, with a section-by-section commentary, can be found in the publication *Current Law Statutes Annotated*. So the trick here is to find your subject heading and work forward from there.

11.13   Still this research has limitations. Searching by subject may be altogether too broad for your purposes. Suppose you want to find out how a particular case mentioned in the textbook you used first has fared as an authority in the courts since the text writer stopped work. This might happen because the case seems particularly relevant as a precedent for your problem. What you need here is the *Case Citator* facility within *Current Law*. There are three volumes of the *Scottish Current Law Case Citator* covering 1948–1976, 1977–1997 and 1998–2001 respectively, and case citator sections (the Cumulative Table of Cases) in the *Current Law* monthly parts from 2002 onwards. These provide alphabetical lists of cases for each of England and Scotland, in which you find the case you are interested in. What the citator then gives you is a list of references to other cases in which your case has been cited. The references are in the form of the year of the volume of *Current Law* in which the other case was first digested, followed by its number in that volume. If, for example, you look up *Donoghue v Stevenson* 1932 SC (HL) 31 in the Scottish section of the *Citator* for 1948–1976, what you find is that it was 'distinguished 51/3988; 52/4290: applied 56/11829; 75/3994: followed 76/3296'. These are all Scottish cases; you will get the first as case number 3988 in the 1951 volume of *Current Law*. If you then turn to *Donoghue* in the English section of the *Citator*, you will find several more references in which the case has been discussed. Remember, however, that you will have to look at all the citators to get a complete picture on the subsequent history of a case because the case decided in, say, 1955, can be cited at any time up to the present. (See further below, para **11.24**, for tracing comment on a case in the secondary literature.)

11.14 A similar facility exists in respect of legislation, with four volumes of the *Legislation Citator* covering the periods 1948–1971, 1972–1988, 1989–1995 and 1996–1999, and extensions from 2000 onwards in the *Current Law* monthly parts. There are both chronological and alphabetical listings of the statutes, through which you can find details of amendment and repeal by Parliament, consideration of sections in cases, and what statutory instruments have been issued under an Act. There is also a *Statutory Instrument Citator* with three volumes so far (1993–1995, 1996–1999, and 2000–2001), and monthly updates thereafter. The fate of Acts of Parliament can also be traced in the alphabetical-by-subject *Index to the Statutes*, published annually and giving all Acts in force at the date of publication. The *Chronological Table of the Statutes* is a historically arranged list, published annually, and giving details of amendment and repeal. There are equivalent guides to statutory instruments, respectively the *Index to Government Orders* and the *Table of Government Orders*. (See further below, para **11.24**, for tracing comment on a statutory provision in the secondary literature.)

11.15 As noted in the previous chapter (see above, para **10.40**), a key point with a statute is whether or not, or the extent to which, it is in force. The annual publication *Is It in Force?* gives statutes passed in the preceding 25 years alphabetically by year, along with details of the extent to which they have become or ceased to be law. Current texts, often with the legislative history attached, can be found in *The Parliament House Book* and the other looseleaf *Encyclopaedias* now available in many subject areas dominated by statute. The looseleaf format is adopted to allow the librarian to insert new material when published and to remove old material when it ceases to be the law. What you always have to check with such publications, however, is the date when the last group of inserts was released, and then go on to find out if there has been any later development which has not yet found its way into the encyclopaedia in question.

11.16 Another limitation of research in *Current Law* and other manual sources arises from the gap between composition of each part and its publication. For legislative and government material this can be overcome by reference to the daily, weekly, monthly and annual lists of publications produced by The Stationery Office (TSO). These are especially useful in chasing up the most recent statutory instruments which may not yet be on the LexisNexis and Westlaw databases (but note that the Daily List is available at the TSO's on-line bookstore (http://www.tso.co.uk/bookshop/bookstore.asp)). For statutes or statutory instruments issued within the last two weeks, consult HMSOnline's New Legislation link, http://www.hmso.gov.uk/legislation/whatsnew.htm. A weekly publication called WHISP (What's Happening In the Scottish Parliament) lists business at Holyrood and can be consulted at http://www.scottish.parliament.uk/business/whisp.html. For cases, turn first to the unbound parts for each series of law reports (see above, para **10.10, 10.17**). Each unbound part usually has two subject indices, one indicating the content of that part, and another indicating the contents of at least a number of preceding parts. The subject headings are normally like those in *Current Law*. Since 1986 there has also been *Green's Weekly Digest* (GWD), the weekly parts of which summarise very recent Scottish cases under *Current Law*-style subject headings. Some of the serious newspapers publish law reports which are more detailed than those in GWD but are still summaries rather than full reports. They usually appear within a few days of the decision being made. The main example is *The Times*, which produces a law report almost every week day during the court terms. These are mainly decisions of the English courts, but do also include Scottish, Community and European Court of Human Rights cases. An annual looseleaf volume, *Times Law Reports*, gathers all the reports together and helpfully indexes them. A much less extensive service is also provided by *The Independent, The Daily Telegraph, The Financial Times* and *The Guardian*. All of these are of course also available on-line (see below, para **11.29**). Court websites have facilities listing the cases most recently put up for users, and this is probably as up-to-date as you can get (although sometimes English decisions of which you know from other sources take a surprisingly long time to appear on the Court Service site).

11.17   For older cases, on which the databases may be not so good, there are a number of manual aids to be searched. Most important of these is the *Faculty Digest*, which lists and summarises cases under subject headings as well as providing a citator of cases and legislation referred to. There are six volumes, covering the period 1868 to 1922 and including a very useful index giving not only the *Digest's* subject headings but also other legal terms and phrases used in the cases. Six further volumes, each spanning a decade, bring the *Faculty Digest* down to 1980. The *Scots*

Digest covers House of Lords cases from 1707–1947, and other higher court decisions from 1800–1947, while for pre-nineteenth century cases you should consult *Morison's Dictionary* under the appropriate subject heading (see above, para **10.15**). *Tait's Index* covers the *Dictionary* and its supplements.

11.18   There are also English digests of cases in addition to *Current Law*. For instructions on how to use these, see Clinch, *How to Use a Law Library*, pp 122–127.

RESEARCHING FOR AN ESSAY OR OTHER PROJECT WORK

11.19   When you are researching an essay or other project, you are setting out to give a more general survey of a topic than is necessary in dealing with a problem. Nevertheless the research techniques just described will still be highly relevant. You will still need to find out what the relevant legal sources are, and how they have been handled over the years. Probably you will have more need for wide subject-based research techniques, but often in dealing with more specific points the more narrowly-based updating approach will be required.

11.20   In an essay, however, you will also need to research the secondary sources, that is, the monograph and journal literature on your topic, official publications, and the media. Of course this might also be relevant and helpful in tackling a problem, but the answer to the problem must rest first and foremost on the sources for the law itself rather than on sources describing and analysing the law. An essay, on the other hand, may be more critical or speculative, and if so ought to take account of other criticisms and speculations. It is likely to be less doctrinal in nature than a problem answer, especially if it adopts a historical, comparative, philosophical or sociological approach. In this section, therefore, we turn to how you find this secondary material.

Finding monograph and periodical material

11.21   There are a number of aids to finding the published literature. Again textbooks can be of help here, especially if they have bibliographies or contain literature references in footnotes. Library catalogues should be used. Again, where the catalogue is on computer, this can speed up and extend the range of searching considerably, especially when you can put in key words that are likely to turn up in the title of a book. The obvious way of going about this is through the subject and/or title catalogues, but if you know that an author is an expert in the field of interest, it is worth consulting the author catalogue to see what appears under the name in question. These searches, whether or not on computer, can of course turn up material which is irrelevant to your needs, or miss things which are relevant, and this is where the unscientific browse in the relevant subject section of the library itself can often prove worthwhile.

11.22   Catalogues and browses tell you what is in the library, but the library's coverage is not necessarily comprehensive. Often you can access the catalogues of other libraries through the Internet or computers, or by means of microfiches or other copies, held in your library. It is possible to order material held in other libraries through the inter-library loan service, although there will normally be a charge for this. The service extends to both books and articles in journals (you are usually supplied with a photocopy of the latter). You do not have to identify a library where the work is held to use the service, since most material is obtained from the British Library. It is also usually possible to request the library to order a copy of the work in question to be held in its own permanent stock. You should ask a member of the library or teaching staff how to do this.

11.23   But even this does not exhaust all possibilities. There are a number of bibliographies which list published law books and are regularly updated: examples are *Law Books in Print*, *Lawyers' Law Books*, and *International Legal Books in Print*. It is well worthwhile to cast an eye over the book review and books received sections of recent issues of the law journals to see what the latest publications are. Law publishers' catalogues can enable you to anticipate publication of new works or new editions of established works, as well as providing a check on the backlist of already published ones, and should not be treated as merely marketing material. Most law publishers have also established searchable websites giving details about their publications, as have good bookshops; indeed there are bookshops, such as Amazon, which exist only on the Internet. If you are on the hunt for whether or not a book has been published, or are trying to find out what has been written by a particular author or on a particular topic, websites like these are extremely helpful. It is also worth searching on Internet search engines such as Google, Yahoo, Alta Vista and Ask Jeeves, using titles and author names for the search: a number of academics have personal websites on which their works are listed, and sometimes copies are available there to be downloaded.

11.24 There are special problems in researching the state of the periodical literature. For a start, although a catalogue will tell you what journals are held in the library, it will not usually tell you what their contents are. Since a great deal of the most important critical and discursive legal writing is found in journals rather than in monographs, there are other reference tools to help you track down relevant material in these sources. The most useful, useable and up to date of these are electronic. On Westlaw, 'Legal Journals Index' indexes articles from 1986 in over 430 English language law journals published in the United Kingdom and Europe, and can be searched by key word, author, and case or legislation discussed. Some journals can also be accessed in full text at 'United Kingdom Law Journals': they include *European Human Rights Law Review*, *European Law Review*, *European Intellectual Property Review*, *Intellectual Property Quarterly*, *Journal of Business Law*, and *Scots Law Times (News)*. There is also a much more extensive collection of US law reviews, with full text facilities mostly beginning in the mid-1990s. LexisNexis also has a 'UK Journals' button, which features full texts of a number of journals, mostly English practitioner-oriented, but some of use to the Scots lawyer and the student: for example, *Journal of the Law Society of Scotland*, *Oxford Journal of Legal Studies*, *Industrial Law Journal* and the *International and Comparative Law Quarterly*. LexisNexis also has a very long-established collection of US law journals in full text. Back in the hard copy world, *Current Law* lists books and journal articles under its subject headings in its monthly parts, but in the *Yearbook* they are grouped in a section towards the back of the volume, albeit still under subject headings. An American publication, *Index to Legal Periodicals*, lists journal articles, covering not just the USA but also the United Kingdom, Australia, Canada and New Zealand back to 1908. The *Index* is complemented by the *Index to Foreign Legal Periodicals* which, beginning in 1960, lists articles in journals published in the non-Anglophone world. The significance of this index may be greater in Scotland than in England as a result of the Civilian tradition of Scots law. In general, the easiest way to use these now is through databases accessible on the Internet. Thus *Index to Legal Periodicals* is on a database called FirstSearch, and *Index to Foreign Legal Periodicals* is on Eureka. An increasing number of law journals are available online through their publishers – indeed, some are *only* available online (see further below, para **11.27**) – and if your library has a hard-copy subscription you may well also have online access through the law school computers.

11.25   There are non-law bibliographies which cast their net over many fields of knowledge including or potentially relevant to law. A good example is BIDS (Bath Information and Data Services), which will probably be available on networks in your law library. This leads you to databases such as the *Social Sciences Citation Index* and the *Art & Humanities Citation Index*, through which you may find articles in fields likely to be relevant to legal studies such as criminology, economics, history, politics and sociology. Remember, too, that searches on the Internet with the aid of Yahoo, Alta Vista and Ask Jeeves, using titles and author names for the search, can take you to the institutional and personal websites of academics where their publications are listed, and sometimes copies may be downloaded. In this connection, note too an interesting project called SHERPA (Securing a Hybrid Environment for Research Preservation and Access), which may eventually make available on the Internet for research use a huge database of academic articles published in the UK (see http://www.sherpa.org/).

11.26   Any index will be a little behind the most recent publications in the periodical field, and your final port of call in the trawl for material in the library should be at the place where the most recent issues are held and (usually) displayed. Many journals clearly identify their subject area in their titles, and this can either give you the ones you need or tell you which ones are unlikely to be worth investigation. Many law journals are fairly generalist in nature, however, and the list of contents (sometimes given on the cover) often repay scanning. In Scotland this is particularly the case, and you should check the following if you are working on a Scottish subject: *Juridical Review*, *Edinburgh Law Review*, *Scots Law Times* (News section), *Journal of the Law Society of Scotland*, *Scottish Law Gazette* and *SCOLAG Bulletin*.

11.27   In addition, the following English, Welsh and Irish journals not only often provide material on Scots law, but also give good general comparative and English coverage: *Law Quarterly Review, Modern Law Review, Legal Studies, Cambridge Law Journal, Oxford Journal of Legal Studies, Current Legal Problems, Cambrian Law Review, Northern Ireland Legal Quarterly, Irish Jurist, New Law Journal, International & Comparative Law Quarterly*.

Note also the journals published only on the Internet, such as: *Web Journal of Current Legal Issues*, available at http://webjcli.ncl.ac.uk, *Journal of Information Law and Technology* (http://elj.warwick.ac.uk/jilt/), *Oxford*

University Comparative Law Forum (http://ouclf.iuscomp.org/), *Electronic Journal of Comparative Law* (http://law.kub.nl/ejcl/), and *SCRIPT-ed* (http://www.law.ed.ac.uk/ahrb/script-ed/index.asp).

Official publications other than legislation and court decisions

11.28   It is not only law books and articles in legal journals which may be of interest to lawyers. Official publications from The Stationery Office, which include Scottish Law Commission, Royal Commission and other reports, will be found in the *Lists* already referred to (see above, para **11.16**) as well as on governmental, Parliamentary, Stationery Office and Law Commission websites[1], which now commonly also provide freely accessible full texts. This is also true of the European Commission website (http://europa.eu.int/comm/index_en.htm). Parliamentary debates and committee proceedings, whether at Westminster, Holyrood or Strasbourg, can be accessed on the Parliamentary websites, often in audiovisual form (live or recorded) as well as in text. These often provide fascinating insights into the cross-currents of policy and opinion lying behind legislation and other governmental activity (or inactivity, as the case may be).

1   The Law Commission websites are (Scottish) http://www.scotlawcom.gov.uk/, and (England and Wales) http://www.lawcom.gov.uk/. For other official websites referred to here, see above, paras **10.31**, **11.16**.

The media

11.29   The media – newspapers and broadcasters – provide a means of tracking current affairs and opinion across a whole range of topics interesting to lawyers and to law students with essays to write, and the Internet now provides an easy means by which a researcher can access, not only what is going on today, but also, through easily searchable online archives, what has already happened or been said. In the United Kingdom, the most comprehensive site is that of BBC News Online (http://news.bbc.co.uk/), and access to its archive is free, unlike that for most of the major newspapers (although most of these do allow you free access to the last seven days' material). The newspapers most likely to give you relevant information are the 'broadsheets': *Times, Guardian, Financial Times, Daily Telegraph, Independent, Scotsman, The Herald,* and 'Sundays' such as *The Observer, Sunday Times, Sunday Independent,*

Sunday Telegraph, *Scotland on Sunday* and *The Sunday Herald*. Serious news magazines are often also very informative on legal topics: *The Economist*, *The New Statesman* and, for the doings of the Scottish Parliament and Executive, *Holyrood*. You can set Internet search engines like Google to give you 'news alerts' on topics of interest to you, although this can be a bit of a hit and miss affair. LexisNexis and Westlaw also enable you to search for news. The global reach of the Internet means that the research possibilities do not stop at the shores of Britain; equally, however, you should remember the local press, which often has websites (see eg the *West Highland Free Press* at http://www.whfp.com/), and may throw a different light from that of the nationals on issues before the courts or the legislature. And it should not be forgotten that one of the most important of the early cases about the Internet involved the competing websites of two Shetland newspapers (*Shetland Times v Wills* 1997 SC 316; 1997 SLT 669; 1997 SCLR 160; [1997] FSR 604; [1997] EMLR 277; Edwards and Waelde (eds), *Law and the Internet: A Framework for Electronic Commerce* (2000), p. 185).

Research in EC and international law

11.30   For research in European Community law, consult Clinch, *How to Use a Law Library*, pp 241–272. Note again the databases for European Community Law available online and on CD-Rom (above, para **10.18**). Much Community law is also accessible through the LexisNexis and Westlaw databases. You should also take note of SCAD (*Service central automatisé de documentation*), which is a bibliographic database giving details and short summaries of official Community documents and publications, and of articles from over 2,000 journals. From 1992 there is also *European Current Law*, in monthly parts with a *Yearbook* (see above, para **11.12**). For research in international law, Elizabeth Beyerly, *Public International Law: A Guide to Information Sources* (1991) is now a little out of date. A useful starting point for information is John P Grant, J Craig Barker and Clive Parry, *Parry and Grant Encyclopaedic Dictionary of International Law* (2nd edn, 2004). Each year *The British Year Book of International Law* has an article on that year's UK-related materials on international law, with references to primary sources for materials. The website of the American Society of International Law (http://www.asil.org) has a 'Resources' section and also a specifically 'ERG' section ('Electronic Resources Guide'), providing a useful guide to other international law materials available on-line. Other helpful sites include http://www.llrx.com/ international_law.html, http://library.kent.ac.uk/library/lawlinks/ international.htm, and, for links to all jurisdictions, http://www.worldlii.org. Further, every major international organisation has its own website, often with useful further links (eg the United Nations site at http://www.un.org/ english/).

Research in Scottish legal history and Roman law

11.31 The starting point for finding out what research materials can be used in the pursuit of Scottish legal history is still *The Sources and Literature of Scots Law*, the first volume in the series of Stair Society publications. For secondary literature on legal history since 1936 consult H L MacQueen and W J Windram, 'The sources and literature of Scots law: a select critical bibliography 1936–1982', (1983) 4(3) *Journal of Legal History* 1, David Sellar, 'Legal history in Scotland' (1987) *Zeitschrift für Neuere Rechstgeschichte* 74, and W M Gordon, 'Roman law and Scots law – a bibliography' in *The Civil Law Tradition in Scotland* (Stair Society, supplementary series vol 2, 1995). D M Walker's *The Scottish Jurists* (1985) combines bibliography with biography and history, but needs some care in respect of historical detail. The Stair Society has a website at http://www.stairsociety.org, with links to other website resources in legal history. An excellent Roman Law Resource webpage run by Ernest Metzger of the Aberdeen Law School is available at http://iuscivile.com/.

Empirical research

11.32 The assumption to date in this chapter has been that the research in which you are engaged is essentially doctrinal; that is, concerned with ascertaining the state of the law considered as a body of rules. But this is by no means the only way of looking at law. Empirical or socio-legal methods employ some of the techniques of the social scientist in studying law as a social phenomenon. While this kind of research can and does rely on written material, it also seeks to generate information as part of the research process. For example, it might be that you would wish to find out what the social attitudes of judges are. In order to find this out, you are at the very least going to have to talk to judges and ask them questions, perhaps by a mixture of oral interview and formal written questionnaire. This will, if the judges cooperate, produce the material from which you can draw your conclusions. But already written material will probably still be important. For example, it might be that the social background of the judges plays a part in forming their social attitudes, and you could derive information about this from publicly-available sources. This book has quoted several statistics about lawyers, courts and others in Scotland, most of which were obtained from an examination of published material such as the annual reports of government and other organisations, and law directories. Empirical work can be very instructive and rewarding, and it is surprising how cooperative data subjects can be. A few years ago, some of my students embarked on 'empirical' research on standard form contracts. Some wrote to well-known companies and were successful in obtaining copies of their standard contracts and comment from managers on how they used them in business. Others entered into contracts with organisations using standard forms and tried to find out directly how willing the organisations were to negotiate individual terms. Others downloaded copies of the 'click-wrap' standard forms available on the Internet from companies engaged in electronic commerce. The results were interesting, although the samples were too small to permit any very strong conclusions. It also threw a new light on the significance of contracts for the students concerned. Although it would be unwise to embark upon a programme of empirical research without guidance from law school staff experienced in the use of these techniques, it is certainly worth considering their use. For further comment on the subject, with useful ideas on how results of the research can be presented in charts, graphs and tables, see A Bradney *et al*, *How to Study Law*, (4th edn, 2000) chapter 6.

CHAPTER 12

Essays and examinations

INTRODUCTION

12.01 The immediate goal of formal study is assessment. In the nineteenth century the institutional writer Bell, who was also Professor of Scots Law at Edinburgh, thought that 'public examination is not a fair test of a man's knowledge of the subject of his studies', and that examinations were particularly inappropriate in law because 'the pupils are more advanced; many of them are of an age, and in a situation, in which it is not pleasant to submit to examinations, and not decorous or proper to shun them; the subject is not peculiarly well fitted for examination, as a test of knowledge; and there is not time, with due regard to the extensive business of the course, to carry on examinations with any hope of advantage'[1]. Be that as it may, in the modern world of legal studies, assessment is usually carried out by written exams and essays, although oral examination is by no means unknown. This chapter gives a few suggestions as to how to prepare for and go about your written assessment exercises. Written assessment generally takes one of two forms: the essay researched and written by the student in his or her own time (subject to a deadline of some sort), and the examination written at a specific time. Although some forms of assessment can hover somewhere between these two categories – the 'take-home' exam, for instance (see below para **12.17**) – the structure of this chapter is based upon them.

---

1   Found quoted in T StJ N Bates, 'Mr M'Connachie's notes and Mr Fraser's confessional', (1980) 25 *Juridical Review* 166 at 178–179.

12.02   Before getting down to this, however, it is worth saying a word or two about the purpose of assessment exercises. One basic point is that they show how much you have learned from taking the course. This is not just a matter of showing specific quantities of knowledge, although clearly this is one of the elements to be expected in any assessment. The assessment should also show the extent to which you have mastered the subject in terms of handling your knowledge of it in specific ways: for example, in answering problems or in developing a critical view of the sources. With essays you are showing research and writing skills as well as the ability to reason and argue critically using legal materials. In all this, therefore, there are goals beyond the immediate one of your passing or failing. The process of assessment is also one in which you develop and manifest skills which will be helpful in later professional life. Assessment may also be *formative* (ie practice to develop the necessary skills, with feedback afterwards from the marker) or *summative* (ie contributes to your final grade for the course). What is said below is equally applicable to both.

WRITING ESSAYS

12.03   The previous chapter discussed the research methods which you can deploy in working on an essay or dissertation. Here, therefore, we will focus on writing up the research. The first and obvious point, given what has just been said about the purposes of assessment, is that it is not enough simply to record what your research has turned up. Instead, you have to use your research material as the building blocks of an argument in which you draw conclusions on issues which emerge from the research. Some guidance on what you are to do may be apparent from the essay title which you have been set, especially if it is in the form of a question. Alternatively you may have been given a general subject area to work on but have been left to decide for yourself what aspects to cover. In these circumstances it can be worth thinking of the various possible general approaches, and whether any of them seem particularly appropriate or useful in the light of your research on the topic. Is it an area of law of great social concern? Are there aspects which are controversial or in need of reform? Would a comparative or historical approach help to explain the current state of the law?

Starting to write

12.04 It is often difficult to know how to begin. The blank sheet of paper (or, these days, the blank screen of the word processor monitor) is an intimidating sight. It is unlikely that you will be able to start writing with a clear picture in your head of exactly what you want to say and how you are going to say it. How do I know what I want to write until I know what I have written? In my own writing, I have often found it helpful to start with one small thing which has caused me difficulty when reading the sources. The effort involved in explaining the difficulty to myself often triggers insights as to other issues posed by the material and provides a foundation for the essay as a whole. Then slowly the argument and the structure of the piece begin to take shape, and although frequently revised as I proceed, the essay is underway. Indeed, I would suggest that it is a good idea to start writing as your research proceeds, and not to wait until you think you have finished your library work. Often the process of writing and thinking about what to write stimulates a particular line of inquiry, making your research much more focused on particular points and meaning less time wasted in digging up material which ultimately you do not use.

Writing clearly and well

12.05 Writing is a means of communication. You should always remember that you write to be read by others. This means that your reader has to be able to understand what you are saying. F W Maitland, a great English law professor of the nineteenth century, used to read his drafts aloud to himself so that he could sense how the words would be received by an audience, and he is remembered and read today as one of the finest legal writers of all. Another great stylist among English lawyers who has explained in print how he set about writing was the late Lord Denning (see his *The Family Story* (1981) pp 207–208). We cannot all be Maitlands or Dennings, however, and there are a number of other points which, kept in mind, can help you achieve this end of clarity.

Some do's and don'ts

12.06 The rules of grammar and syntax are basic to the goal of making yourself understood in writing. On these, you can gain a great deal from dipping into such general classics as Gowers' *Complete Plain Words*,

Fowler's *Modern English Usage*, and the very useful *Style and Usage Guide* published by *The Times* newspaper. More specifically aimed at lawyers, albeit US ones, is Bryan A Garner, *The Elements of Legal Style* (2nd edn, 2002). Punctuation is also an important way of conveying (or obscuring) meaning, as is apparent from the very title of Lynne Truss's amusing, yet sound and extremely helpful, *Eats, Shoots and Leaves: The Zero Tolerance Approach to Punctuation* (2003)[1]. Use introductions and conclusions to summarise, respectively, the questions you wish to raise in your essay and your conclusions. These can be written once you have finished the main body of the work, but should not be synopses or summaries of the paper. Define technical terms the first time you use them. On the other hand, avoid pomposity of the type associated with legal discourse. There is a difference between what is customary courtesy in court and what is needed in good writing. Do not argue 'with the greatest (or all due) respect' to the 'learned judge/professor' with whom you disagree, or 'submit' your views. If you have to refer to yourself (and it is better not to, as a general rule), do not do so in the third person (for example, as 'the writer') but in the first (singular 'I' and 'my', rather than 'we' and 'our'). But do not be colloquial or chatty. Avoid clichés, the kinds of phrase you are used to seeing and hearing in everyday speech and in print and broadcast journalism (eg phrases mentioning level playing fields, moving goalposts, this moment in time, things coming out of the woodwork, babies and bathwater, bottom lines, or the end of the day). Metaphors, the transfer of a name or an image to something to which it is not properly applicable, are often clichés; moreover, once admitted to your prose, they tend to multiply and become mixed (eg 'she grabbed the bull by the horns and ran with it'). Adverbs, such as 'absolutely', 'basically', 'clearly', 'hopefully', and 'obviously' should also be approached with grave suspicion, as should adjectives, especially colourful ones. Do not say that things are 'interesting', 'significant', or 'important'; rather, demonstrate their interest, significance or importance. Resist all temptation to use exclamation marks. Short sentences are a good idea. If you must have a subordinate clause, try not to let others creep in. Readers easily become lost if asked to hold too much in their minds at once. Sometimes, of course, it is impossible to express complex ideas and concepts in a simple fashion. But there may be ways of presenting such complexities in a more attractive and intelligible way. Tables or graphs of statistical information, flow-charts showing the logical structure of a legal rule, and diagrams to illustrate multi-party relationships are three examples of this kind of thing. Headings and sub-headings, perhaps with numerals or letters of the alphabet to identify them, are very helpful to the reader in seeing the structure of your argument. Dividing the piece up in this way can also be helpful to you in trying to see what it is that you want to say. Once you have begun to insert and use headings, you can also begin to see that material is not relevant in one place but would be very helpful in another.

1   Truss is also good on the problem of the apostrophe 's', which seems to trouble many students: see pp 35–67 of her book.

12.07   One further point to follow this paragraph. Do as I say in it, rather than what I do elsewhere in this book!

Read what you have written

12.08   The acid test of intelligibility comes when someone tries to read your work. Obviously when you have completed a draft you should read it over carefully with the points just made firmly in mind. But it can be very difficult to read what you have written with a suitably objective perspective. First, you never write quite what you want to say. In this way, every writer is his or her harshest critic. On the other hand, the writer knows exactly what each sentence means, and is rarely able to see what would strike every other reader as ambiguous or obscure. So it can be a good idea to get someone else to read your piece over with intelligibility in mind. If you look at the first or last footnotes in academic articles, or at the preface to books, you will see that it is commonplace for the author to thank friends, relatives or colleagues, sometimes in embarrassingly effusive or personal terms. It is easy to poke fun at this sort of thing but in fact the gratitude is usually genuine enough. At the very least the people thanked will have helped the writer to a better expression of his or her thoughts, and often they will have corrected errors and omissions as well. As a student, you may have more difficulty than the typical academic in getting someone to look at drafts of your work. If the essay is for formal assessment, you may not want to give your good ideas and materials away to your fellow students, and you may not be allowed to seek more than minimal assistance from a teacher or tutor. Parents and other friends may be willing, but are they able? It is best to have someone with at least an inkling of legal method and reasoning for the purpose. Nowadays there is increasing acceptance in the law schools of the idea that even in assessed essays you can submit a first draft to your tutor for critical comment to be taken into account in a second and final draft. Having experienced such a system (although not in Scotland), I can say that it made the final versions much more pleasurable to mark. I also think that the students benefited, because they were shown how both the research and the writing might be improved. This enhanced their skills in both fields, and that was, after all, one of the main purposes of the whole exercise.

Referencing: footnotes and endnotes

12.09   An important part of writing up research is foot- or endnoting, which can be easily done with all worthwhile word-processing programs. The purpose of such notes is to show from what source the information in the text has been derived. This enables the reader to go to the source thus identified, and check whether the proposition for which it has been cited is in fact borne out by what it says. The note should therefore give the reader sufficient information to permit ready identification of the source and its location. Footnotes are to be preferred, because it is easier for the reader to move to them from the main text than is the case with notes placed after the end of the main text. If you use endnotes, ensure that they begin on a fresh page and that the main text and the notes are stapled separately from each other. This is because the two documents can then be read side-by-side, making it possible to see quickly and painlessly what sources you have been using and whether you have used them correctly or not.

12.10   There are several systems for foot- and endnotes. You will come across many of them in your reading of legal and other academic literature. The most common in law is to indicate a note by a superscribed number at the relevant point in the main text. The number is then the first element in the note. Here is how to write the reference that follows:

(a)   **Case** — name in italics, followed by citation. If quoting a particular passage in a judicial opinion, give judge's name and page reference. If there are several references to a case in your essay, it is permissible after the first reference to use an abbreviated form (eg the first-named party in the case), preferably having identified what it is in the first reference.

(b)   **Statute** — short title, followed by chapter number, and section number.

(c)   **Book** — Author's initials and surname, book's title in italics, edition if later than first, place and date of publication (for these details check title pages), page or paragraph reference. An example: W A Wilson, *The Scottish Law of Debt*, 2nd edn (Edinburgh, 1991) p 104. Again, you can use an abbreviated form for subsequent references; eg Wilson, *Debt*, p 96.

(d) **Article** — Author's initials and surname, title of article in inverted commas, date and, if appropriate, volume number of journal, journal title in italics, first page, and page of reference. An example: H L MacQueen, 'Desuetude, the cessante maxim and trial by combat in Scots law', (1986) 7 *Journal of Legal History* 90 at p 94. Subsequently this might be referred to as 'MacQueen, 'Desuetude', or as 'MacQueen (above, note [*insert the number of the note at which the article was first cited*])'.

12.11 Another system of referencing, known as the Harvard system, tries to get round publishers' dislike of footnotes and the desire of writers and readers to have them by inserting a very brief form of note into the text itself. The note takes the form of an abbreviated reference to the source (typically by author's surname and date of publication, followed where appropriate by a page reference). Here is an example: 'It is indicative of the conservatism of Scots law that *Regiam* remained its principal text until near the end of the seventeenth century [Cooper 1936: p 80]'[1]. In this system, it is essential to have a bibliography attached to the essay in which the abbreviated reference is expanded as fully as in a more conventional note. Thus, in the example just given, consultation of the bibliography shows that 'Cooper 1936' is T M Cooper, '*Regiam Majestatem* and the auld lawes', in *An Introductory Survey of the Sources and Literature of Scots Law*, published by the Stair Society in Edinburgh in 1936. The system, although neat, can be rather irritating to the reader when it breaks up sentences, or when there are multiple references for a particular point[2]. Its naming as the Harvard system should not lead to confusion with the Harvard Law Review Association's *Uniform System of Citation*, 14th edition (Cambridge Mass: Harvard Law Review Association, 1986), which gives the standard system used in American law reviews and legal texts.

1 For this sentence see J W Cairns, T D Fergus and H L MacQueen, 'Legal humanism in Renaissance Scotland', (1990) 11 *Journal of Legal History* 40 at p 42; also, as 'Legal humanism and the history of Scots law: John Skene and Thomas Craig', in *Humanism in Renaissance Scotland*, ed J MacQueen (Edinburgh, 1990) 48 at p 50. This footnote is also intended to illustrate further techniques in footnoting with regard to edited works.

2 See in illustration of these points Cairns et al, 'Legal humanism', above, note 1, at p 44.

12.12   Two other points may be made about foot- and endnotes. It is permissible to use them to make brief comments which are relevant but which would interrupt the flow of argument if inserted in the main text at this particular point. However, in general, I try to follow what I was taught by a distinguished professor, which still seems good advice to me: discursive material which cannot be firmly bonded into the text should be ruthlessly discarded, at least from the current piece of work. (You might be able to use it in another essay later.) Notes should not become a way round a word limit. The other point is that you can use notes to make cross-references to other parts of your essay. Indeed notes can cross-refer to each other to explain abbreviated references. For example you might say in a note 'See Wilson, *Debt* (cited above, note 4), p 63', where note 4 was the place where the reader could find the full citation of the work in question. Remember that the note should enable the reader to find the source you used.

Two great sins: plagiarism and ignoring the arguments of others

12.13   In legal writing, not to say writing generally, there are two great sins which you must avoid: plagiarism, sometimes politely called unacknowledged use of sources, and failure to take account of arguments opposed to your own. *Plagiarism* is copying what someone else writes and passing it off as your own. The word stems from the Latin *plagium*, which is still the technical term in Scots criminal law for kidnapping someone else's child. Plagiarism is regrettably common, not just among students, but among lawyers and indeed other professionals generally, facilitated by the ease with which material can be 'cut and pasted' from digital sources on the Internet. The reason for this is, of course, that in law it is important to be exact, and if the law is embodied in the language of a statute or has been well and accurately stated by a judge or legal writer, you may go wrong if you try a reformulation in other words. This reformulating is, however, what you have to do, and this is why you have to think very hard about the precise meaning of words when you write about law. You are allowed to quote what other people say, but you must always make it clear when you are quoting. This can be done with inverted commas or, where a quotation is more than a sentence in length, by a separate and indented paragraph. The limits of decency (and perhaps of copyright law) in quoting will be found round about the 100-word mark. In all cases you must give a foot- or endnote reference to the source. It is not a good idea to hand in an essay which is a string of quotes with brief linking passages. Although there is skill and labour in this sort of thing which is useful for a lawyer, it does mean that one of the essentials – your ability to communicate in your own words – is missing from the essay.

12.14 Failure to *take account of opposite views* is the second sin to be avoided. If you do not meet these contrary arguments, then again you are not showing one of the skills which essay-writing tests, namely, the ability to argue for a particular position in a matter of debate. Indeed, having an argument or view to oppose can make an essay easier to write. You can spend a lot of time showing the weaknesses in the other side's position and the countervailing strengths of your own. In the end, this is what it means to have an academic approach. You can form a view in your own words which is based solidly on evidence obtained by means of research, and that is proof against counter-arguments which you have taken fully on board. These are, of course, also invaluable skills to bring to the legal profession.

Layout and presentation

12.15 The last words in this section are about layout and presentation of the finished piece of work. I have already referred to the use of headings and sub-headings (para **12.06**). The use of paragraphing and the general desirability of breaking up blocks of text might also be mentioned. The basic test of when to paragraph is, have you finished dealing with a particular point? As Gowers put it in *Complete Plain Words*: 'Every paragraph must be homogeneous in subject matter, and sequential in treatment of it' (p 258). Again, thinking about these matters carefully can actually be of help in working out the substance of your argument. Lines should be double-spaced and margins should be wide, to enable the marker to write comments. A bibliography is generally required and may indicate, for example, works to which you have referred but not had occasion to cite directly in the foot- or endnotes. A bibliography is essential if you have adopted the Harvard reference system. It can be divided up, for example into legislation, cases, government publications, monographs and periodical publications. Within such divisions it is conventional to use alphabetical ordering.

12.16   Unless you are an exceptionally clear handwriter, essays must be typed or produced on a word processor. It is not a good idea to irritate the marker of an essay by handing in quasi-legible script or worse (as is all too often the case). Remember that student handwriting can deteriorate terribly as a result of high-speed note-scribbling in lectures and libraries. You can employ professional typists and word processors at a reasonable charge, or do the job yourself. If you choose the latter, it is worth learning in some detail the formatting facilities available on the standard word-processing packages, as appropriate use will make your work look professional and impress the examiner. Universities and colleges now generally provide computer laboratories for student use. You may well think it worthwhile to buy your own personal computer (look out for machines on sale in the university, many second-hand and therefore cheaper), or be able to persuade some well-disposed relative to make you a gift of one. If so, ensure that any machine and software packages you obtain are compatible with the university systems. The great advantage of word processors over typing and handwriting is that you can change your text innumerable times right up to the last moment and still produce what looks like an immaculate piece of work. Also, with many word processing software packages you get a spell checker and a word counter, both extremely useful facilities. The danger is that you lose control of what you are writing because it is so easy to change bits here and there, or move parts around. In all cases, you should run a careful final check over the script before you hand it in to make sure that all is as you would wish to have it if were you the marker. Attention to detail will repay you every time.

EXAMINATIONS

12.17   There are a wide variety of different types of examination. The traditional form is the unseen three-hour written paper. But there are many variations on the theme. In law exams it is common to allow you to have access to relevant statutory materials. With a so-called 'open-folder' exam you are allowed to bring in notes and refer to them during the course of the examination. If you have statutory materials, you may be permitted to use copies which you have personally annotated. There are also 'open-book' exams where you can bring in textbooks, but these are not so popular with examiners because not every student has the resources to make the necessary purchases. The 'take-home' exam, which has already been mentioned, is one where you are given the paper to prepare in advance of the examination, perhaps a week or a few days before an answer is written in exam conditions. Normally your answers in any of these exams would take the form of a connected piece of prose, but multiple-choice papers where you simply mark one of several alternative answers given in the questions can be used. Finally there is the oral examination, where there is no written work at all.

Preparation: revision

12.18 The preparation you undertake for an exam obviously depends to some extent on its precise nature. For most, however, it will be necessary to go through the process of acquiring (or re-acquiring) and absorbing a fairly large body of knowledge in the subject to be examined. As Alexander Bayne, first professor of Scots Law at Edinburgh University, wrote in 1726, 'It is not enough in the study of law to know and comprehend the rules and principles of it; but we must be at pains to fix them on the memory' (*A Discourse on the Rise and Progress of the Law of Scotland, and the Method of Studying It*, p 173). The great complaint against law exams has always been that, no matter what professors like Bayne and his successors might say, the only faculty which they tested was that of memory. The development of the different forms of examination described in para **12.17** has been an effort to meet that criticism. But it should also be said that it is not entirely inappropriate that the ability to remember quite detailed matters should be tested. There are some basic things every lawyer ought to know; the structure of the legal system is one example. It is a poor lawyer who carries no law in his or her mind, or who in consultation with a client cannot recall the details of the client's case. Lawyers need a good memory, and it is no good challenging this element in the assessment process with the comment that 'in practice you can always look it up'. That is unfortunately not the case.

12.19 Allowing statutes, notes and texts into the exam hall is one way of lessening the need to remember vast amounts of specific detail such as exact statutory wording, or the names and facts of cases. But the material you have with you will be of little help unless you have a pretty good idea of how to get around in it, and of what you are looking for. If you do no preparation for an exam because you will have statutes and notes with you, in the exam hall you will not find the answers with mere hopeful turning of the pages of the materials. In other words, you need to know the law fairly well before having the support material is of much use to you. All this is equally true of the 'take-home', where, although you have the run not only of your notes and books but also of the whole library and Internet, if you do not know where to look and what to look for, your task will be like finding the needle in the proverbial haystack.

12.20   Preparation for an examination really begins at the start of the course, the whole of which constitutes, among other things, a process of acquiring the relevant body of knowledge. If you work steadily on the course throughout its duration, you will already have a fair grasp of it by the time you begin revision in the weeks before the exam takes place. The problems are, of course, that you are usually working on several courses at once, and that an academic year is a long time, making it difficult by the end to remember clearly what you were doing at the beginning. So revision of an intensive kind is necessary for most, reading, re-reading and thinking about the year's material. Previous exam papers will be held in the library (ask if you do not know where), and are well worth consulting for at least the last two or three years. But do not worry if your immediate reaction to such old papers is that you cannot do them; this is common. A little reflection with your course materials also at hand usually reveals what the questions are about. If you have problems in understanding some or all of the course or the past papers, talk to the course teachers and your fellow students as well as consulting the usual printed sources. Try and get a clear picture of the course structure, and of the structure of the different parts of the course; it is often easier to understand detailed points if you have grasped the general thrust and concepts of the area of law in question.

Question-spotting

12.21   Because there is so much law in any course, the temptation is strong to try and anticipate what questions will be asked, especially where, as is usual, you can choose which of the questions in the paper you will answer. Having done this, you then engage in selective revision of the topics you think will come up, leaving the rest out. This is one way of making things manageable for yourself, and is not necessarily bad, given that the aim is solely to pass the exam. But the obvious danger is that your 'spots' do not turn up in the exam, or that not enough of them come up, or that you leave out some bit because it is difficult rather than because it is unlikely to be in the exam. You are then left high and dry without enough questions to answer, and almost certainly fail the exam. I would suggest that selective revision is an emergency measure only, and that if you employ it, do so on the basis of rational calculation rather than on the basis of bits you like and bits you don't.

Read the paper: essay questions

12.22 When you get to your place in the exam hall, read the whole paper with care. There are usually three types of question in a law exam: the 'short notes' question, the 'essay' question, and the 'problem' question. The 'short notes' question, where you are asked to write such answers on a selection of specific topics, is not very common these days. Such questions mainly test knowledge and understanding of what are usually difficult concepts. You are expected to cite relevant authorities in statutes and cases. A second is the 'essay' question, which again tests knowledge and understanding, but which by virtue of the way the question is put requires you to handle your material in a way other than the mere regurgitation of what you have learned.

Example of an essay question

12.23 This example of an essay question is from an exam on the law of Delict:

> 'Comment on the scope of the duty of care (a) to prevent third parties from committing wrongs against another person; (b) not to cause nervous shock to another person. Why is the law concerned to limit the scope of the duty in such cases, and how has it achieved this limitation?'

The answer to this question must be divided into at least two parts, dealing with (a) and (b). The temptation to which weak students may succumb is to embark upon a description of the law – mainly cases in this example – relevant to each head. But that is not enough. In both cases you are asked first to comment upon the *scope of the legal duty* involved. As the second sentence in the question actually says, the law of delict restricts liability for failing to prevent third parties from injuring others, and for causing nervous shock. The discussion in relation to the first sentence should therefore illustrate the limitations of the liabilities involved, perhaps starting with those cases where the courts have said there was *no* liability for these types of wrongdoing, and following up with the most extreme examples of where liability *has* been imposed. This then enables you to move smoothly into explaining why there are problems with both types of case, and to explain the legal tests which have been developed to determine when there is and when there is not liability in cases of this kind. It is not necessary to describe or cite every case there has ever been on the subject. The lesson is the great importance of reading the question carefully, and of structuring your answer accordingly.

Read the paper: problem questions

12.24   The 'problem' question tells a story in which problems arise for one or more of the characters. You are then asked to advise a character or to discuss how a court would deal with this problem. Often there is a subsidiary question, or a group of questions, in which the originally stated facts are varied in some way, and you are asked to state how these changes affect the first set of conclusions you drew. The 'problem' question is like the tutorial problems which you will have been set during the year, and the approach required is much the same as well (see above, para **9.12**). Again, knowledge and understanding are important, but you are being asked to put that knowledge and understanding to work, either in the interests of the character you are to advise or in solving the problem in the way that a court would. There is a difference between these two approaches. When you are advising a character, you need to work out what he or she is likely to be looking for, and direct your 'advice' to that end. But when you are discussing a problem more generally, there is less need to find the interpretation that best suits one character.

12.25   Problem-solving is of course an important lawyerly skill, so the use of problems in exams is to be expected. What will the examiners be looking for? It may sound obvious, but what is wanted is an answer to the question asked (which may be different from the question you want to answer). So again it is crucial to read the question carefully. First, you have to identify the area of law relevant to the problem. This is not as easy as in the 'essay' or 'short notes' question, because the 'problem' question may well not mention any legal topic in its wording. There are one or two traps into which to avoid falling when you are identifying what the topic is. The problem facts may look like those of a leading case in a particular subject. Do not rush to start your answer with a lengthy narrative of that case; note the parallels and keep thinking. Problems usually deal with several legal points, and are unlikely to focus on a single authority. It may be helpful to take a sentence-by-sentence approach at the outset and jot down any points or authorities which occur to you as you read each one. The other trap is that once you think you have identified what the topic of the problem is, you start writing down everything you know about that topic. Remember that you are NOT being asked what you know about the topic, but to apply what you know to this set of facts. This means that you have to decide what is relevant to the problem and what is not. This is where the sentence-by-sentence analysis suggested a moment ago may come in useful again.

12.26 As you start to apply the law to the facts of the problem, it may become apparent that you need to have more information about the circumstances before you can come to a firm conclusion in law. That is one of the skills being tested, so you should include such points in your answer. Similarly some of the facts may be irrelevant to the answer. The best way of dealing with this is generally to say which facts you regard as irrelevant. On the other hand, it may not be entirely clear whether a fact is or is not relevant. If so, it is probably going to be worth a few marks to discuss this uncertainty.

12.27 Again, you are expected to display knowledge of the relevant sources of the law. Cases and statutory sections with a bearing on the answer to the problem should be cited; where you have supporting material in the exam hall, they assist you to be accurate in this respect. (See further below, paras **12.32–12.33**.)

Example of a problem question

12.28 This example of a 'Problem' question is from a delict exam:

'Faith Good is a lecturer in Investment Law at Glasburgh University. She is also a director of studies, in which capacity she gives students advice on the curriculum and other pastoral matters. For carrying out this work the University pays her an honorarium of £1,000 per year, which is included in her December salary payment and is subject to deductions of tax but not national insurance. Lecturers at Glasburgh are not contractually bound to become directors of studies. One of Faith's directees is Desiree Bland, a mature student who is financing her studies from her investments in the Stock Market. Faith gives Desiree advice on her investments, along with advice on her study programme and other personal problems. Desiree's investments turn out badly, and she blames Faith's negligent advice. Comment on the University's potential vicarious liability.'

12.29   In answering this problem, first note the last sentence, which gives you the angle from which you are to approach the legal issues thrown up by these facts. It is the liability of the university, not that of Faith, which we are discussing. The question is about *vicarious liability*, which is the liability of an employer for the negligence of an employee acting in the course of his or her employment and causing injury. So there are at least three issues that are likely to be of concern here: (i) Is Faith negligent? (ii) Is her relationship with the university one of employment? (iii) Was Faith acting in the course of her employment? The issues of greatest concern to the university are (ii) and (iii), and these should be dealt with first. It seems clear that as a lecturer in the university she is an employee. But is the position as a director of studies a separate matter? The facts about the methods of payment and the absence of an obligation to act as a director are relevant to this. Is Faith in the course of her employment? You are told in the problem what directors normally do. Does giving investment advice come within the scope of 'pastoral matters'? How important is it that Desiree finances her studies from her investments? Even if the advice is not a 'pastoral matter', might it be within the course of an investment law lecturer's employment? What is the relevance (if any) of the fact that Desiree is a mature student? Are there special responsibilities on the director/lecturer in such cases? In considering these issues, you would refer to legal authorities which suggest what the answers might be, perhaps with particular emphasis on any suggesting either a sure way out for the university or that it was likely to lose the case. A final defence might be that Faith had not been negligent, and some brief discussion of this in the light of the law on liability for negligent advice would bring the answer to a good conclusion. Here, as in the earlier points, you would want to refer carefully to the facts of the problem in order to determine which were relevant to this particular issue. The emphasis would fall on the relationship between Faith and Desiree, rather than on the details of Faith's contract with the university and how she was paid.

Some do's and don'ts during the exam

12.30   There are a number of points to bear in mind when you are actually writing the exam. Make sure you write all necessary details about yourself and the exam on the cover of the script book at the start. Try to write legibly and in intelligible language (not in text-messaging style). Although an exam answer cannot be a finished piece of prose in the way that a prepared essay can, it will not get marks if it cannot be read or understood. Remember that the examiner has the right to give no marks for illegible script. Some students want to write as much as possible in the time available, but it is rare for speed to be coupled with a legible script. There is also the danger that if you are writing all the time a great deal of what you say may not be relevant to the question. Start the answer to each question on a fresh page (this makes it easier for the examiner to find the question to be marked). Do not write in the margins, because often the examiner finds it helpful to use these for annotations which help thought on what the mark should be. These notes are often also helpful later when the examiner explains a failure to the student. As with essays, write in short sentences. It is easy to lose control of what you are saying if you have too much going on. Here is a sentence from a script I have marked:

'Frustration is a means whereby a contract may be discharged but it is because performance has been rendered impossible due to something which is outwith the control of the contracting parties and that they have not known about this or accounted for this in the contract, for example in the event of war breaking out, which is outwith their control and if they foresaw the risk of a war breaking out and allowed for it in their contract then their contractual obligations would not have been frustrated.'

It would be much better for the reader if this stream of consciousness was broken up, perhaps thus:

'Frustration is a means of discharging a contract. It occurs when performance becomes impossible due to circumstances beyond the parties' control. An example may be the outbreak of war. [*Some case examples would be useful here, incidentally.*] The contract is not frustrated by the event, however, if the contract contains relevant provision for it.'

12.31 A crucial point is to take account of time. You have to answer so many questions in so many hours. The time spent on each question should be proportionate to the number of marks which each is worth in relation to the paper as a whole. It may be that the question you have 'spotted' and prepared for comes up, but in tackling it first do not lose sight of the fact that one question with high marks does not guarantee a pass, especially if you are only able to give limited or no attention to the last question through lack of time. I have seen many papers which were fails as a result of this unbalanced approach.

12.32 Do not copy out (a) the question; (b) statutory provisions; or (c) any notes you may have with you. With regard to (b), it is of course necessary to be alert to the precise language of the statute, but it is usually possible to incorporate this into the flow of your own sentence structure and, in problems, the advice you are giving to a character. Thus, for example, it is time-consuming and gains few marks to say:

'Section 75 of the Consumer Credit Act 1974, which is relevant, reads as follows: "If the debtor under a debtor-creditor-supplier agreement falling within section 12(b) or (c) has, in relation to a transaction financed by the agreement, any claim against the supplier in respect of a misrepresentation or breach of contract, he shall have a like claim against the creditor, who, with the supplier, shall accordingly be jointly and severally liable."'

This also tells the examiner nothing to show that you understand this rather complex provision. Much better to say, supposing D to be a customer who has bought defective goods from S paying with a credit card provided by C:

'D has a claim against S for breach of contract in respect of the defective goods. D's credit card contract with C was a debtor-creditor-supplier agreement under CCA s. 12(b), being a restricted-use agreement to finance a transaction between D and a supplier such as S other than the creditor C (see also CCA s 11(1)(b)). It follows that D can claim for the defective goods against C as well as S; C and S are jointly and severally liable (CCA s. 75).'

This shows that you can apply CCA section 75 to the problem, and that you can follow the cross-references set up by the section. It cross-refers to section 12, which in turn cross-refers to section 11. This shows that you understand the Act; all that is left now is to explain the significance of 'joint and several liability'.

12.33 Another bad idea is to give a laborious narrative of the facts of cases which you cite as authority in your answer. Remember that what is important in a case is its *ratio decidendi* (see above, para **10.22**). This is not to say that the facts of previous cases are never relevant to an answer. There may be a fact in the problem before you which has a direct parallel in the previous case law. It may be that you will want to distinguish the problem before you from a previous case on the basis of some materially different fact, but you should confine yourself to that fact. Suppose a sale of goods problem in which you are asked to advise the buyer of a new car with various minor defects such as leaks in the power steering and flecks of rust on the bodywork what rights he has against the seller. A good answer might say:

> 'Under the legislation before 1994 it was held that a new car with leaks in the power steering is merchantable (*Millars of Falkirk v Turpie*). But in that case the leak was the only defect and it was easily repairable. Where there were several minor defects, it was later held that the buyer could reject the car and get the price back from the seller (*Rogers v Parish Motors*). And the Sale and Supply of Goods Act 1994 now specifically provides that the existence of minor defects makes goods of unsatisfactory quality entitling a consumer buyer to reject them.'

Notice also that it is not necessary here to provide a full citation for the cases mentioned, nor indeed would it be necessary to give their full names. In the two mentioned above, it would be enough to say '*Millars*' and '*Rogers*'. It is helpful, however, if you underline the names of cases and statutes, because that helps the examiner see whether or not you are picking up the relevant authorities.

12.34 Once you think you have finished, make sure you write on the cover of the script book the numbers of the questions you attempted. This helps the examiners, whose goodwill you need. The last thing to do – and this is only if you have time – is to read your script over at the end of the exam, to correct mistakes, and add in notes on points which occurred to you after you finished a particular question. If at all possible, add in your further material at the end of your answer to the relevant question – another reason for making sure that you start each question on a fresh page (see above, para **12.30**). This correction and addition can be very hard to do; it is even worse than trying to read your own essays for sense and style. But it can save you from disaster and add some extra marks, so it is worthwhile. Whatever you do, do not spend the last few minutes of the exam sitting and staring vacantly at your neighbour's back.

If you fail

12.35 Should you have the misfortune to fail an exam, do not be hesitant in seeking the reasons why from the examiner. Often it is not so much lack of knowledge and understanding as lack of exam technique which trips you up. This may seem unfair, but remember that the exam is not just a test of knowledge and understanding but also of certain other skills, most of which are of importance in later life and in particular in the legal profession.

CHAPTER 13

Homily and epilogue

INTRODUCTION

13.01 There is a long tradition in books of this kind to adopt a somewhat paternalistic approach to their readers and give them homilies on the lifestyle which it is necessary for law students to adopt if they wish to be successful. In his *Direction, or Preparative to the Study of Law* published in 1599 the English Civilian William Fulbecke required his readers to observe 'temperance', which he defined as 'a restraint of the mind from all voluptuousness and lust, as, namely, from covetousness, excess of diet, wantonness, and all other unlawful delights'. He also advised students to work in the morning rather than at night after dinner: 'for when the stomach is full and stuffed with meat, the thick air being round about us, stopping the pores, the great store and abundance of humours is carried, as Aristotle saith, to the head, where it sticketh for a time, and layeth as it were a lump of lead upon the brain, which maketh us drowsy and prone to sleep'. More recently, Professor Glanville Williams also recommended the morning as the best time to work, as well as warning that 'alcohol is inconsistent with study' (*Learning the Law*, (12th edn, 2002) p 84). Others will tell you that you should subscribe to a 'good' newspaper, meaning usually any newspaper that is not a tabloid (although the distinction has increasingly less content these days).

13.02 For good or ill, however, experience suggests that law students, like all students and not a few practising lawyers, can get by quite well without observing these rules too closely. A monastic existence will serve you just as badly as one of hedonistic self-indulgence. Although law and lawyers are often accused of being detached from social reality, law ultimately springs from and is dependent upon social activity of all kinds. The subject matter of law studies offers you a particular perspective on a wide range of things that go on in the world, often deepening your understanding of it; but at the same time your comprehension of the law will be enriched if you observe what is going on around you in daily life and make the effort to understand how the law fits in. To take an example from my own experience, the Consumer Credit Act 1974 can seem almost meaningless if you attempt to understand it merely from reading the statute. An example of its prose style can be found in the previous chapter (see above para **12.32**). But it all becomes much more real if you go into the shops and look out for all the signs showing that customers can use credit cards or obtain other credit deals which will enable them to buy goods. Now ask yourself how these signs comply with the Advertising Regulations under the Act. If you yourself have to borrow money from a bank to fund your studies, or apply for a credit card, you will see how the forms you have to fill in comply with the Act. Once you realise that credit card users can only run up debts to a particular limit on the card, but that they can decide how much they are going to repay each month, the Act's concept of 'running-account credit' becomes easier to grasp. The same is true of 'debtor-creditor-supplier agreements' once you realise how people often pay the supplier for goods or services with money borrowed from another person specifically for the purpose.

13.03   The lesson is, then, not to cut yourself off from the world to pursue your legal studies but rather to immerse yourself in it as part of the whole process of an education in law. As an aspect of this, and despite the comment at the end of para **13.01**, (cf para **11.29**), it is a good idea to get into the habit of reading one or more of the daily broadsheets (which you can do on the Internet), or check BBC News Online. Tabloids may put you in touch with popular sentiment and are certainly not irrelevant to the lawyer, but 'serious' newspapers still see themselves to some extent as organs of record, and so they contain each day a great deal of legally useful information over and above the main news stories. We have already seen how many have law reports which are of little interest to anyone other than readers with a legal background (para **11.16**). In addition, most will carry reasonably detailed accounts of proceedings in the Westminster and Holyrood Parliaments, which may include the progress of Bills designed to change the law. The business pages contain information on the financial and other markets, knowledge of which is of the greatest importance to practising lawyers for professional reasons, and can often throw interesting light on legal topics. In addition there will be comment and debate in features and letters pages which frequently touch on matters of legal interest, and some papers have a regular Law page or supplement. For a Scots lawyer it is probably necessary to take one of the Scottish papers as well as one of the 'national' dailies, as the latter often fail to deal fully with issues in Scotland (some do now have Scottish editions, however). Television and radio should not be ignored; Parliamentary proceedings from both Westminster and Holyrood are broadcast in both media, as well as on the Internet. Much can be learned from news, current affairs, financial and consumer programmes on the broadcast media, as well as from documentaries.

13.04 Professor Glanville Williams suggests a course of reading in fiction, drama, biographies and other material in which there is some legal interest (*Learning the Law* (12th edn, 2002), pp 265–274). This is certainly worth a look, especially as he includes Scottish material such as the novels of Sir Walter Scott and Robert Louis Stevenson (both advocates). It was Scott, indeed, who in *Guy Mannering* put in the mouth of his character Peter Pleydell the advocate the aphorism with which Glanville Williams begins: 'A lawyer without history and literature is a mechanic, a mere working mason; if he possesses some knowledge of these, he may venture to call himself an architect'. But some may find the prescribed diet is rather heavy going in places. In the following paragraphs some lighter or more Scottish additions are made to the list.

13.05 Splendidly gossipy works which every Scots lawyer ought at least to dip into are the numerous personal writings of the eighteenth-century advocate, drinker, womaniser, and author, James Boswell (most readily sampled in John Wain, *The Journals of James Boswell 1762–1795* [1991]); Lord Cockburn's *Memorials of His Time* (first published 1856); Lord Stott's *Diary* (three volumes covering the period 1954–1973 and published 1991, 1995 and 1998); and Sir Randall Philip's *Journal 1947–1957* (1998). Cockburn was a contemporary of Scott, and the *Memorials* draw a fascinating (if not entirely reliable or objective) picture of the hard-drinking Bench and Bar in late eighteenth- and early nineteenth-century Scotland. Thus he wrote of the Court of Session judge Lord Hermand (who, like Boswell, had obviously not read his Fulbecke):

'Common-place topers think drinking a pleasure; but with Hermand it was a virtue ... he had a sincere respect for drinking, indeed a high moral approbation, and a serious compassion for the poor wretches who could not indulge in it; with due contempt of those who could, but did not ... No carouse ever injured his health, for he was never ill, or impaired his taste for home and quiet, or muddled his head; he slept the sounder for it, and rose the earlier and the cooler. The cordiality inspired by claret and punch was felt by him as so congenial to all right thinking ...'

The diaries of Lord Stott, who was Lord Advocate in the 1960s and then a Court of Session judge, do not quite rival this sort of thing, but in an often humorous way reveal a lot about the Scots lawyers of his time (some still living, others certainly within living memory of your older teachers and practising lawyers), and about the nature of a successful advocate's practice. Sir Randall Philip was a prominent QC in the 1940s and 1950s, and he likewise reveals quite a lot about well-known figures, notably Lord President Cooper, as well as attending a lot of congenial dinners with his brother advocates of the period.

13.06   From a slightly later era comes the first part of the scabrous memoirs of Sir Nicholas Fairbairn QC, *A Life is Too Short* (1986), which begins with his recollection of the discomforts of his birth, surveys a chequered career as a law student and advocate of the Scots Bar (amongst other activities), and concludes as he becomes a Tory MP in 1974. Although Sir Nicholas died in 1995, the second part of his memoirs has yet to see the light of print. For a view of the law from more or less the other end of the political spectrum, see the memoirs of Ian Hamilton QC, *A Touch of Treason* (1990) and *A Touch More Treason* (1994). In a highly varied career, Hamilton is most famous for his leading role in the snatching of the Stone of Destiny from Westminster Abbey at Christmas 1950 (when he was a law student at Glasgow). This incident is also described at length in his *The Taking of the Stone of Destiny* (1952, reprinted 1991). Hamilton subsequently was involved in the leading constitutional case of *MacCormick v Lord Advocate* 1953 SC 396, which is discussed in *A Touch of Treason* and also in the now out-of-print autobiography of the petitioner in the case, John MacCormick, *The Flag in the Wind* (1955), chapter 26. MacCormick was a Glasgow solicitor, and a number of other Glasgow lawyers have also produced interesting memoirs, mainly about their criminal law practices: for example, Lawrence Dowdall, *Get Me Dowdall: From the Casebook of* *a Criminal Lawyer* (1979); Joseph Beltrami, *The Defender* (1988); and Len Murray, *The Pleader* (2002).

13.07 Judicial memoirs tend to be less entertaining than those of the lawyers who appear before them. Thus Lord Brand's brief *An Advocate's Tale* (1995) is mainly of interest for his highly critical view of Lord President Cooper and his unstinting praise of Lord President Emslie, from whom he never felt compelled to dissent when they sat together in the First Division of the Court of Session or the High Court of Justiciary. Lord Justice-Clerk Wheatley had a more distinguished career, but tells his story in rather stolid fashion in *One Man's Judgement* (1987). The best modern Scottish judicial autobiography, even although a rather self-satisfied one, remains Lord Macmillan's *A Man of Law's Tale* (1952). When Sheriff Nigel Thomson was on the bench in the 1980s and 1990s, he gained a reputation for an innovative and imaginative approach to sentencing; and his memoirs, *In and Out of Court: The Legal and Musical Times of Sheriff Nigel Thomson* (2001), are also as distinctive and lively as the title suggests. There have been few worthwhile biographies of Scottish judges, but Brian D Osborne, *Braxfield: The Hanging Judge? The Life and Times of Lord Justice-Clerk Robert McQueen of Braxfield* (1997), salvages the reputation of one eighteenth-century figure whose character had been travestied in Cockburn's *Memorials* and further darkened by its fictionalisation in Robert Louis Stevenson's *Weir of Hermiston*. Braxfield's contemporary Lord Kames has also been the subject of a lot of work because of his role in the Scottish Enlightenment, as a mentor of Adam Smith and David Hume the philosopher[1]: see eg Ian S Ross, *Lord Kames and the Scotland of his Day* (1972), a heavyweight but fascinating work.

1   And uncle of the jurist of the same name, for whom see above, para **1.48**.

13.08 If your taste is more for fiction than biographies, memoirs and diaries, you might like to note that Joan Lingard's *Second Flowering of Emily Mountjoy* (1979) is probably the only novel to open with the settlement of a conveyancing transaction in an Edinburgh solicitor's office. This is not as unpromising a start as it sounds. Rebecca West's feminist classic *The Judge* (1922, reprinted 1980) also starts off in the office of an Edinburgh solicitor, but leaves it far behind by the time the novel ends. If you prefer thrillers and crime, the Rebus novels of Ian Rankin, also set in Edinburgh, are amongst the best of the genre, with lawyers (and MSPs) often featuring amongst the bad guys; but with some knowledge from your LL.B programme you may also be entertained by Rankin's little mistakes about the Scottish legal system. The connections with Scots law become pretty tenuous in Alexander McCall Smith's gently humorous Botswana novels featuring Mma Ramotswe and the Ladies No 1 Detective Agency, but the author is Professor of Medical Law at, and a graduate of, the Edinburgh Law School. His collections of short stories about Professor von Igelfeld of Regensburg are also worth reading for the fun they have with academic pretensions (and not just German ones). Another Scottish law teacher who successfully turned his hand to fiction is Francis Lyall, Professor of Public Law at Aberdeen, who wrote such detective novels as *A Death in Time* (1987), *Death and the Remembrancer* (1988), *The Croaking of the Raven* (1990), *Flying High* (1991) and *Death in the Winter Garden* (1993). A final addition to Glanville Williams' list of fiction is the four detective novels of Sarah Caudwell, in which the narrator-detective (whose sex is never revealed) is a legal academic who deploys former pupils now practising at the English Bar from Lincoln's Inn to solve crimes by the application of scholarship from the armchair (or, more often, as yet another non-follower of Fulbecke, from the Corkscrew wine bar). Caudwell's Scottish connection is her Aberdeen Classics degree; she became a barrister specialising in tax planning, which technical and difficult area of law is often at the heart of her none the less highly amusing stories.

13.09   Law can also be the subject of political and campaigning writing. An excellent example, written by a Scot who is alas! an English QC, is Helena Kennedy's *Eve Was Framed: Women and British Justice* (1992). In fact, while the book makes occasional forays into Scotland, it is mostly about English justice, although the message is equally applicable north of the border. Partly as a result of the book's publication, there has been some progress on the issues raised by Kennedy, and it forms interesting background to such Scottish cases as *Lord Advocate's Reference (No 1 of 2001)* 2002 SLT 466 and *Galbraith v HM Advocate (No 2)* 2002 JC 1. Kennedy's latest book, *Just Law* (2004), criticises what she sees as the erosion of civil liberties in Britain, and considers issues about immigration, asylum and terrorism in this context. Another Scot who has moved to a foreign jurisdiction is James Boyle, Professor of Law at Duke University in the USA: his *Software, Shamans and Spleens* (1996) attacks with vigour and humour what he sees as the repressive nature of the legal rules being developed for the information society, his analysis ranging from blackmail, through insider dealing, to the ownership of human body parts. You will learn a lot, entertainingly, about the information society as well as about politics, economics and law from this book. A rather different perspective on the information society – its exciting implications for the practice of law and the way people get to know about the law – comes from yet another Scots law graduate now working outside the jurisdiction: Richard Susskind, a leading consultant in London following his books *The Future of Law: Facing the Challenges of Information Technology* (1996, pbk 1998) and *Transforming the Law: Essays on Technology, Justice and the Legal Marketplace* (2000, pbk 2003) (and see his website, http://www.susskind.com/).

13.10 In the most recent edition of Glanville Williams' *Learning the Law*, the editor adds film-going to the list of possible recreations for law students, and makes a number of excellent viewing recommendations. To these might be added:

— *The Devil's Advocate* (1997), in which the newest attorney in New York's most powerful law firm (Keanu Reeves) discovers that Satanic support from his senior partner (Al Pacino) is why he never loses a case (Charlize Theron plays the attorney's long-suffering wife);

— *Erin Brockovich* (2000), about using the law as a weapon in an environmental campaign, with Julia Roberts as an unlikely assistant in a law firm;

— *Black and White* (2002), a film about the 1950s trial of an Australian Aborigine, Max Stuart, for the rape and murder of a small girl; the Scottish actor Robert Carlyle plays Stuart's lawyer, and the film skilfully shows how the forensic process fails to get to the truth, whatever that may have been.

13.11 It is a pity that none of these films are about Scottish situations or involve Scots law or lawyers. The fact that *Erin Brockovich* and *Black and White* arose from real cases does show, however, that what happens in and out of court is the stuff of real drama and deep human interest. More could be made by modern film-makers of the raw material to be found in famous Scottish cases. Novelists have shown the possibilities: Robert Louis Stevenson's version of the Appin murder case of 1752 and its consequences in *Kidnapped* and its sequel, *Catriona*; Frank Kuppner's brilliant fictionalisation in *A Very Quiet Street* (1989) of the story of Oscar Slater, convicted of a murder he did not commit and imprisoned for nearly 20 years before being rescued by Sir Arthur Conan Doyle (see above, para **1.19**)[1]; and John Robertson, who won the Saltire Scottish Book of the Year Award in 2003 with his powerful novel *Joseph Knight* (2003), based upon *Knight v Wedderburn* (1778) Mor 14545, in which the Court of Session held that Scots law did not recognise the institution of slavery. The famous

Glasgow case of Madeleine Smith, against whom the charge of poisoning her clandestine lover and social inferior Pierre Emile l'Angelier was found not proven in 1857, seems full of dramatic possibilities[2]. Could something also be made of *Donoghue v Stevenson* (see above, para **10.26**)? We now know a great deal about the background to the case, thanks to the undernoted research on the rather sad figure of Mrs Donoghue, her campaigning solicitor Walter Leechman, and their opponent, the unfortunate ginger beer manufacturer David Stevenson[3].

1   See further on the Slater case Thomas Toughill, *Oscar Slater: The Mystery Solved* (1993) and Richard Whittington-Egan, *The Oscar Slater Murder Story: New Light on a Classic Miscarriage of Justice* (2001).

2   See Douglas McGowan, *Murder in Victorian Scotland: The Trial of Madeleine Smith* (1999).

3   See G Lewis, *Lord Atkin* (1983), ch 3; A F Rodger, 'Mrs Donoghue and Alfenus Varus', (1988) 41 *Current Legal Problems* 1; W W McBryde, 'Donoghue v Stevenson: The Story of the 'Snail in the Bottle' Case', in A J Gamble (ed), *Obligations in Context: Essays in Honour of of David M Walker* (1990); P T Burns and S J Lyons (eds), *Donoghue v Stevenson and the Modern Law of Negligence: The Paisley Papers* (1991). A memorial to the case stands at the junction of Wellmeadow Street and Lady Lane in Paisley, the site of the Minghella cafe where Mrs Donoghue and her friend took their fateful refreshment in August 1928.

13.12   The point of all this is that law and legal study can be an entertaining and interesting way of life as well as hard work. The two must be held in balance to get the most out of your study. The realisation that law touches on nearly every aspect of human activity may also help you if you decide in the course of your studies that a career as a professional lawyer is not for you. Your education does not then go to waste, but is rather capable of being deployed in almost any walk of life that involves capacity for taking a balanced view fairly based on all available evidence and a careful analysis thereof. Many law students enter jobs in government (local and central), business, finance, social work, librarianship and teaching. They do so and succeed because the law degree, properly approached and understood, is not a narrow, dryly vocational training, but a general education in the world as it is and why it is. If studying Scots law is your choice, it is a good one.

Useful addresses

University applications

Universities and Colleges Admission Service (UCAS)

PO Box 28
Cheltenham
GL52 3LZ

Applicant enquiries: 0870-1122211, email enquiries@ucas.ac.uk for an automated response
General enquiries: 01242 222444
http://www.ucas.ac.uk

Universities offering LL.B degrees

UNIVERSITY OF ABERDEEN

School of Law
Taylor Building
Old Aberdeen
AB9 2UB

Tel: +44 (0) 1224 272441
Fax: +44 (0) 1224 272442
http://www.abdn.ac.uk/law/

UNIVERSITY OF ABERTAY DUNDEE

Bell Street
Dundee
DD1 1HG

Tel: +44 (0) 1382 308412
Fax: +44 (0) 1382 308400
http://www.tay.ac.uk

UNIVERSITY OF DUNDEE

Department of Law
Scrymgeour Building
Park Place
Dundee
DD1 4HN

Tel: +44 (0) 1382 344028
Fax: +44 (0) 1382 224419
http://www.dundee.ac.uk/law/

UNIVERSITY OF EDINBURGH

School of Law
Old College
South Bridge
Edinburgh
EH8 9YL

Tel: +44 (0) 131 650 2007
Fax: +44 (0) 131 662 4902
http://www.law.ed.ac.uk
For admissions, contact College of Humanities and Social Science
Admissions Office, Tel: +44 (0) 131 650 3565, Fax: +44 (0) 131 650 4678,
email: hssug@ed.ac.uk

UNIVERSITY OF GLASGOW

School of Law
Stair Memorial Building
Glasgow
G12 8QQ

Tel: +44 (0) 141 330 6075
Fax: +44 (0) 141 330 4900
email: faculty@law.gla.ac.uk
http://www.gla.ac.uk

GLASGOW CALEDONIAN UNIVERSITY

Division of Law, School of Law & Social Sciences
Cowcaddens Road
Glasgow
G4 0BA

Tel: +44 (0) 141 331 8657
Fax: +44 (0) 141 331 3439
email lss@gcal.ac.uk
http://cbs1.gcal.ac.uk/law/

NAPIER UNIVERSITY

School of Law
Sighthill Campus
Edinburgh
EH11 4BN

Tel: +44 (0) 131 455 3488
http://www.napier.ac.uk/law/

THE ROBERT GORDON UNIVERSITY

Department of Law, Aberdeen Business School
Garthdee Road
Aberdeen
AB10 7QE

Tel: +44 (0) 1224 263800
Fax: +44 (0) 1224 263838
email Aberdeen.business.school@rgu.ac.uk
http://www.rgu.ac.uk/abs/aboutabs/page.cfm?pge=5852

UNIVERSITY OF STRATHCLYDE

The Law School
Stenhouse Building
173 Cathedral Street
Glasgow
G4 0RQ

Tel: +44 (0) 141 548 3738
Fax: +44 (0) 141 552 4264
email: contact-law@strath.ac.uk
http://www.law.strath.ac.uk/

The University of Stirling (for details of which see **Appendix 2** below) is
understood to be seeking Law Society accreditation for an LL.B degree,
to start in 2005.

Professional bodies in Scotland

The Law Society of Scotland

26 Drumsheugh Gardens
Edinburgh
EH3 7YR

Tel: +44 (0) 131 226 7411
Fax: +44 (0) 131 225 2934
email: lawscot@lawscot.org.uk
http://www.lawscot.org.uk

The Faculty of Advocates

Advocates' Library
Parliament House
Edinburgh
EH1 1RF

Tel: +44 (0) 131 226 5071
Fax: +44 (0) 131 225 3642
http://www.advocates.org.uk/

Professional bodies in England

The Law Society (of England and Wales)

The Law Society's Hall
113 Chancery Lane
London
WC2A 1PL

Tel: +44 (0) 207 242 1222
Fax: +44 (0) 207 831 0344
email: info.services@lawsociety.org.uk
http://www.lawsociety.org.uk (this site provides useful information and
links on qualification in England)

The Bar Council (of England and Wales)

3 Bedford Row
London
WC1R 4DB

Tel: +44 (0) 207 242 0082
http://www.barcouncil.org.uk/

Other addresses

Citizens Advice Scotland

Spectrum House
2 Powderhall Road
Edinburgh
EH7 4GB

Tel: 0131 550 1000
Fax: 0131 550 1001
email: info@cas.org.uk
http://www.cas.org.uk/

Scottish Qualifications Authority (SQA)

Hanover House   Ironmills Road
24 Douglas Street   Dalkeith
Glasgow   Midlothian
G2 7NQ   EH22 1LE

Tel: 0845 279 1000
Fax: +44 (0) 141 242 2244
email: customer@sqa.org.uk
http://www.sqa.org.uk

The information in this Appendix was correct at the time of writing (April 2004) to the best of the author's knowledge and belief, but its absolute accuracy is not guaranteed, and details may have changed since publication.

BA Degrees in Law

These degrees are available at Abertay Dundee University, Glasgow Caledonian University, Napier University, Paisley University, The Robert Gordon University, and Stirling University. Further information is available from these institutions (addresses below). The entrance requirements for all are lower than those for the LL.B degree, and they do not satisfy the entrance requirements of either the Law Society of Scotland or the Faculty of Advocates. The degrees are typically aimed at the Qualified Conveyancer or Executry Practitioner, Legal Executive or 'para legal', or the manager in either the private or the public sector who requires knowledge of law to carry out management functions.

Universities offering degrees in legal studies which are not LL.Bs

UNIVERSITY OF ABERTAY DUNDEE

Bell Street
Dundee
DD1 1HG

Tel: +44 (0) 1382 308412
Fax: +44 (0) 1382 308400
http://www.tay.ac.uk

NAPIER UNIVERSITY

School of Law
Sighthill Campus
Edinburgh
EH11 4BN

Tel: +44 (0) 131 455 3488
http://www.napier.ac.uk/law/

GLASGOW CALEDONIAN UNIVERSITY

Division of Law, School of Law & Social Sciences
Cowcaddens Road
Glasgow
G4 0BA

Tel: +44 (0)141 331 8657
Fax: +44 (0) 141 331 3439
email lss@gcal.ac.uk
http://cbs1.gcal.ac.uk/law/

UNIVERSITY OF PAISLEY

High Street
Paisley
PA1 2BE

Tel: 0800 027 1000
email: uni-direct@paisley.ac.uk
http://www.paisley.ac.uk/courses/ug-courseinfo.asp?courseid=388

THE ROBERT GORDON UNIVERSITY

Department of Law, Aberdeen Business School
Garthdee Road
Aberdeen
AB10 7QE

Tel: +44 (0) 224 263800
Fax: +44 (0) 224 263838

email Aberdeen.business.school@rgu.ac.uk
http://www.rgu.ac.uk/abs/aboutabs/page.cfm?pge=5852

UNIVERSITY OF STIRLING

Department of Accounting, Finance & Law
University of Stirling
Stirling
FK9 4LA

Tel: +44 (0) 1786 467280
Fax: +44 (0) 1786 467308
email: accountancy@stir.ac.uk
http://www.stir.ac.uk/Departments/Management/Accountancy/

The information in this Appendix was correct at the time of writing (April 2004) to the best of the author's knowledge and belief, but its absolute accuracy is not guaranteed, and details may have changed since publication.

Funding

Government funding

Student Awards Agency for Scotland (SAAS)

Gyleview House
3 Redheughs Rigg
Edinburgh
EH12 9HH

Tel: +44 (0) 131 476 8212
http://www.student-support-saas.gov.uk/

Student Loans Company Ltd

100 Bothwell Street
Glasgow
G2 7JD

Tel: Freephone 0800 405010
http://www.slc.co.uk/index.html

Charities

The Carnegie Trust for the Universities of Scotland

Cameron House
Abbey Park Place
Dunfermline
Fife
KY12 7PZ

Tel: +44 (0) 1383 622148
Fax: +44 (0) 1383 622149
email: jgray@carnegie-trust.org
http://www.carnegie-trust.org/grant6.htm

The Clark Foundation for Legal Education

Messrs Tods Murray
Solicitors
66 Queen Street
Edinburgh
EH2 4NE

http://www.todsmurray.com/recruitment/clark-foundation.htm

The WS Society Educational Scholarship

The General Manager
The WS Society
Signet Library
Parliament Square
Edinburgh
EH1 1RF

The Pritchard Educational Trust

The Secretary
The Law Society of Scotland
26 Drumsheugh Gardens
Edinburgh
EH3 7YR

Career Development Loans

For further information, consult http://www.lifelonglearning.co.uk/cdl/

Educational Trusts and Endowments

The Scottish Council for Voluntary Organisations (SCVO) maintains a Directory of Grant Making Trusts at http://www.scvo.org.uk/essentials/directories/grant_making_trusts/. The SAAS maintains a register of charities offering educational endowments which it will search on behalf of any student not in receipt of an award from public funds. This service does not appear to be available online.

SOCRATES

http://europa.eu.int/comm/education/programmes/socrates/erasmus/what_en.html

http://www.erasmus.ac.uk/index.html

The information in this Appendix was correct at the time of writing (April 2004) to the best of the author's knowledge and belief, but its absolute accuracy is not guaranteed, and details may have changed since publication.

Latin phrases

ab initio: from the beginning

ad hoc: for this purpose only (sometimes with the sense of improvised)

ante: before

avizandum: the period during which the court considers its judgment in a case

bona fide: good faith

consensus: agreement

consensus in idem: agreement to the same thing

contra: against

damnum: damage, loss

de facto: in fact

de jure: of law

de minimis: trivial

dictum (plural *dicta*): a saying or statement, usually judicial

dominium: ownership

ejusdem generis: of the same kind

esto: suppose it to be so

ex facie: on the face of it (usually referring to a document)

ex gratia: freely, gratuitously, without a legal obligation

ex post facto: after the event

fructus: fruit

hinc inde: on the one hand and on the other

ibid: at the same place (used in footnotes to refer to work already cited in previous note)

idem: the same person (used in footnotes to refer to another work by the same author as that as the last-cited work)

in dubio: on a doubtful point

in extenso: in full

in modum probationis: in the way of proof

in solidum: for the whole amount

in toto: in total, in full

infra: within (in footnotes, equivalent to 'later' or 'below')

injuria: wrongful act

inter alia: amongst other things

inter vivos: between living persons

jus: right (sometimes 'law')

jus ad rem: right to a thing (personal right)

jus in personam: personal right

jus in rem: right in a thing (real right)

jus quaesitum tertio: right acquired by a third party (under a contract between two other parties)

lex: law (often written law)

locus: place

mala fide: bad faith

mens rea: wicked mind

mortis causa: on account of death or in anticipation of death

obiter dictum (plural *obiter dicta*): statement(s) or saying(s) not essential to the main point; of judicial statements, meaning not part of the *ratio decidendi* (see below)

ope exceptionis: as a defence

pactum: agreement

pari passu: equally

per: by; used in footnotes and headnotes to indicate that a statement was made by somebody (e.g. a judge) who is named immediately afterwards

per se: by itself

post: after, later, below (in footnotes)

prima facie: at first sight

pro rata: proportionately, by shares

pro tanto: for so much

prout de jure: by any legal form of proof (usually the context is that proof is not confined to written evidence)

quantum: amount

quantum lucratus: amount of enrichment

quantum meruit: amount it (goods/services supplied) was worth (usually market value)

quoad ultra: as regards everything else

quid juris?: what is the law? how is the law to be applied? (often used in examination questions)

ratio decidendi: the rule for which a case stands as authority

rebus integris (or, *rebus stantibus*): things standing as they do just now

res: thing, the object of an action

res gestae: things done, the circumstances of the case

res non sunt integrae: things do not stand as they did

restitutio in integrum: restoration to the original position *sine die*: indefinitely

status quo: the current position

status quo ante: the position as it was before

supra: above

uberrima fides: the utmost good faith

unum quid: a whole

veritas: truth

vide: see

vitium reale: an inherent flaw in the title to something (eg stolen goods)

See further *Trayner's Latin Maxims* (4th edn, 1993, with foreword by A G M Duncan).

Books

This appendix contains a list of introductory works on various branches of Scots law. It is neither comprehensive or intended to be a guide as to relative quality. Practitioner and more advanced works have been omitted unless there was no other book on the subject. For the most part I have listed the books under the headings of the compulsory subjects of the Law Society of Scotland and the Faculty of Advocates. It will always be necessary to up-date a textbook, and you should also check for any new editions of the books listed here.

General

The Stair Memorial Encyclopaedia of the Laws of Scotland (continuing)

H MacQueen and others (eds), *Gloag & Henderson's Introduction to the Law of Scotland* (11th edn, 2001)

C Ashton and others, *Fundamentals of Scots Law* (2003)

N Busby and others, *Scots Law: A Student Guide* (2nd edn, 2003)

K Norrie (ed), *The 100 Cases that Every Scots Law Student Needs to Know* (2001)

Scottish legal system

A A Paterson and T StJ N Bates, *The Legal System of Scotland: Cases and Materials* (4th edn, 1999)

D M Walker, *The Scottish Legal System* (8th edn, 2001)

R White and I D Willock, *The Scottish Legal System* (3rd edn, 2003)

W A Wilson, *Introductory Essays on Scots Law* (2nd edn, 1984)

Scots private law

J M Thomson, *Family Law in Scotland* (4th edn, 2002)

A M O Griffiths and L Edwards, *Family Law* (1997)

E Sutherland, *Child and Family Law* (1999)

H MacQueen and J Thomson, *Contract Law in Scotland* (2000)

S E Woolman and J Lake, *An Introduction to the Scots Law of Contract* (3rd edn, 2001)

J A K Huntley, *Contract: Cases and Materials* (2nd edn, 2003)

W J Stewart, *An Introduction to the Scots Law of Delict* (3rd edn, 1998)

F McManus and E Russell, *Delict: a Comprehensive Guide to the Law* (1998)

J M Thomson, *Delictual Liability* (3rd edn, 2004)

R Evans-Jones, *Unjustified Enrichment: Vol 1 Enrichment by Deliberate Conferral: Condictio* (2003)

H L MacQueen, *Unjustified Enrichment* (2004)

M A Hogg, *Obligations* (2003)

A McAllister and T G Guthrie, *Scottish Property Law: An Introduction* (1992)

P Robson and K Miller, *Property Law* (1992)

K G C Reid and others, *The Law of Property in Scotland* (1996)

K Reid, *The Abolition of Feudal Tenure in Scotland* (2003)

R Rennie, *Land Tenure Reform* (2003)

D R Macdonald, *An Introduction to the Scots Law of Succession* (3rd edn, 2001)

K McK Norrie and E Scobbie, *Trusts* (1991)

J Chalmers, *Trusts: Cases and Materials* (2002)

Conveyancing

A J McDonald, *Conveyancing Manual* (7th edn, 2004)

J H Sinclair, *Handbook of Conveyancing Practice in Scotland* (4th ed, 2002)

G L Gretton and K G C Reid, *Conveyancing* (2nd edn, 1999; 3rd edn anticipated 2004)

Commercial/mercantile law

F Davidson and L Macgregor, *Commercial Law in Scotland* (2003)

N Grier, *Commercial Law Basics* (2nd edn, 2003)

N Grier, *Company Law* (2002)

A D M Forte (ed), *Scots Commercial Law* (1997)

A D M Forte and D J Cusine, *Cases and Materials on Scottish Commercial Law* (1987; 2nd edn anticipated December 2004)

Public law

Lord Reed (ed), *A Practical Guide to Human Rights Law in Scotland* (2001)

Lord Reed and J Murdoch, *A Guide to Human Rights Law in Scotland* (2002; 2nd edn anticipated September 2004)

C Himsworth and C O'Neill, *Scotland's Constitution: Law and Practice* (2003)

J Munro, *Public Law* (2003)

J McFadden and M Lazarowicz, *The Scottish Parliament: An Introduction* (3rd edn, 2003)

Criminal law

C H W Gane and C N Stoddart, *Casebook on Scottish Criminal Law* (3rd edn, 2000)

T H Jones and M G A Christie, *Criminal Law* (3rd edn, 2003)

R A McCall Smith and D Sheldon, *Scots Criminal Law* (2nd edn, 1997)

Evidence

M Ross, *Walker and Walker's Law of Evidence in Scotland* (2nd edn, 2000)

F Raitt, *Evidence* (3rd edn, 2001)

D Sheldon, *Evidence: Cases and Materials* (2nd edn, 2002)

Taxation

Consult C J Tyre's article on 'Revenue' in volume 19 of *The Stair Memorial Encyclopaedia* together with updating supplement.

European Community law

D A O Edward and R C Lane, *European Community Law: An Introduction* (2nd edn, 1995; 3rd edn forthcoming 2004)

J Usher, *General Principles of EC Law* (1998)

J Usher, *EC Institutions and Legislation* (1998)

S Weatherill and P Beaumont, *EU Law* (3rd edn, 1999)

Jurisprudence

M D A Freeman, *Lloyd's Introduction to Jurisprudence* (7th edn, 2001)

Consult also D N MacCormick, 'General Legal Concepts', in volume 11 of *The Stair Memorial Encyclopaedia*.

International private law

E Crawford, *International Private Law* (1998)

Consult also R D Leslie's article 'Private International Law' in volume 17 of *The Stair Memorial Encyclopaedia*.

Roman law

Justinian's Institutes, trans P Birks and G McLeod (1987)

B Nicholas, *An Introduction to Roman Law* (1962)

A Borkowski, *Textbook of Roman Law* (2nd edn, 1997)

Useful diagrams

Fig 1   The structure of the Scottish courts (simplified)

(Note also the procedure of reference to the European Court of Justice.)

(a) Civil courts

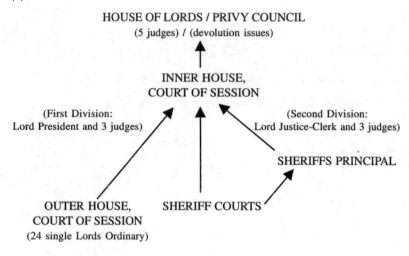

HOUSE OF LORDS / PRIVY COUNCIL
(5 judges) / (devolution issues)

INNER HOUSE,
COURT OF SESSION

(First Division:
Lord President and 3 judges)

(Second Division:
Lord Justice-Clerk and 3 judges)

SHERIFFS PRINCIPAL

OUTER HOUSE,   SHERIFF COURTS
COURT OF SESSION
(24 single Lords Ordinary)

(b) Criminal courts

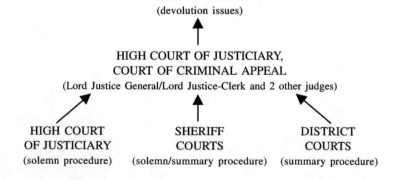

PRIVY COUNCIL
(devolution issues)

HIGH COURT OF JUSTICIARY,
COURT OF CRIMINAL APPEAL
(Lord Justice General/Lord Justice-Clerk and 2 other judges)

HIGH COURT   SHERIFF   DISTRICT
OF JUSTICIARY   COURTS   COURTS
(solemn procedure) (solemn/summary procedure) (summary procedure)

Fig 2 Qualifying as a solicitor

LLB DEGREE
(2/3/4 years)

PRE-DIPLOMA TRAINING CONTRACT
(4 years max; Law Society of Scotland exams)

DIPLOMA IN LEGAL PRACTICE
(1 year)

ENTRANCE CERTIFICATE

POST-DIPLOMA TRAINING CONTRACT
(2 years: admission after first year)
TPC and PCC

DISCHARGE AND ENROLMENT CEREMONY

Fig 3 Qualifying as an advocate

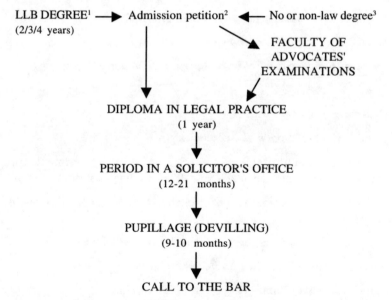

LLB DEGREE[1]   Admission petition[2]   No or non-law degree[3]
(2/3/4 years)

FACULTY OF
ADVOCATES'
EXAMINATIONS

DIPLOMA IN LEGAL PRACTICE
(1 year)

PERIOD IN A SOLICITOR'S OFFICE
(12-21 months)

PUPILLAGE (DEVILLING)
(9-10 months)

CALL TO THE BAR

1   The LLB degree may be preceded by a non-law degree.
2   There are no specifications as to when an admission petition should be made.
3   Any outstanding required examinations are taken at this stage.

Some useful websites

For University Law School and Department websites, all of which have invaluable further links to sites of legal relevance, see Appendix 1.

Parliaments

Westminster Parliament: http://www.parliament.uk/

Scottish Parliament: http://www.scottish.parliament.uk/

European Parliament: http://www.europarl.eu.int/home/default_en.htm

Courts

Scottish Courts: http://www.scotcourts.gov.uk

Appellate Committee of the House of Lords: http://www.publications.parliament.uk/pa/ld199697/ldjudgmt.htm

Judicial Committee of the Privy Council: http://www.privy-council.org.uk/output/page5.asp

England and Wales Court Service: http://www.courtservice.gov.uk

European Court of Justice: http://curia.eu.int/en/

European Court of Human Rights: http://www.echr.coe.int/

Governments

Scottish Executive: http://www.scotland.gov.uk/

Scotland Office: http://scottishsecretary.gov.uk/index.htm

Advocate General for Scotland: http://www.scottishsecretary.gov.uk/ags.htm

UK Government Online: http://www.ukonline.gov.uk/Home/Homepage/fs/en

Directgov: http://ukonline.direct.gov.uk/Homepage/fs/en

European Commission: http://europa.eu.int/comm/index_en.htm

10 Downing Street: http://www.pm.gov.uk/

UK Cabinet Office: http://www.cabinet-office.gov.uk/

UK Foreign and Commonwealth Office: http://www.fco.gov.uk/

UK Home Office: http://www.homeoffice.gov.uk/

UK Treasury: http://www.hm-treasury.gov.uk/

UK Department for Constitutional Affairs: http://www.dca.gov.uk/

UK Department for Culture Media and Sport: http://www.culture.gov.uk/

UK Department for Education and Skills: http://www.dfes.gov.uk/

UK Department for Environment, Food and Rural Affairs: http://www.defra.gov.uk/

UK Department for Trade and Industry: http://www.dti.gov.uk/

Other public bodies

Crown Office: http://www.crownoffice.gov.uk/

Scottish Law Commission: http://www.scotlawcom.gov.uk/

Law Commission for England and Wales: http://www.lawcom.gov.uk/

Scottish Legal Aid Board: http://www.slab.org.uk/

Public Defence Solicitors Office: http://www.pdso.demon.co.uk/pdso_home.htm

Scottish Criminal Cases Review Commission: http://www.sccrc.org.uk/

Judicial Appointments Board for Scotland:
http://www.judicialappointmentsscotland.gov.uk/

Scottish Council for Law Reporting: http://www.scottishlawreports.org.uk/

Scottish Legal Services Ombudsman: http://www.slso.org.uk/

Registers of Scotland: http://www.ros.gov.uk/

Scottish Information Commissioner: http://www.itspublicknowledge.info/

Citizens Advice Scotland: http://www.cas.org.uk/

British and Irish Legal Information Institute: http://www.bailii.org.uk

Companies House: http://www.companies-house.gov.uk/

UK Patent Office: http://www.patent.gov.uk/

UK Information Commissioner:
http://www.informationcommissioner.gov.uk/

Child Support Agency: http://www.csa.gov.uk/

Criminal Injuries Compensation Authority: https://www.cica.gov.uk/

Motor Insurers Bureau: http://www.mib.org.uk/index.asp

Professional bodies

Law Society of Scotland: http://www.lawscot.org.uk/

Faculty of Advocates: http://www.advocates.org.uk/

WS Society: http://www.signetlibrary.co.uk/

Royal Faculty of Procurators in Glasgow: http://www.rfpg.org/

Scottish Paralegal Association: http://www.scottish-paralegal.org.uk/

Legal Services Agency: http://www.lsa.org.uk/

Legal publishers in Scotland

LexisNexis UK Scotland: http://www.lexisnexis.co.uk/scotland/

W Green: http://www.wgreen.co.uk/

Edinburgh University Press: http://www.eup.ed.ac.uk/

Avizandum: http://www.avizandum.com/

News, entertainment and information

Scots Law News: http://www.law.ed.ac.uk/sln

Scottish Law Online: http://www.scottishlaw.org.uk/

Absolvitor: Scots Law Online: http://www.absolvitor.com/

Scottish Legal Action Group: http://www.scolag.org/

Stair Society: http://www.stairsociety.org/

Note that website addresses change, and the accuracy of the above references cannot be guaranteed over time.

Index

[all references are to paragraph number]